P9-CTB-403

ESSENTIALS OF
PERSONNEL
MANAGEMENT

Mitchell S. Novit
Indiana University

PRENTICE-HALL, INC., ENGLEWOOD CLIFFS, N.J. 07632

Library of Congress Cataloging in Publication Data

Novit, Mitchell S
  Essentials of personnel management.

  (Essentials of management)
  Includes bibliographies and index.
    1. Personnel management. I. Title. II. Series.
HF5549.N65   658.3   78-11217
ISBN 0-13-286617-X
ISBN 0-13-286609-9 pbk.

Prentice-Hall Essentials of Management Series
Stephen P. Robbins, **editor**

Editorial/Production supervision: Esther S. Koehn
Interior and cover design: Christine Gadekar
Buyer: Harry Baisley

10 9 8 7 6 5 4 3 2

Printed in the United States of America

Prentice-Hall International, Inc., *London*
Prentice-Hall of Australia Pty. Limited, *Sydney*
Prentice-Hall of Canada, Ltd., *Toronto*
Prentice-Hall of India Private Limited, *New Delhi*
Prentice-Hall of Japan, Inc., *Tokyo*
Prentice-Hall of Southeast Asia Pte. Ltd., *Singapore*
Whitehall Books Limited, *Wellington, New Zealand*

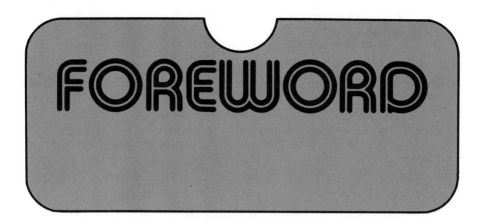

FOREWORD

With the rapid growth in recent years of courses in such areas as personnel, organizational behavior, production, decision science, labor relations, and small business management, there has developed an increased need for a viable alternative to the standard 500- or 600-page, casebound textbook. The Essentials of Management Series has been designed to fill that need. The Series consists of brief, survey books covering major content areas within the management discipline.

Each book in the Series provides a concise treatment of the key concepts and issues within a major content area, written in a highly readable style, balancing theory with practical applications, and offering a clarity of presentation that is often missing in standard, full-length textbooks. I have selected authors both for their academic expertise and their ability to identify, organize, and articulate the essential elements of their subject. So, for example, you will find that the books in this Series avoid unnecessary jargon, use a conversational writing style, include extensive examples and interesting illustrations of concepts, and have the focus of a rifle rather than that of an encyclopedic shotgun.

The books in this Series will prove useful to a wide variety of readers. Since each covers the essential body of knowledge in a major area of management, they can be used alone for introductory survey courses in colleges and universities or for management development and in-house educational programs. Additionally, their short format makes them an ideal vehicle to be combined with cases, readings, and/or experiential materials by instructors who desire to mold a course to meet unique objectives. The books in this Series offer the flexibility that is either not feasible or too costly to achieve with a standard textbook.

Stephen P. Robbins
Series Editor

for
my wife,
Judy,
my son, David, and my daughter, Amy

CONTENTS

PREFACE   xi

PART
1

INTRODUCTION   1

1
THE PERSONNEL FUNCTION   3

NATURE OF THE PERSONNEL FUNCTION   4
DEVELOPMENT OF PERSONNEL MANAGEMENT   5
PERSONNEL FUNCTIONS   7
ORGANIZATION OF THE PERSONNEL FUNCTION   14
DUAL FUNCTIONS OF PERSONNEL MANAGEMENT   17

2
PERSONNEL MANAGEMENT AND PUBLIC POLICY   20

EVOLUTION OF PUBLIC POLICY   21
CURRENT LEGISLATION AFFECTING
THE EMPLOYMENT RELATIONSHIP   24

Contents

PART

&2&

PLANNING FOR HUMAN RESOURCES   33

3

HUMAN RESOURCE PLANNING   35

QUANTITATIVE FORECASTING	36
QUALITATIVE HUMAN RESOURCE PLANNING	41
ANALYZING LABOR AVAILABILITY	42
MONITORING AND INTEGRATING THE PERSONNEL PROGRAM	44

4

ORGANIZATION STAFFING LEVELS   47

WORK MEASUREMENT	48
USING COMPARATIVE DATA	49
THE BUDGETING PROCESS	53
LABOR ORGANIZATIONS AND PERSONNEL LEVELS	54

PART

&3&

RECRUITMENT AND SELECTION   57

5

RECRUITMENT OF PERSONNEL   59

DEFINING THE LABOR MARKET	60
METHODS AND SOURCES	60
INTERNAL RECRUITMENT	64
PUBLIC POLICY	65

6

THE SELECTION PROCESS   68

BASIC ELEMENTS IN SELECTION	69
THE PROCESS OF VALIDATION	75
EVALUATING CANDIDATES	81

Contents

MAKING THE SELECTION DECISION   85
ORGANIZING FOR SELECTION   88

7

PUBLIC POLICY
AND PERSONNEL SELECTION   92

DEVELOPMENT OF PUBLIC POLICY
AGAINST DISCRIMINATION   92
LEGISLATION AND EXECUTIVE ORDERS   93
JUDICIAL DECISIONS AND THEIR IMPACT   97
AFFIRMATIVE ACTION PROGRAMS   100
SYSTEMIC DISCRIMINATION   103

PART
4 3

DEVELOPMENT AND APPRAISAL   107

8

TRAINING   109

TRAINING AS BEHAVIOR CHANGE   110
THE FORMAL TRAINING PROCESS   111
ORGANIZING FOR TRAINING   121
PUBLIC POLICY AND TRAINING   122

9

MANAGEMENT DEVELOPMENT
AND CAREER PLANNING   125

ORGANIZING THE DEVELOPMENT FUNCTION   126
ANALYZING THE MANAGERIAL JOB   127
IDENTIFYING AND SELECTING MANAGERS   129
THE ASSESSMENT CENTER   129
ANALYZING CANDIDATES   131
CAREER PLANNING   132
DEVELOPING OBJECTIVES
AND ACTION PLANS   133
ACTIVITIES FOR DEVELOPING MANAGERS   134

MONITORING AND EVALUATING
THE PROGRAM   136
PUBLIC POLICY AND MANAGEMENT DEVELOPMENT   137

10

PERFORMANCE APPRAISAL   139

DEFINING PERFORMANCE   140
SETTING GOALS   140
COMMON ERRORS   141
METHODS OF APPRAISAL   143
WHO DOES THE APPRAISAL?   149
FREQUENCY AND TIMING   150
ORGANIZING FOR APPRAISAL   151
PROVIDING FEEDBACK   151
INNOVATIONS   152
PUBLIC POLICY AND APPRAISAL   154

PART 5

COMPENSATION AND PRODUCTIVITY   157

11

WAGE AND SALARY ADMINISTRATION   159

GOALS IN WAGE AND
SALARY ADMINISTRATION   160
THE GENERAL WAGE LEVEL   161
THE VERTICAL WAGE STRUCTURE   164
DETERMINING THE ACTUAL
WAGE STRUCTURE   168
HANDLING SPECIAL PROBLEMS   169
WAGE INCENTIVES   171
PUBLIC POLICY AND COMPENSATION   172

12

PRODUCTIVITY AND LABOR COSTS   177

WHAT IS PRODUCTIVITY?   178
THE UNIT LABOR COST   179
PROGRAMS FOR IMPROVING PRODUCTIVITY   182

Contents

PART

6

EMPLOYEE MAINTENANCE

189

13

EMPLOYEE BENEFITS AND SERVICES

191

DEVELOPMENT OF BENEFITS
AND SERVICES   192
PROTECTION AGAINST DEATH
AND DISABILITY   193
RETIREMENT   195
PROTECTION AGAINST JOB LOSS   196
PAY FOR TIME NOT WORKED   197
EMPLOYEE SERVICES   199
ADMINISTRATION OF BENEFIT PROGRAMS   200
FLEXIBLE COMPENSATION   200

14

EMPLOYEE SAFETY AND HEALTH

203

EXTENT OF THE SAFETY AND
HEALTH PROBLEM   204
ORGANIZING THE SAFETY AND
HEALTH FUNCTIONS   205
MEASURING SAFETY AND HEALTH COSTS   207
MEASURING ACCIDENTS AND ILLNESSES   208
OCCUPATIONAL SAFETY AND HEALTH ACT   209

PART

7

LABOR ORGANIZATIONS

215

15

LABOR-MANAGEMENT RELATIONS

217

EXTENT OF ORGANIZED LABOR TODAY   218
STRUCTURE AND GOVERNMENT   219
THE ROLE OF LAW   221

COLLECTIVE BARGAINING   222
POLITICAL AND INSTITUTIONAL NATURE   224
MANAGEMENT ORGANIZATION   226
PUBLIC SECTOR COLLECTIVE BARGAINING   227
EVALUATING THE LABOR RELATIONS FUNCTION   228

PART 8

THE FUTURE

231

16

PERSONNEL MANAGEMENT IN THE FUTURE

233

DEMOGRAPHIC CHANGES AND THEIR IMPACT   233
CONTINUING GOVERNMENT REGULATION   236
DEMANDS FOR BETTER WORK PRACTICES   237
INCREASED ROLE FOR PERSONNEL MANAGEMENT   237

PREFACE

This book is addressed to two groups: those with career interests in staff personnel administration and those with career interests in general management. The concepts of effective personnel management are essential for both. I had five objectives in writing the book:

1. To provide an up-to-date text that can be used as a main or supplemental source for college, university, and continuing management education courses and programs in personnel administration and general management (as well as organizational behavior courses where there is a need to add functional personnel material).
2. To provide a concise, readable, yet authoritative coverage of the fundamentals of personnel management—one that would offer an alternative to the voluminous treatments currently available.
3. To offer a comprehensive look at public policy and government regulation—the critical areas of personnel management today.
4. To provide a useful source of personnel information in concise form for practicing managers. Today the management of people is more challenging than ever. The book's contemporary approach ought to prove valuable to the manager on the job.
5. To demonstrate that sound personnel management is not confined to the private sector, but is applicable to all types of organizations. Examples used have been chosen from both the public and private sectors.

Many persons have contributed to this project. The series editor, Steve Robbins, has a keen eye for the written word. His ability not only to spot weaknesses in the manuscript but to supply the right remedy proved invaluable. The book is much better for his contribution, though its deficiencies are solely the responsibility of the author.

Bob Meldrum of Prentice-Hall expressed interest and encouragement when the book was little more than an idea and a rough outline. It meant so much at the time. Ted Jursek assumed editorial duties in the management area at Prentice-Hall after the book was underway. His telephone conversations were always supportive as he made helpful suggestions and encouraged me to complete the project.

Marcie Moriarty showed a remarkable knack for transforming

scratched up sheets into polished, typed pages. She managed, always cheer-fully, to meet my typing deadlines of "immediately" or "sooner, if possible." Trina Marlin and Cindy McLochlin ably provided service of the same high quality when they were needed.

Two of the most wonderful people I know contributed more to this undertaking than they will ever know—my children, David and Amy. My greatest wish is that their cups runneth over with all the blessings life can bestow.

And, finally, there is the person who has meant everything to this and all my endeavors—my wife, Judy. We have shared so much over the many years. This is my inadequate way of saying just how much our relationship has meant.

Mitchell Novit

PART

1

INTRODUCTION

THE PERSONNEL FUNCTION

⟸ IDEAS TO BE FOUND ⟹
IN THIS CHAPTER

- Development of personnel management
- Major personnel functions
- Organization of the personnel department
- Line–staff conflicts
- Productivity and organizational maintenance

All organizations, whether profit seeking or not, exist for some purpose. They exist in a modern industrial society to produce and distribute goods and services that are needed and desired by the society's members. To produce and distribute these goods and services it is necessary to put human mental and physical energies to productive use.

Putting human energy to productive use is what personnel management is all about. The tasks necessary to accomplish the organization's purposes must be specified, and broken down into workable units that can be performed by one individual. The efforts of each individual must be coordinated with those of others.

Persons with the needed skills and abilities must be acquired. Once acquired they must be motivated to perform. As skills become obsolete, training in new skills must occur. Corrective action must be taken if work does not meet prescribed standards. Measures must be instituted to retain the services of those who make a positive contribution.

Personnel management exists to perform these and related activities. This chapter looks at the nature and development of personnel management, and examines the major personnel functions.

NATURE OF THE PERSONNEL FUNCTION

Personnel management exists in the organization in two related but distinct forms, which may sometimes be confused. The first is the *relationship between a manager and his or her subordinates*. With only minor exceptions, being a manager implies responsibility for directing and supervising the work of others. In this sense every manager is a personnel manager.

The second form is the existence of personnel management as a *specialized staff department*. Staff departments provide supporting services for the organization. Legal and market research departments are some other typical staff functions. Functions directly related to production and distribution of the organization's goods or services are referred to as line or operating departments.

Persons in the personnel department are staff personnel specialists. Often these individuals, with the exception of the managers within the department itself, do not themselves have subordinates to directly supervise. It is the job of the staff personnel department to provide assistance and support to the rest of the organization in dealing with the myriad problems involved in developing and maintaining a cohesive and productive work force.

Personnel management is often thought to exist only in large organizations where the staff personnel department is clearly identified on the organization chart. This is not the case at all. All organizations, large or small, have a personnel function. In large organizations the functions of personnel management are performed by specialists who may devote themselves only to one area such as college recruiting. In an organization employing only a few people, all the functions may be done by one person whose principal responsibilities lie elsewhere.

Nor is personnel management confined to profit-seeking institutions. The municipal police department, the state university, the United States Air Force, the public school system—all have a personnel function. It is surprising how little impact the profit-seeking factor has upon the concepts and operations of good personnel administration. All organizations exist for some purpose, and it is the factor of goals and purpose rather than the measurement of success by profits that determines the need for personnel management.

In understanding personnel management it is important to keep in mind the distinction already mentioned—the shared responsibility that exists between the staff personnel department and the manager who has direct responsibility for his or her subordinates. The nature of this shared responsibility will be discussed in this chapter and will be alluded to frequently.

But far more important than this structural arrangement are the many functions which must be performed in the proper management of personnel.

It is these functions involved in the acquisition, development, nurturance, and utilization of the organization's human resources which are the principal concern of this book. Complex relationships evolve in the necessary sharing of this responsibility between operating managers and the personnel department. But these are simply additional complicating factors which make the management of personnel an endlessly fascinating and challenging aspect of organizational life.

DEVELOPMENT OF PERSONNEL MANAGEMENT

If one looks back at personnel management as it was practiced at the turn of the century, it is difficult to see the beginnings of the field as we know it today. "Personnel management" is perhaps too grandiose a term to describe the primitive actions that secured employees and put them to work. In the manufacturing facility the foreman would do the hiring by cursory visual inspection at the factory gate. Training was practically nonexistent except for on-the-job instruction by a fellow worker. Performance appraisal and management development were unheard of. Recordkeeping was almost nil. Health insurance, paid vacations, pensions and other benefits did not exist. Discipline was arbitrary and sudden firings without recourse were commonplace. The concept of due process for the employee had not yet arisen. Discrimination based on race, ethnic background, sex and religion was an accepted way of life.

Changing the Employer-Employee Relationship

It is impossible to isolate one or two forces as being primarily responsible for the vast changes that have occurred in managing workers since that time. All the forces which transformed or accompanied the transformation of this country from an agricultural nation of rural dwellers to a highly developed, urban, industrial society played an important role. Among these were the development of large-scale, mass-production enterprises; the explosion in technology; the proliferation of the automobile and the accompanying road and highway system; mass communications in the form of radio and, later, television; the replacement of unskilled immigrant laborers by a more educated populace; the steady movement from blue-collar to white-collar work; developments in the social sciences; rising levels of affluence on a scale never before seen; the growth and influence of trade unions; the expansion and increasing scope of governmental activity—all these factors played an important role in redefining the relationship between employer and employee.

Paralleling the change in the methods of managing workers was the development of the organizational specialty known today as personnel management or personnel administration. It had its origins in the early decades of the twentieth century and grew along with other staff functions which began to appear at this time.

The Staff Function Emerges   At the turn of the century organizations, particularly industrial corporations, began to grow and expand. Large organizations found that greater efficiencies could be obtained by borrowing a concept thought to have been pioneered by the Prussian Army under Bismarck. This was the practice of centralizing certain ancillary service functions in a separate unit. This unit would provide the service for the entire organization. Instead of each operating unit buying its own supplies and materials, it was more economical to have this done by one specialized unit. These units became staff departments.

In the personnel area each foreman would no longer do the recruiting, screening, and hiring. It was more efficient to have at least the first two functions performed by a central department charged with providing assistance. With this initial start additional factors began operating to increase the size and scope of the personnel function.

One was the development of the field of industrial psychology. Early industrial psychologists began the process of individual measurement and the determination of factors associated with successful job performance. With the famous Hawthorne experiments that began in the 1920s, systematic investigation was brought to bear on the relationship of environmental factors to worker performance. Personnel departments grew because greater expertise could be obtained by putting these functions in the hands of specialists.

The spread and growth of labor unions added to the forces creating growth and expansion. Organizations with labor unions found it necessary to standardize their personnel policies. This helped reduce conflict with the union. To avoid arbitrary decisions which might run counter to the labor agreement, authority was taken away from the operating supervisors. This was especially true with regard to discipline. Authority was given instead to staff personnel administrators who could better insure standardized treatment of employees.

By the same token, organizations without labor unions found it desirable to standardize personnel policies to keep unions out. More responsibility and authority was given the personnel department. It became personnel's responsibility to create a climate not conducive to the formation of labor unions.

A critical factor spurring growth, and one still operating today, was increasing governmental regulation of the employment relationship. Beginning with early protective labor legislation such as child labor laws and workman's compensation, government regulation meant more extensive recordkeeping and monitoring of the organization. With the impetus provided by additional legislation such as the Wagner Act during the 1930s, personnel departments were given greater responsibilities and additional staff to cope with them.

The transformation of the labor force as it became increasingly skilled and better educated also played an important role. Shortages of skilled labor developed during the 1940s and continued during prosperous times in the decades to follow. This necessitated increasingly sophisticated personnel programs.

Personnel Management Today   Like all ancillary organizational functions, personnel administration has gone through periods of growth and increased status and periods of retrenchment and decline. What seems true today is that the field is achieving an importance greater than it has ever known. Much recent literature about personnel administration deals with this theme.[1]

The overwhelming reason is the growth in government regulation of the relationship between worker and organization. Society is demanding greater equity and due process in the employment relationship. Employee safety and health have become strong concerns. New laws have been passed with a resultant increase in regulatory agencies to implement them.

This greater demand for equity and better treatment occurs at a time when rising expectations from workers seem sometimes to create infinite demands for organizational rewards that are only finite. Also the nature of the organization and its role in society are being questioned perhaps as never before. At the same time competitive pressures on a world-wide basis are becoming more intense.

There seems little likelihood these pressures will decrease; in fact, there is every reason to believe the opposite is true. Thus there is every reason to anticipate an increasingly critical and important role for personnel administration in the years to come.

PERSONNEL FUNCTIONS   The major functions of personnel management center around providing and maintaining a cohesive and productive work force. Within this overall purpose several distinct areas emerge. Later chapters will deal with each of these functions in detail.

---

[1]For example see Fred K. Foulkes, "The Expanding Role of the Personnel Function," *Harvard Business Review*, March–April, 1975, and Herbert E. Meyer, "Personnel Directors Are the New Corporate Heroes," *Fortune*, February, 1976.

Human Resource Planning   Human resource or personnel plan-
                                     ning are newer and more acceptable
terms for the organizational function traditionally known as manpower planning. Despite the increasing attention it has received in recent years, it is
still one of the least developed areas in personnel management. In one sense
all organizations must engage in some type of human resource planning. The
extent to which this is formalized tells whether it can be recognized as a
separate and distinct function.

Basically, human resource planning is concerned with the organization's long and short term goals and how these relate to the available and
needed human resources. A police department, for example, can make an
assessment of future needs based on projected growth in its geographic area
and some estimate of the funding it is likely to receive. By assessing its
present personnel in terms of such factors as age, skill levels, and potential
for advancement, and by including an estimate of losses, the organization can
make forecasts of its future needs.

A business corporation plans for its personnel needs in a similar fashion. The major difference in private sector planning is that the organization
typically has greater control over choices it makes about the kind of organization it wants to be. Organizational choices in the public sector are limited
by the legislative and political process.

Human resource planning also has an important qualitative aspect in
terms of the type individual needed in the future. This, too, is a function of
the organization's goals, strategic planning, and assessment of its future
environment. If the police department anticipates a greater role in dealing
with so-called white-collar crime and a diminishing role in combatting vio-
lence in the streets, it may have to recruit, select, and train a different type
individual than those who have been utilized in the past. Legal requirements
calling for a change in the personnel mix also have to be accounted for.

Human resource planning is the basic function in a personnel program.
Good planning for personnel involves an integrated approach which ties all
the personnel functions together into a comprehensive program that fits the
organization's total planning process.

                Organization   Determination of proper staffing
               Staffing Levels   levels for organizations is rarely
                                          treated in the literature as a separate
personnel function. This omission may result from its not showing up on
organization charts as separate and distinct from other personnel areas.

Nonetheless, determining the proper numbers of persons needed is a
critical factor which must be incorporated into the personnel system. Too
many people and the organization incurs excessive costs; too few people and

the organization risks poor quantity and quality of the goods and services it provides.

Determining personnel levels is a function not always placed in the staff personnel department. Sometimes it is a line responsibility that is administered as part of the total system of cost control. As is true for most personnel functions, it is best handled as a shared responsibility between operating and staff managers.

Recruitment and Selection   Recruitment and selection are two functions usually thought of in conjunction; more than any others they are associated with personnel management. Recruitment consists of finding applicants for positions the organization is trying to fill. While less complex than other functions, recruitment still requires skill, particularly when unique jobs must be filled. It is also more difficult when the labor market is tight or when the organization lacks the financial resources to compete readily for personnel.

Selection consists of making choices among applicants to choose those most qualified. It is important because certain skills and traits are either impossible or difficult to acquire through training and development. Organizational discretion in this area has been greatly restricted in recent years by laws pertaining to equality of employment. For this reason, proper management of the selection process, always important, is even more critical today.

It is easy to think that understanding selection today is a matter of understanding the law. This is far from the case. Even without legal considerations, selection is very complex. It begins with the process of defining exactly what tasks the worker performs, ascertaining the difference between successful and unsuccessful performance, and then relating characteristics in the individual to the performance desired. The chapter on selection discusses this in detail.

Personnel Training   The contribution of training in helping provide workers with the proper skills and abilities is so obvious that this function comes readily to mind when discussing personnel administration. The negative effects of having poorly trained employees and the positive effects of having well-trained employees are apparent in practically all organizations.

Training is often thought of in terms of teaching someone to do something either on the job or in a classroom. This is a very limited view. Training is more accurately thought of as the process of behavior change or behavior modification. This means that all of the stimuli in the organization from year-end bonuses to nods of approval or disapproval by supervisors are having impact upon individual behavior. Training is thus a continuous process that is occurring with or without organizational awareness.

Management Development and Career Planning   Closely related to the training function is that of management development. Training is usually thought of in connection with the hourly employees while management development is associated with college recruiting and other attempts to provide an adequate supply of future managers. The development of a pool of talented personnel available to undertake more demanding jobs is not left to chance in organizations which have good personnel programs. Such a talent pool could result by accident, but more often it is the result of careful planning.

In recent years management development has been affected by the necessity for providing females and minorities with opportunities to move into managerial ranks instead of being clustered in lower level jobs. This has meant increasing attention to these programs to make sure they meet organizational needs as well as social objectives for equality of opportunity. There is little reason to believe that these objectives will be incompatible in well-run programs. It probably does mean, though, that greater sophistication will be required to meet these dual objectives.

Management development is not just college recruiting and training on and off the job. It is the entire process of recruitment, selection, placement, job rotation, performance appraisal, wage and salary administration—in a word, the entire personnel arsenal—to insure that future managers are available in the proper quality and quantity.

In recent years a new personnel function has arisen as an adjunct to management development. It is new enough so that it is just now beginning to make an appearance in some of the larger and more progressive organizations. This is the function of career planning which is undoubtedly due for greater growth.

Career planning is new enough that it does not lend itself to precise definition. Basically it involves balancing the organization's needs for workers, supervisors and managers with the needs and desires of the individual employees. Formerly it was assumed that the organization's needs were paramount and that employee desires automatically followed those of the organization.

Career planning challenges this assumption. It assumes that some nurses in the hospital will wish to become administrators. Others will prefer a career of professional nursing. Some corporate engineers will want to become managers of engineering units. Others may want to become general managers. Still others may wish to pursue totally different careers. It is obviously impossible to meet the desires and expectations of everyone. Career planning seeks to achieve a better balance.

Performance Appraisal   Performance appraisal is essential for a well-run organization. Job performance must be monitored so that performance meets some desired standard. Penalties must be attached to performance which is below standard. Exceptional performance needs to be recognized and rewarded.

Good performance appraisal is important for insuring that the most qualified persons rise to the top of the organization. It also helps insure that those with lesser qualifications do not advance past their capability level.

It is natural and inevitable for humans to assess and evaluate one another. The personnel appraisal process formalizes this natural tendency so that it may best serve organizational purposes.

Wage and Salary Administration   Along with recruitment and selection, wage and salary administration is probably the area most closely identified with personnel management. In an economy which uses money as the principal means of exchange, people must be paid for their work. Numerous constraints exist in this simple sounding process. Many things must happen to effectively realize this objective.

A relationship must be established between the employee's contribution and the wage or salary received. This means that jobs must be ranked in some fashion that corresponds to their contribution. Workers must also perceive their compensation as having a relationship to what they feel is their contribution. This perception is based on concepts of equity in terms of others in the organization as well as others outside the organization.

Consideration in compensation must also be given workers who perform in a superior fashion. The same is true for workers of average performance as well as those below average or unsatisfactory. (This obviously has a relationship to the performance appraisal function which is just one example of the interrelatedness of personnel management processes.)

The organization's wage scale must be related to the external market. Payments must not be made in excess of what the job is worth. At the same time the wage and salary scale must not be so low that it fails to attract or retain workers. Making these determinations when a labor union is involved adds a complicating dimension. All in all, wage and salary administration is one of the more challenging personnel functions.

Productivity and Labor Costs   Productivity does not show on organization charts as a separate and distinct function. This is true even though productivity in a broad sense is the ultimate aim of personnel activities. Productivity is the relationship of input to output. Labor costs are an important component in the overall productivity of the organization. The critical factor is not the absolute dollars paid to workers. It is the relationship of the output received for the dollar paid.

In recent years new programs have begun appearing dealing with worker productivity. They have been brought about by concern with either stagnant or declining productivity levels. Work in the behavioral sciences has contributed to their development.

The programs referred to are job enrichment, behavior modification, organizational development, and changing work schedules. They are designed to foster more positive attitudes towards work and to reduce feelings of malaise and dissatisfaction. They permit greater autonomy and individual decision making. They are supposed to reduce organizational conflict.

They have come about in response to alleged job "alienation," concerns about the "quality of life" and the "new values" of today's worker. By no means is there universal agreement that something called alienation actually exists, that the values of today's worker are radically different, or that the quality of life is a major problem. But there has been concern that industrial societies may be witnessing the disintegration of the social fabric that has generated productive effort under often unpleasant conditions for countless generations. Such programs as those mentioned are attempts to come to grips with this issue. Thus far they have been mostly restricted to the larger business corporations. Where they exist the personnel department usually has responsibility for administering them and monitoring their effectiveness.

Benefits and Services   Programs of fringe or supplementary benefits have become an increasingly important part of the wage and salary package in recent years. They are of two types. Some are required by law and others are offered voluntarily by the employer or obtained through collective bargaining.

Most organizations today also offer many services to their employees. These include such things as credit unions, bowling and softball leagues, subsidized cafeterias, and retirement counseling.

Safety and Health   The Occupational Safety and Health Act of 1970 has had such dramatic impact upon questions of worker safety and health that it is easy to think this function began with its passage. This is not the case at all. Safety as an organizational function has been around for a long time, though mostly confined to manufacturing operations in the private sector.

Safety and health has not always been identified with personnel management. Many organizations in the past have included it as a line function under the production department. The increased emphasis on safety and health brought about by the Occupational Safety and Health Act is changing this. Personnel departments are finding themselves more and more involved in matters of worker safety and health. It also means that organizations other than just those involved in manufacturing are beginning to recognize this as a major function.

Labor Relations   Proper management of the labor relations function is critical for any organization that must bargain collectively with employee organizations. Labor relations exists as a separate function whenever the organization has formally recognized the right of a labor union or union type organization (such as a professional association) to represent and bargain for the workers over wages, hours, and working conditions.

It is critical because decisions made in this area can have such enormous impact. Mistakes made on the side of leniency can saddle the organization with excessive costs which it may have to live with for a long, long time. Attempts to be too strict can result in collective action such as slowdowns and strikes which can be extremely costly. The nature of dealing with a labor organization is such that mistakes are extremely hard to rectify once committed.

Labor relations occurs on two related but separate planes. One is the *negotiation* of the labor contract or agreement. This consists of bargaining over the terms of all the matters that are summed up under the heading of wages, hours and working conditions. It is a well-known process because in the negotiations which occur between large unions and employers, as in the automobile industry, the events are well reported in the media.

The other process is the *administration* of the labor agreement. This is the daily process by which the parties mold from the general terms of the negotiated agreement, the concrete operating particulars of working together. It almost always involves the grievance procedure as hundreds and even thousands of disagreements are resolved over such matters as which worker is entitled to the better paying job.

Practically all organizations that bargain with labor or labor-type organizations centralize much responsibility for this function in the staff personnel or labor relations unit. The union makes it mandatory that policies and procedures be standardized and uniform to an unusually high degree. This involves, as a general rule, limiting the discretion of individual supervisors and placing it in the hands of staff specialists. Especially is this true for matters involving worker grievances.

In the past labor unions were largely confined to the private sector but this has dramatically changed in recent years. Public sector organizations of union type organizations for teachers, police officers and fire departments are quite common.

ORGANIZATION OF THE
PERSONNEL FUNCTION
All organizations have their unique ways to organize the personnel function. Nonetheless, most will show an organization structure related to that shown in Figure 1.

The personnel function is centralized in a personnel department and is a staff function. This department is considered the focal point of personnel activities.

Personnel departments are headed by individuals who bear a variety of titles—personnel manager, director of personnel, personnel administrator, director of industrial relations, and employee relations supervisor for instance. Organizations which bargain with labor organizations often make the distinction between the personnel managers of the unorganized (or nonbargaining unit) personnel and the organized portion.

Personnel departments are typically broken down into smaller specialties that cover the major functions discussed earlier. Large organizations have a combination centralized-decentralized structure. This means a personnel department at central headquarters and separate personnel departments at various subunits such as divisions and plants. Personnel departments at decentralized locations usually have small staffs; the personnel manager may perform all of the personnel functions and is known as a *personnel generalist*. At centralized locations the duties become much more specialized.

In addition to establishing relationships with workers and managers in the organization, the centralized-decentralized nature of the staff personnel function also means that relationships must be established between the headquarters personnel department and the various sub-unit departments. Some organizations give much authority and autonomy to the decentralized units with the central department assuming a coordinating and facilitating role. In other cases authority is retained centrally and the subunits are permitted little discretion.

Line–Staff Relationships
Complicating an understanding of the personnel function and complicating the utilization of the personnel department is the familiar line–staff conflict. The problems of line and staff have been around since the development of modern organizations. Despite numerous attempts in both management theory and practice to eliminate the problem, it still exists, though often in disguised form.

One of the oldest tenets of management theory, the principle of unity of command, suggests that each person in the organization should report to one superior only. The reasoning behind this principle is obvious. More than one superior in the hierarchy can place the subordinate in an untenable

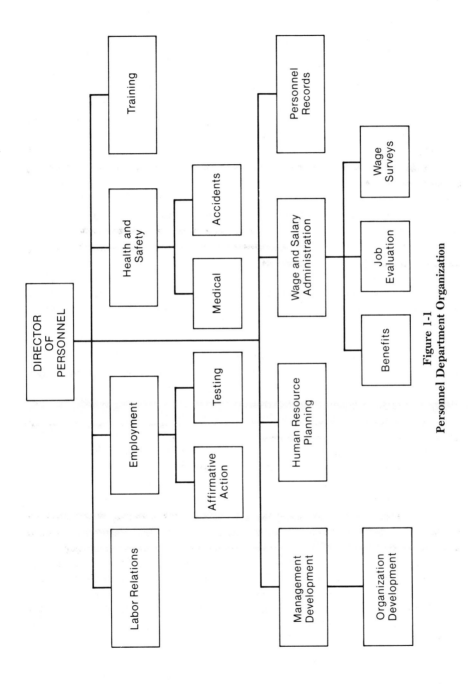

Figure 1-1
Personnel Department Organization

15

position in case of conflicting instructions. Such conflicts have been seen as dysfunctional for the organization.

The staff department such as personnel violates this tenet because in effect it shares responsibility and authority for the organization's personnel with the various operating managers. In years past attempts have been made in management theory to get around this by suggesting that staff departments have an "advisory" function only and that ultimate decision-making power rests with the operating departments. It is generally recognized today that this is a fiction.

In numerous areas staff departments exert direct authority over operating departments. Some staff functions, such as quality control in a production operation, have far more authority than other staff functions such as market research. To account for this some management writers have divided staff departments into three types: advisory, service, and control.[2]

Of all the staff functions the personnel department probably best represents a combination of all three. It is advisory in any matters where an operating manager wishes consultation for a personnel problem. It provides service in numerous ways such as performing wage surveys, recruiting and screening applicants for selection, and assisting employees obtain medical benefits.

In addition the personnel department also acts in a control capacity. It insures compliance with organizational personnel policies. It sees that operating managers abide by federal and state laws. It has direct authority over managers who violate terms of the union contract by doing such things as firing employees without authorization.

It is this control function that produces much of the conflict between the personnel department and the organization. While the extent of this conflict may be exaggerated, it does exist and is something that has to be reckoned with. The problem is exacerbated by the conflict between the dual roles of advisory and control. The advisory role requires a relationship between the personnel department and the operating managers of trust and openness. Assistance in personnel matters is sought only where mutual trust and respect exist. The control function almost automatically establishes an adversary relationship which is not conducive to trust and openness.

It is a fallacy to assume that such conflict in the organization is undesirable. If not carried to excess, such conflict can actually be beneficial. Just as is true of the American political system, organizations are carefully structured systems of checks and balances. The absence of all internal conflict may well signal a breakdown in organizational functioning. At the same time, excessive conflict can be dysfunctional.

[2]Leonard R. Sayles, and George Strauss, *Managing Human Resources*. Englewood Cliffs, N.J.: Prentice-Hall, 1977, Chapters 2 and 3.

DUAL FUNCTIONS OF
PERSONNEL MANAGEMENT

There is another little-understood aspect of personnel management which can produce strained relationships between the personnel department and the organization. Organizations have two major goals for the management of personnel: (1) *productivity*, and (2) *organizational maintenance*.[3] The productivity goal is as the name implies the goal of obtaining maximum output from employees in relationship to cost. Profit making organizations survive in competitive environments by besting competitors through high employee output (in relation to cost). Non-profit making institutions are also concerned with productivity, especially when budgets come under scrutiny and financial resources are diminishing.

The organizational maintenance goal is less obvious. This is the goal of maintaining the organization as a cohesive force in the face of internal and external stress. It has additudinal dimensions relating to worker satisfaction with the job and the organization. It has behavioral dimensions relating to turnover, absenteeism, and positive actions such as courtesy toward organizational clients instead of negative actions such as deliberately damaging equipment.

In the best of all possible worlds these goals would coincide. In fact the early human relations movement was largely based on such an assumption. It was assumed that happy workers are productive workers. Organizational maintenance efforts to make workers more contented with their jobs would also make them more productive.

In more recent years this concept has been discarded as far too simple an assumption for a very complex phenomenon. Most management writers today, particularly in the behavioral sciences, do not accept the doctrine that contented workers are automatically the most productive workers. Studies indicate some positive relationship between satisfaction and turnover and absenteeism. But a consistent relationship between satisfaction and productivity has never been established in studies to date.

Workers may be satisfied because they receive high pay in relation to what is required of them. But the organization may not survive if competing organizations are obtaining higher output at lower cost. The remedy that suggests itself is placing additional demands upon the workers. This may result in some decrease in satisfaction while it increases productivity. But if the organization goes too far and its demands become excessive, workers may retaliate by quitting, absenteeism, work stoppages or other actions which damage productivity.

All organizations whether profit seeking or not walk a tightrope be-

---

[3]John B. Miner, and Mary Green Miner, *Personnel and Industrial Relations: A Managerial Approach*, 3rd ed. New York: Macmillan, 1977, Chapter 1.

tween productivity and organizational maintenance. To a large extent the degree to which the organization strikes a proper balance between these two goals determines whether or not it will be successful in the long run. The personnel decisions that must be made in balancing the two are among the most difficult any organization faces.

For the personnel department this conflict complicates its existence and puts it in an ambivalent position. In effect it must wear two hats. To assist in accomplishing the productivity goal it represents the organization. It helps *monitor workers* to make sure that performance standards are met.

At the same time it has responsibility for organizational maintenance. Here it must represent the worker. It *monitors the organization* to make sure that supervisors do not mistreat and abuse workers.

All organizations are faced with continual internal and external stress, that these goals help create. It is an inevitable fact of existence. The amount of stress will vary from one organization to another. It will also vary within a single organization from one time period to another.

The personnel department becomes the focal point for many of the subtle relationships that exist as a result of this continual tension. Staff personnel managers have a special responsibility for being the buffer and neutralizer of the myriad conflicts that inevitably arise. Rarely are organizations aware this process is occurring. The time this process takes is resented. Personnel departments are criticized for not spending time on "productive" activities which can be tangibly measured.

Nonetheless, the maintenance of that delicate balance between productivity and organizational maintenance represents in many ways one of the greatest contributions that the personnel department makes to the organization. It remains that elusive quality, almost impossible to measure, which seldom receives the recognition it should. It does, however, help distinguish the first rate personnel department from the ordinary.

SUMMARY   The role of personnel management is to provide for the acquisition, maintenance and utilization of the organization's human resources. Personnel management exists in two forms. One is the relationship between the individual manager and his or her subordinates. The other is a staff function which had its origins at the turn of the century when the staff concept was first introduced into modern industrial organizations. All organizations regardless of size have a personnel function. Only when an organization reaches a certain size does it formally appear as a staff function on the organization chart.

There are many functions in personnel management including human resource planning, recruitment and selection, training, management development, career planning, wage and salary administration, performance appraisal, and labor relations. Some of the newer functions in personnel management are in areas such as organization development, which is devoted to improving the relationship between the worker and the work performed, and job enrichment, a process designed to increase individual autonomy and decision making.

Personnel staff departments are organized in a variety of ways. A distinction is often made between the personnel manager of the workers not organized into a labor union and the labor relations or industrial relations director in charge of the organized sector of the labor force. Large organizations, particularly business corporations with decentralized operations, have both centralized personnel departments at corporate and division headquarters and centralized departments at the plant and branch locations.

Personnel departments have all the traditional problems associated with line–staff conflict in organizations. The job of personnel is particularly complicated by the responsibility it has for the personnel goal of organizational maintenance while much of the line organization is concerned with the goal of productivity. These two goals can conflict and put the personnel department in an ambiguous position.

SELECTED REFERENCES

GLEUCK, WILLIAM F., *Personnel—A Diagnostic Approach*, rev. ed. Dallas, Texas: Business Publications, 1978.

MARSHALL, WILLIAM R., *Administering the Company Personnel Function*. Englewood Cliffs, N.J.: Prentice-Hall, 1976.

MINER, JOHN B. and MARY GREEN MINER, *Personnel and Industrial Relations: A Managerial Approach*, 3rd ed. New York: Macmillan, 1977.

ROBBINS, STEPHEN P., *Personnel: The Management of Human Resources*. Englewood Cliffs, N.J.: Prentice-Hall, 1978.

SAYLES, LEONARD R. and GEORGE STRAUSS, *Managing Human Resources*. Englewood Cliffs, N.J.: Prentice-Hall, 1977.

SIKULA, ANDREW F., *Personnel Administration and Human Resources Management*. New York: John Wiley, 1976.

2

PERSONNEL MANAGEMENT AND PUBLIC POLICY

⟸ IDEAS TO BE FOUND ⟹
IN THIS CHAPTER

- Evolution of public policy
- Protective labor legislation
- Compensation, selection and hiring laws
- Retirement, training and safety and health legislation
- Laws governing labor relations

No area in personnel administration has become as important in recent years as that of government policy. Federal and state legislation has been growing rapidly. The rulings of quasi-judicial regulatory agencies have multiplied. From the trial, appellate and high courts of the federal and state governments come seemingly endless decisions. Rather than showing signs of diminishing, there is every indication the trend will continue.

Legislation and litigation dealing with employee relations have been around since this country's earliest days. (The first recorded prosecution of striking workers took place in 1806.) Developing an acceptable public policy has not proved easy. The nature of this country's constitutional government, imbued with the philosophy of Adam Smith and free enterprise, has not provided a climate readily adaptable to government regulation. Many of the issues are still being wrestled with.

This chapter provides a survey of legislation dealing with the employer–employee relationship; later chapters examine this legislation in more detail. The evolution and development of public policy is also examined.

EVOLUTION
OF PUBLIC POLICY

Seeing the historical development of public policy within this country's economic, social, and legal climate helps us understand public policy today.[1] For convenience, it is helpful to think in terms of: (1) an *early* period of protective labor legislation beginning in the nineteenth century and lasting through the 1930s, (2) a *transition* period from the 1940s to the early 1960s, and (3) a *modern* period beginning in the early 1960s.

The Early Period

The United States economy has historically been organized around the concepts of a market society. A pure market system implies the absence of regulation, competition providing the mechanism by which the production and distribution of goods and services takes place.

Among many problems created by unregulated competition is the pressure placed upon employers to take actions that may not be consonant with the best interests of employees. Using low cost child labor, not paying compensation for job related injuries, and cutting wages during periods of labor surplus are some of the harmful results necessitated by the relentless pressure of competition to hold down costs.

Thus, the earliest laws dealing with employer–employee relations were designed to protect workers from the hazards of unrestrained competition. From this came the descriptive term *protective labor legislation*. The period of protective labor legislation began in a rudimentary form early in the nineteenth century and extended through the 1930s. The major issues of this period were: (1) the use of children in factories and mines, (2) work-connected deaths and injuries, (3) low wage levels for women and children, (4) persons too old to work, and (5) unemployed persons unable to find work.

Child labor legislation began as concern for the education of working children. Connecticut passed the first law in 1813, though it was never enforced, and Massachusetts passed the first effective law in 1838. Both acts required that working children receive a specified minimum level of education. In addition to education, by 1853 seven states had passed laws limiting the hours of work for young persons under a certain age.

By 1910 approximately one-third of the states had child labor laws. There was wide variation as to how restrictive the laws were and how well they were enforced. There was concern that states were using such laws or their lack as a competitive weapon to attract or retain industry. To standardize such laws various groups supported a federal child labor measure.

Congress enacted a child labor law in 1917. In 1918 the U.S. Supreme

[1] For the best historical source on public policy see U.S. Department of Labor, *Growth of Labor Law in the United States*, Washington: U.S. Government Printing Office, 1967.

Court struck it down as unconstitutional.[2] The Supreme Court ruled that the Constitution does not specifically grant the power to regulate industrial relations to the federal government. It said this power does not exist since the tenth amendment reserves to the states all powers not expressly granted the federal government.

Congress made several attempts to circumvent the ruling but all were struck down. In 1924 Congress passed a child labor amendment; by 1930 only six states had ratified it. It never received enough support to become part of the Constitution.

In 1938 the issue was resolved when Congress passed the *Fair Labor Standards Act*. This act, which included child labor provisions for firms engaged in interstate commerce, was found constitutional in 1941.[3]

Another issue that surfaced in the nineteenth century was the question of who should bear the costs if a worker were injured or killed on the job. With the growth of industry and increasing hazards of the work place, this became a serious problem. Under early doctrine the worker or the estate in case of death could collect monetary damages only by taking the employer to court and proving negligence. But even so, the employer had numerous defenses under common law.

In the latter part of the nineteenth century a movement began to adopt a concept pioneered in Europe that compensated the worker without regard to fault. This concept reached fruition in the form of *workmen's compensation* laws (referred to in recent years as "workers' compensation"). These laws required the employer to insure workers against job related injuries or death without regard to negligence or responsibility. The federal government enacted the first such law for certain federal employees in 1908. Wisconsin in 1911 had the first state law to take effect, and by 1920 all but six states had such laws on their books.

Early *minimum wage* laws were passed under the inherent police power of the state. This power grants the state the right to pass laws to protect the citizenry. By putting a floor on the compensation level for women and children, the minimum wage was intended to provide protection for these two groups. The first minimum wage law was enacted by Massachusetts in 1912. By 1923 a total of seventeen states had enacted such laws, all dealing with women and children.

In that year the U.S. Supreme Court struck down a District of Columbia minimum wage law saying it was in violation of the fourteenth amendment to the Constitution.[4] This amendment prohibits deprivation of "life, liberty or property without due process of law." The court in effect said the

---

[2]*Hammer v. Dagenhart*, 247 U.S. 251 (1918).

[3]*United States v. Darby*, 312 U.S. 100 (1941).

[4]*Adkins v. Children's Hospital*, 261 U.S. 525 (1923).

minimum wage was an illegal interference in the right of employer and employee to freely enter into an employment contract of their own choosing.

In 1937 the Supreme Court reversed its stand of 1923 in a case from the state of Washington.[5] A year later in 1938, with passage of the Fair Labor Standards Act, Congress established a minimum wage for private sector firms in interstate commerce. (Earlier action by Congress had established a minimum wage for employees of the federal government as well as some government related employment.)

Social Security, so taken for granted today, was a daring concept when passed by Congress in 1935. Its premise was that employers and employees should be taxed to provide some financial assistance for workers when they retired. It was a form of retirement insurance provided by the federal government from matching contributions paid by employer and employee. While many changes have occurred in Social Security since that time, the basic premise remains operative today.

Unemployment insurance, another radical concept when enacted, was passed as part of the same measure. It was paid by employers as a tax on payrolls and was designed to assist employees during periods of involuntary unemployment. The system is basically the same today.

The Transition Period

The 1930s closed with the concept of protective labor legislation well established at both the state and federal levels and with the major legal hurdles surmounted. With the 1940s came a two-decade period in which programs were strengthened and expanded. It also marked a transition between the long struggle of the early period and the programs of modern times.

While the 1940s and 1950s were a relatively quiescent time, they were still marked by a peculiar measure that was enacted in 1946. Many economists believe it to be one of the most influential economic measures of recent decades.

The legislation referred to is the *Employment Act of 1946*, popularly known as the "full employment" bill. It had no enabling provisions. No regulatory agencies were established. Nothing was prohibited. It said simply that the government should take action to maintain employment at high levels, but only in a manner designed to foster free enterprise.

The act in effect pledged all future administrations to take an active role in economic affairs. It provided Congressional sanction for a different role for government from the early philosophy of laissez-faire and it helped build the climate that would eventually result in such recent legislation as that dealing with equal employment opportunity.

Other than this somewhat unique measure, the transition period was

[5]*West Coast Hotel v. Parrish*, 300 U.S. 379 (1937).

not noted for any innovative legislation. This was to change with the 1960s when there was a distinct turn in public policies and programs.

The Modern Period The modern period of public policy began with the administration of John F. Kennedy in 1961 and it was continued by his successor in office, Lyndon B. Johnson. Because government activity was greatly increased, it is often referred to as the period of an "active" public policy.

The new public policy was designed primarily for those who had never had adequate access to the labor force—the Appalachian mountaineer, the black in the ghetto, persons of Hispanic origin, the unskilled, females, the handicapped—all those persons and groups who were to become categorized by the term "disadvantaged." This period was characterized by three major objectives outlined in the 1964 Manpower Report of the President:

1. the creation of jobs
2. developing the ability of workers
3. matching workers with jobs

There is a danger of oversimplification to see in the modern period a sharp break with the past. Many programs to accomplish these objectives had been enacted long before and during the Depression. Land grant colleges were founded in the 1840s, vocational education was started in 1917, jobs were created by such programs as the Works Projects Administration and the Civilian Conservation Corps during the 1930s.

But it did represent a break in signaling a greater government commitment to bring disadvantaged persons into the mainstream of American economic life. Much modern legislation including attempts to end discrimination can be traced to this commitment.

CURRENT LEGISLATION AFFECTING THE EMPLOYMENT RELATIONSHIP Much legislation dealing with the employment relationship is duplicated at the federal and state levels. In some cases federal law applies exclusively to organizations in interstate commerce and state law to organizations in intrastate commerce. This is largely true, with some exceptions, of legislation dealing with labor organizations.

In other cases there is overlapping jurisdiction. This usually means the higher or more restrictive standard (from the employer's point of view) applies. This is the case with equal opportunity laws. Minimum wage laws are similar. States can require a higher (but not a lower) minimum wage for firms in interstate commerce.

In yet other situations there is joint administration between the federal

24

and state governments. For unemployment insurance the federal government establishes minimum standards and some supplemental financing but the programs are largely under state control and financing.

Compensation The principal federal legislation in the compensation area is the *Fair Labor Standards Act* (1938) also known as the *Wage–Hour Act*. It is administered by the Wage–Hour Administrator in the Department of Labor and stipulates minimum wages which must be paid persons who work in organizations which come under its jurisdiction. It also specifies that persons who work in excess of forty hours a week must be paid at the rate of time and one-half for overtime.

Additionally there are numerous other statutes dealing with minimum wages and other matters. the *Walsh–Healey Public Contracts Act* (1935) requires minimum wage payments and overtime pay for government contractors with contracts over $10,000. The *Davis–Bacon Act* (1931) provides certain stipulated minimum wage payments for mechanics and laborers on public projects. The *National Foundation on Arts and Humanities Act* (1940) is a little known piece of legislation which covers performers, laborers, and mechanics employed directly for the foundation or certain contractors and subcontractors receiving federal assistance. It requires that workers doing similar work as that in the local labor market be paid the same rate of pay.

The *Work Hours Standards Act* (1962) covers mechanics and laborers employed on public works and those connected with dredging or rock excavations in any river or harbor. It requires overtime pay at the rate of time and one-half for hours in excess of forty. The *Service Contract Act* (1965) covers employers with government service contracts in excess of $2,500. It requires payments at the local rate but at no less than the minimum wage. The *Copeland Anti-Kickback Act* (1954) covers employees on any federally financed public project and prohibits the use of coercion in requiring employees to give up part of their compensation.

Discrimination in matters of compensation is covered by the *Equal Pay Act* (1963). This act prohibits differences in compensation based on sex and is administered by the Wage-Hour Administrator.

At the federal level garnishment of wages is covered by Title III, *Consumer Credit Protection Act* (1968). It limits garnishments of paychecks to 75 percent of the employee's disposable earnings or thirty times the federal minimum hourly wage, whichever is greater. It also prohibits discharge for a single garnishment. *State Measures:*

In addition to federal measures, a majority of the states have minimum wage legislation. Most states also have provisions for overtime pay. There is considerable variation among the states in the scope of these laws. All states provide for some regulation of wage garnishments.

Additionally, nearly all the states have laws regulating the payment of wages. These deal with such matters as the frequency with which employees must be paid, the method of payment, wage payments upon termination of work, and wage payments if an employee dies. Over half of the states also have their own equal pay statutes.

Selection and Hiring   At the federal level the primary selection legislation is Title VII, *Civil Rights Act* (1964). This act bars discrimination based on race, color, religion, sex, or national origin and established the Equal Employment Opportunity Commission (EEOC) which is the regulatory body charged with enforcing its provisions. It was amended in 1972 by the *Equal Employment Opportunity Act*. This amendment expanded coverage of Title VII to state government employees and provided limited enforcement powers for the EEOC (which had none under the 1964 act).

Discrimination against workers between the ages of 40 and 70 is prohibited by the *Age Discrimination in Employment Act* (1967).[6] The *Vocational Rehabilitation Act* (1973) has provisions to assist in the hiring, placement, and advancement of handicapped persons. It also requires government contractors and subcontractors to have affirmative action programs for the handicapped. The *Veterans' Readjustment Act* (1974) provides for employment opportunities for veterans and handicapped veterans of the Vietnam war period.

In addition to this legislation a series of Presidential Executive Orders has been issued beginning with Lyndon Johnson. These provide for anti-discrimination and affirmative action programs by government agencies and government contractors and subcontractors. The Office of Federal Contract Compliance (OFCC) was established under Executive Order.

Hiring of minors is regulated by the *Fair Labor Standards Act*. It requires a minimum age of 16 for most jobs and establishes 18 as the minimum for hazardous jobs. Employment of those younger than 16 is limited to certain non-manufacturing and non-mining occupations. Minors under 16 also cannot be employed in farm work during school hours.

Another category dealing with hiring practices is that concerning veterans of the armed forces. These rights have been established by numerous *Selective Service Acts* and date back to World War II. They specify that a veteran is entitled to be rehired into a former job or position of similar nature.

In addition to legislation at the federal level, over thirty states have laws similar to Title VII of the Civil Rights Act. All states also have legislation regulating child labor.

---

[6]As originally passed age limits were 40 to 65, but a 1978 amendment increased the upper limit to 70.

Training   In 1973 Congress passed the *Com-*
                                              prehensive Employment and Training
Act (CETA) which amended and replaced the *Manpower Development and Training Act* (1962). This legislation provides a broad range of training and job opportunities for disadvantaged, unemployed, and underemployed persons. It has provisions for financial assistance to employers who provide entry level training for disadvantaged persons and retraining for those whose skills have become obsolete.

Apprenticeship training for the skilled trades is provided under the *National Apprenticeship Act* (1937). This is a program that for several decades has been a cooperative venture participated in by government, business, and labor unions. Under the act the government establishes standards and provides assistance for a combination of on-the-job and off-the-job training and study to increase the supply of skilled workers.

At the state level the major training legislation of significance is that enacted by twenty-nine states which have established apprenticeship agencies which work in close cooperation with the federal government's apprenticeship system. These programs supplement and complement the national program.

Safety and Health   Employee safety and health are cov-
                                             ered by the relatively new *Occupa-*
tional Safety and Health Act (OSHA) of 1970. Basically the act empowers the federal government to establish safety and health standards for the work environment. Implementation and enforcement are provided for through a number of advisory and regulatory commissions, agencies, and committees.

The Occupational Safety and Health Act is federal legislation, but it does provide that any state which desires to assume responsibility for safety and health matters within its jurisdiction can submit an operational plan to the Secretary of Labor. Specific criteria which must be met are specified and the state plan must be at least as effective as the federal program. Numerous states have submitted such plans, but not all have passed enabling legislation. Some have been withdrawn after submission.

Through the Social Security program the federal government provides another form of protection for workers who are under its coverage. For the worker who becomes partially or totally disabled and is unable to work, or is unable to work on a full-time basis, Social Security payments are made to replace at least a portion of lost income. In cases of permanent, total disability, the payments continue for life.

Workers' compensation comes under state jurisdiction. These programs are designed for protection of the worker against work related accidents and certain occupationally connected illnesses. Compensation is with-

27

out regard to fault or negligence. A portion of medical expenses and lost income are covered. The employer bears all the cost.

Jurisdiction of the State

All states have such programs. There is wide variation as to coverage and benefits. There is also variation in methods of financing. Some states require the employer to insure with a state-managed fund while others give another option of buying insurance from a private company. A few states permit the employer to self-insure. Attempts have been made in recent years to bring workers' compensation under federal control, but such efforts have not been successful.

In addition to workers' compensation, several states have temporary disability insurance programs. These are similar to the disability provisions of Social Security. They provide coverage for nonwork-related disabilities which prevent the employee from working.

Retirement

Retirement assistance for private sector employees is strictly a federal function. Two major pieces of legislation deal with retirement. The older of the two is the *Social Security Act* (1935) which is an extensive program providing financial benefits for persons retiring beginning at age 62. The program is a familiar one since it has been in existence for so long and covers such a large percentage of the workforce. It is financed by matching employer–employee contributions. For organizations which come under its jurisdiction, contributions to the Social Security program are mandatory for both employer and employee. Social Security payments are not intended to provide the sole source of support for retired individuals but are designed as supplements to pensions, personal savings, and other means of support.

The newer legislation in this area is the *Employee Retirement Income Security Act* (ERISA) passed by Congress in 1974. ERISA is a very complex measure and is designed to provide protection for employees who are covered under private pension plans. It was enacted after many years of concern that employees often found themselves for a variety of reasons not receiving their pension benefits upon retirement.

The act specifies certain vesting rights for employees. This means the employee after a designated time period acquires ownership of the funds in the pension plan and does not lose them upon termination. Among its numerous provisions the act also establishes regulations or standards for funding the plans; this helps insure that the funds are available for the employee upon retirement.

Protection Against Unemployment

Primary protection for the worker during periods of unemployment (for reasons not connected with health) is provided by the combined federal–state program of *unemployment insurance*.

This program came into existence in 1935 as part of the Social Security Act. The act provided for a tax on employer payrolls which in effect would be rebated to states which established programs of unemployment insurance which met minimum federal standards. All states have unemployment insurance programs.

While unemployment insurance is a combined federal–state program, primary responsibility in this area rests with the states. Financing is provided by a tax levied on employer payrolls without contribution on the part of the employee. The tax is a graduated one, with levels based on the unemployment or turnover experience of the employer.

Payments to the worker are designed to cover periods of job loss of a relatively temporary nature. Thus, maximum periods of coverage are usually for fifty-two weeks, though sometimes this is extended during periods of high unemployment. Benefits are typically scaled in a range between 50 to 75 percent of base pay, with both benefits, eligibility requirements and other provisions subject to wide variations among the states.

Labor Relations and Collective Bargaining

Two different sets of laws and regulations govern collective bargaining between organizations and unions (as well as associations which bargain collectively for their members). One is the set of laws and enactments for the private sector and the other for the public sector. While there are similarities in the provisions, the applicable statutes and executive enactments are completely distinct.

At the federal level the private sector is under the jurisdiction of the *Labor-Management Relations Act*, passed by Congress in 1935 and known at that time as the *Wagner Act*. This is a comprehensive measure which governs in great detail the relations between employer and employee in private sector firms involved in interstate commerce.

The Labor-Management Relations Act was amended in 1947 by the *Taft-Hartley Act* and again in 1959 by the *Landrum-Griffin Act*. The Labor-Management Relations Act as amended by Taft-Hartley is a comprehensive measure. It establishes the right of employees to select representatives of *(unions)* their own choosing for purposes of collective bargaining and establishes election procedures for implementing this right. Employers are required to recognize the union and to bargain with it over wages, hours, and working conditions when the union wins a supervised election.

The act further establishes the National Labor Relations Board (NLRB) to conduct representation elections and to rule on unfair labor practice charges by both parties. These unfair labor practices for both unions and companies are spelled out in the act and provide the framework under which the parties must operate. The act is quite long and contains procedures for handling national emergency strikes.

The Landrum-Griffin Act basically subjects unions to more internal control by the government. It provides a so-called "bill of rights" for union members, stricter financial reporting and disclosure, rules governing union trusteeships, and rules for the conduct of union elections.

In addition to this legislation, the parties must operate under the body of rulings established by procedures under which the National Labor Relations Board operates. These rulings are subject to review by the courts.

Labor relations in the railroad industry is governed by the *Railway Labor Act* (1926). This is a measure passed prior to the Wagner Act which contains many procedures later adopted when the Wagner Act was passed. It basically provides for collective bargaining between railroad employees and management including representation elections and machinery for resolving disputes. In 1936, the act was amended to include air transport as well as railroads.

In the public sector, there is no comprehensive measure equivalent to the Labor-Management Relations Act. Labor relations for federal government employees are regulated by *Executive Order 10988*, issued by President Kennedy in 1960, and by President Nixon's *Executive Order 11491*, made effective in 1970. These orders provide procedures for federal employees to form unions and to bargain collectively. The primary administrative agencies dealing with these laws are the Federal Labor Relations Council and the Federal Services Impasses Panel.

Jurisdictional questions between the federal government and the states over private sector labor relations are very complex. Both legislation and judicial decisions have provided a framework in this area. Basically state governments can regulate industrial relations for firms in intrastate commerce provided such regulation does not conflict with federal law.

There are a variety of state laws dealing with private sector labor relations. Some have legislation similar to the federal Labor-Management Relations Act. Others restrict labor organizations through "right-to-work" laws prohibiting compulsory union membership.

States also deal differently with state and municipal employees. Practically all have legislation permitting collective bargaining for at least some states and local employees. Some permit collective bargaining for practically all and even permit strikes under certain conditions.

SUMMARY The fastest growing area in personnel management is that of government regulation of the employment relationship. Public policy began in the early nineteenth century with laws designed to protect workers from the hazards of an unrestrained market system. Minimum wage laws, workman's compensation measures, child labor laws, old age assistance, and unemployment protection were passed during this period which lasted through the 1930s. Much early legislation was found unconstitutional, but later decisions changed this.

A transition period lasted from the 1940s to the early 1960s. A more active role for the government in economic matters was set forth in the Employment Act of 1946. The modern period began with the administration of John F. Kennedy. Government activity was greatly increased with primary emphasis upon bringing the disadvantaged into the economic mainstream.

Today legislation of all types governs the relationship between employer and employee. This legislation is found at both the federal and state level, with overlapping jurisdiction in some cases and with clear zones of authority in others. Principal measures of concern are Title VII of the Civil Rights Act, dealing with discrimination in employment; the Fair Labor Standards Act, prescribing minimum wages and restrictions on the employment of minors; the Occupational Safety and Health Act and Workers' Compensation in matters pertaining to employee health and safety; the Labor–Management Relations Act which establishes a framework for collective bargaining in the private sector between union and management; and Social Security and the Employee Retirement Income Security Act which provides assistance and protection for retired workers.

SELECTED REFERENCES

BUREAU OF NATIONAL AFFAIRS, INC., *Policy and Practice Series* (Personnel Management, Labor Relations, Fair Employment Practices, Compensation). Washington, D.C.: BNA, Inc., 1977.

GREENMAN, RUSSELL L. and ERIC J. SCHMERTZ, *Personnel Administration and the Law*. Washington, D.C.: BNA, Inc., 1972.

HAMNER, W. CLAY and FRANK L. SCHMIDT, eds., *Contemporary Problems in Personnel*, rev. ed. Chicago: St. Clair Press, 1977.

MINER, MARY GREEN and JOHN B. MINER, *Policy Issues in Contemporary Personnel and Industrial Relations*. New York: Macmillan, 1977.

TAYLOR, BENJAMIN J. and FRED WITNEY, *Labor Relations Law*, 2nd ed. Englewood Cliffs, N.J.: Prentice-Hall, 1975.

U.S. DEPARTMENT OF LABOR, *Growth of Labor Law in the United States*. Washington, D.C.: U.S. Government Printing Office, 1967.

PART

2

PLANNING
FOR
HUMAN
RESOURCES

3

HUMAN
RE/OURCE
PLANNING

◀━ IDEAS TO BE FOUND ━▶
IN THIS CHAPTER

- Quantitative forecasting of needs
- Qualitative planning
- Labor force analysis
- Need for continuing organizational monitoring
- Integrating the personnel program

The organization requires personnel of the right quantity and quality who are available when needed. Human resource planning exists to accomplish that goal. It integrates the organization's overall planning with the personnel function. The term human resource planning is a newer term for the function traditionally referred to as manpower planning. It is an area that has shown much development in recent years.

Lack of planning for human resources means that organizations are constantly facing crises because of a shortage of talent or because surpluses exist. Either situation is detrimental to the organization's interests. Crisis management can never be avoided completely. But a well conceived plan of where the organization is headed and how its human resources must be adapted to help get it there can contribute greatly to the accomplishment of organizational goals.

Human resource planning involves two parts. One is an analysis for determining the *quantitative* needs of the organization—how many persons will be needed in the future under specified conditions of growth, stagnation, or even decline. The other part is a *qualitative* analysis to determine what the people should be like—what qualities and characteristics will be needed, assuming some idea of the organization's future direction.

Additionally human resource planning involves an analysis of the labor market to determine future labor supply and demand. It requires a continual program of organizational monitoring to evaluate the effectiveness of the personnel function. And, finally, an overall plan is essential for integrating all personnel functions into a cohesive program. This chapter looks at the process.

QUANTITATIVE FORECASTING

There are numerous models available for human resource planning, ranging from the very simple to the extremely sophisticated. Regardless of their degree of complexity, all models must incorporate the basic components shown in Figure 3-1.

As the figure shows, the process involves a census or assessment of the organization's current human resources, an estimate of losses, an assessment of which positions will not be replaced, and an estimate of future growth. From these factors an estimate of the numbers needed for the future can be made.

Assessing Current Talent Available

The first step in quantitative human resource planning is to make an accurate assessment of current talent available. There are many bases on which this can be done. A personnel assessment by age offers a look at possible problem areas because of heavy retirements in the future. An assessment by skill level may show deficiencies in personnel with needed skills (or may show an excess of certain abilities). An assessment by management potential will highlight whether or not the organization has an adequate pool of future executives.

Once the bases for assessment have been determined, the organization must decide what classifications to use. Categories should not be so broad as to be of no value, but not so narrow as to prove unworkable because of the large numbers. An age assessment might be done by five- or ten-year intervals. Skill levels may be broken down into highly skilled, semiskilled, and unskilled. Management might be classified as top management, upper middle management, middle management, and first line supervision. Organizations should use categories that fit their particular needs. Some may find clerical and factory positions useful for classification. Others will use bargaining unit and non-bargaining unit personnel as a starting point.

Additionally, a decision must be made as to how far down in the organization such assessment or inventories should be carried. Global inventories in extremely large organizations may prove so broad as to be of little

36

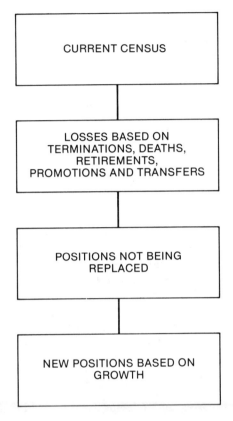

```
┌─────────────────────────┐
│                         │
│     CURRENT CENSUS      │
│                         │
└────────────┬────────────┘
             │
┌────────────┴────────────┐
│     LOSSES BASED ON     │
│  TERMINATIONS, DEATHS,  │
│       RETIREMENTS,      │
│ PROMOTIONS AND TRANSFERS│
└────────────┬────────────┘
             │
┌────────────┴────────────┐
│                         │
│   POSITIONS NOT BEING   │
│         REPLACED        │
│                         │
└────────────┬────────────┘
             │
┌────────────┴────────────┐
│                         │
│  NEW POSITIONS BASED ON │
│          GROWTH         │
│                         │
└─────────────────────────┘
```

Figure 3-1
Basic Components in Quantitative
Human Resource Forecasting

value. But with the overall inventory as a starting point, it may prove useful to carry it out at the division, plant, or even department level.

In Table 3-1 for example, a global inventory of the entire organization indicates that 5 percent of the workforce will be retiring in the next five years. The organization could presumably cope with this very easily. But a breakdown by division shows that Division C has 22 percent of its workforce in that category. This information is important for planning purposes since much effort will be required to cope with a loss of that magnitude.

In addition, the organization may find it useful to break the categories down further. It may be in Division C that the bulk of the 22 percent retiring may be heavily concentrated in skilled workers or in the clerical staff or in the supervisory ranks. Each situation will require different approaches in finding replacements. This underscores the point made earlier. The organization should utilize those classifications which will prove most useful.

Table 3-1
Organizational Retirement Census

	Total Number of Employees	Number Within Five Years of Retirement	Percentage Within Five Years of Retirement
Entire Organization	3480	174	5%
Division A	1287	33	3
Division B	592	41	7
Division C	322	70	22
Division D	1279	30	2

Estimating Losses   The next step is to make an estimate of losses. There are four ways in which losses occur: (1) retirements, (2) promotions and transfers, (3) terminations (voluntary and involuntary), and (4) deaths.

Retirements pose the least problem, especially if the organization has a mandatory retirement policy. A simple count from personnel records will show those reaching retirement age. Those approaching retirement age can be surveyed to see who plans early retirement.

Even without a mandatory retirement age retirement forecasting poses few problems. Retirement decisions are seldom made suddenly. Those at the ages when retirement normally occurs can be surveyed periodically. The estimate derived will be accurate enough for planning purposes.

The other categories under losses pose more difficulties. If it is assumed that conditions in the future will be similar to conditions in the past, an estimate using historical data can be helpful. Table 3-2 shows the type of historical data that can be used.

The data in Table 3-2 is for an organization's most recent five-year period. By taking an average of the five years, it is found that slightly over 2.5 percent of the supervisors have terminated annually. If it is felt that the forecast period will reflect comparable conditions, then this figure can be

Table 3-2
Terminations of First Line Supervisors

Year	Average Number of Supervisors	Terminations	Percentage Terminating
1	2190	31	1.4%
2	2240	48	2.1
3	2260	111	5.0
4	2310	62	2.6
5	2400	56	2.3

used. If expectations are that future conditions will reflect the third year when 5 percent terminated, this percentage would be appropriate.

The same procedure can be used for estimating deaths, promotions, and transfers. There is nothing magic about any of the numbers used. The fact that the arithmetic shows the percentages carried to one decimal place might give a spurious sense of accuracy that does not exist in forecasting. Estimates, no matter how calculated, are nothing more than that.

Positions not being replaced

Estimating Replacements   An estimate must be made of jobs which will be eliminated. Some jobs will no longer exist because of changes in technology. The organization may be reducing its commitment in certain areas. A reorganization of duties may have eliminated the need for certain positions.

If the organization plans transfers or outright dismissals for the affected employees, this can be built directly into the forecast. If the organization plans to follow a policy of attrition by which positions are not filled as people leave, this must be estimated. Often the best way of determining this is a job-by-job assessment of the areas under question. This should be done in conjunction with managers familiar with the areas and with the organization's plans.

The positions not being replaced must be subtracted from losses. They represent a reduction in the number of new persons needed.

Estimating New Position   The most difficult forecast to make is a
Requirements   determination of future members based on expected growth. Few attempts in this area have been consistently successful. Growth and attrition are not necessarily mutually exclusive. Growth in certain areas of the organization may be creating new jobs at the same time that jobs are being reduced in other areas.

The key factor in making growth projections is finding out what measure or measures of the organization relate to the size of the work force. This will differ among industries and from organization to organization. For business firms it would appear that sales volume would be the significant variable. But for many types of business organizations sales volume will have only a limited relationship to the size of the work force. In many organizations once an initial work force has been acquired additional sales can be generated with little additional help.

Production volume would seem on the surface to be closely related to the number of persons needed. But while some relationship may exist, it does not necessarily proceed in a linear or even fashion. For example, an organization may find that anything up to a 15 percent production increase involves only a marginal increase in the number of new persons needed. But if the production forecast calls for a 20 percent increase, it may be necessary to open a whole new assembly line or even a new plant. This could result in a big increase in the numbers required. This figure might hold fairly constant for anything up to an additional 10 percent production increase. At this point another big jump may occur.

In some organizations the number of claims processed or units shipped may be the key variables. In yet others the size of the operating budget may be the critical factor. In most cases where variables can be found it will be necessary to combine two or more in some kind of regression analysis to improve predictive ability.

For the public sector the determination of needs based on growth is both easier and more difficult at the same time. It is easier in the sense that a certain stability exists for most organizations in the public sector that is not always true for the private sector. It is more difficult because funding in the public sector is not only dependent upon demand for services but upon the political process.

In profit-seeking organizations increased demand for product or service is normally translated into increased revenues. These increased revenues are the means for adding staff. By contrast the state public health department may face an increasing demand for its services. But this may be accompanied by a cut in appropriations if the political climate is unfavorable. This complicates any kind of forecasting model.

While it would be desirable to have a mathematical formula by which future members could be determined, many organizations have attempted without success to find some variable or combination of variables which will provide consistently accurate forecasts. In these cases something as simple as canvassing unit managers for their estimates of future personnel requirements may be the best method. Obviously some managers will inflate such estimates in hope of acquiring more people. These inflated estimates will have to be adjusted downward.

Another thing which must be accounted for is changes in labor productivity. This refers to the amount of output obtained for the amount of labor input used. If productivity is increasing, meaning more output for each unit of labor input, then correspondingly fewer persons will be needed. If productivity is decreasing, then additional numbers will be required.

The Outcome

Starting with a current census of whatever category is being forecast, estimating losses, subtracting out the number of positions not being replaced, and then adding in needs based on growth, the organization now has an estimate of its future requirements. The forecast can be made for as many years as desired. The margin of possible error increases with the length of the forecast.

One further matter should be noted in quantitative forecasting. Any forecasting involves assumptions which may prove incorrect. Thus it is desirable that several forecasts be made under different sets of assumptions. This way the organization can plan strategies for various contingencies. It is less likely to be caught by surprise if the assumptions behind any one forecast prove incorrect.

QUALITATIVE HUMAN RESOURCE PLANNING

Assessing the *qualitative* aspects of future needs is an entirely different process from quantitative forecasting. Qualitative forecasting refers to the traits, skills, attitudes, aptitudes and personality characteristics of the future work force. Complexity is added because individuals will not necessarily need the qualities associated with successful performance today. Rather they should have the characteristics associated with successful performance in the future.

The two would be the same if the organization and its environment were to remain static. This type of stability rarely exists. It is the existence of continual change that modifies the organization's jobs. This in turn modifies the characteristics of the persons needed to fill the jobs.

Assessing needs on qualitative dimensions involves two fundamental concepts in personnel management. One is what behaviors or organizational outcomes constitute successful performance. This is called the *job success criterion*. The other is the characteristics in the individual which are related to successful performance. This is the *job specification*.

For simple jobs specifying successful performance may not be too difficult. For example a person might have a repetitive task of welding two parts together. Successful performance could be defined as making neat welds that hold permanently, doing a specified number during a prescribed time period, and meeting acceptable standards in such things as attendance and honesty. For higher level jobs of a supervisory, professional, or executive nature, the problem becomes more complex.

Specifications for the welding job may be a certain score on a manual dexterity test, a literacy level that permits reading simple instructions, elementary calculating skills for completing production records, and evidence of satisfactory attendance on previous jobs. For more complex jobs the specifications will be of a higher level.

For present jobs it is possible to determine empirically which characteristics are associated with successful performance. This is not the case with future jobs since these are not in existence yet. The organization, therefore, has a choice. It can ignore the problem and hope that things work out. Or it can analyze all of the factors expected to affect the organization and its jobs in the future. From this it can make informed judgments of future job specifications.

The latter approach is what is meant by qualitative human resource planning. For the business firm it means a review of strategic goals, markets it hopes to penetrate, anticipated plans of competitors, the expected economic environment, changes in technology, and similar considerations.

For public sector agencies the process is similar. What services will the agency provide in the future? Are the clientele likely to be different? Will technology have an impact? Will there be new competing sources for the service?

An insurance company may decide that its future growth will come from group policies to large organizations instead of sales to individual purchasers. This will require agents who can sell to a more sophisticated buyer. Intellectual skills for such activities as making cost-benefit analyses will likely become more important. Interpersonal skills for establishing rapport with individual consumers will likely become less important.

A mental health agency may anticipate a decline in individual counseling. Research and practice show a greater emphasis upon family and group therapy. This will call for professionals with a different orientation from those employed in the past.

Obviously some guesswork is unavoidable. Uncertainty cannot be eliminated. But the organization's alternative is to continue hiring practices that are working now but may be inappropriate for the future. Systematic assessment of the future is more likely to result in a match between employee characteristics and organizational needs.

ANALYZING LABOR AVAILABILITY

An important part of human resource planning is an analysis of labor force trends. This includes both the supply and demand sides. This is a relatively new area in personnel administration. In years past the implicit assumption was that an adequate labor supply would always be available.

This assumption no longer holds true—if, indeed, it ever did. Population and labor force changes have significant impact upon personnel strategies. This seems obvious for the large organization which employs tens of thousands. But it is also true for the small employer. A factory may employ only 100 persons. But if it draws its labor force from an area with a decreasing labor supply and an increasing demand, then a planned expansion program may not prove feasible.

Assessing Labor Supply

The supply of labor is a function of the labor force. The labor force as measured by the Department of Labor consists of persons either (1) working for

42

wages, self-employed, or in a family business or (2) not working but available for and actively seeking employment. It excludes persons fully retired, full-time students, spouses who are full-time homemakers, institutionalized individuals, and all others not employed and not seeking employment. When expressed as a percentage it becomes the *labor force participation rate*. It is usually depicted as the civilian labor force and excludes persons in the armed forces.

Table 3-3 shows projections for the United States labor force from 1980 to 1990. To make the projections there must be a numerical estimate of each age group and an estimate of how many will be offering themselves for employment.

As Table 3-3 shows, projections vary across different age groups. This reflects the unevenness of various age groups in the population. In the decade from 1980 to 1990 national projections show a big increase of 46 percent in the 35- to 44-year-old group and a decline of 13 percent in younger workers from 16 to 24. Such data is helpful for the very largest employers but of less value for the majority of organizations.

Table 3-4 is an example of the type of local labor market forecast which is of more value for most organizational planning purposes. Most states now have agencies which provide local labor market projections of this type. Many public universities also provide this service.

National trends can be quite misleading as to what is occurring in a given locale. Organizations in the three-county area shown cannot anticipate labor force growth in the 25- to 44-year-olds as is the case for the labor force as a whole. This could be important in planning for future growth in the area.

As shown in the examples, labor supply is broken down by age. Useful projections are also available on other bases such as education and skill levels. For purposes of planning affirmative action programs projections by

Table 3-3
United States Labor Force Projections
for 1980 and 1990
(Numbers in Thousands)

Age Groups	1980	1990	Percentage Change
16–24	25,453	22,139	− 13%
25–34	27,342	32,301	+ 18
35–44	19,516	28,532	+ 46
45–54	16,538	18,733	+ 13
55–64	11,903	11,218	− 5

Source: Data adapted from Department of Labor, *Employment and Training Report of the President* (Statistical Appendix. Table E-3), 1977.

Table 3-4
Labor Force Projections for a Three-County Area

Age Groups	1980	1990	Percentage Change
16–24	17,800	21,450	+ 20%
25–34	28,300	29,500	+ 4
35–44	24,100	24,300	+ 1
45–54	31,400	36,600	+ 16
55–64	18,150	26,300	+ 45

race, ethnic background, and sex are also quite useful. Many agencies also provide this data now.

Assessing Labor Demand   Assessing labor demand involves different considerations. Forecasts of economic activity are important. These forecasts too are readily available for local areas.

Additionally, organizational planners will find it useful to obtain surveys showing hiring plans of organizations in the area where competition for workers will occur. Such surveys can be prepared by organizations either individually or collectively. State economic agencies are becoming increasingly responsive to the need for this kind of information.

Additional information that is helpful involves prospects of new development by private sector firms and government agencies. New organizations can place additional demands on the existing labor supply. If the new organization is large and prominent enough, it may have the opposite effect by attracting new workers to the area. It may also induce persons such as full-time homemakers not presently in the labor force to seek employment.

MONITORING AND INTEGRATING THE PERSONNEL PROGRAM   An additional component of human resource planning is monitoring all phases of the organization's personnel program. This includes terminations, absenteeism, grievances, productivity, labor costs, strikes, health and safety costs, availability of candidates for promotion, pension plan reserves, and any other indicators that measure the organization's personnel health.

This monitoring should be a continuous process. Analysis may show the organization is experiencing high turnover among engineers during the first five years. Those that last five years seem to stay.

Investigation may reveal inadequate wage progression during the first few years. Or it may show that engineers are given only menial and unchallenging assignments during the early period of employment. This could be producing costly turnover.

Monitoring aids in the attainment of the ultimate objective in human resource planning. This is an *integrated personnel program* which ties together all the functional areas. Programs are not conducted in isolation. Their impact on all other activities is accounted for. Instead of pursuing activities that solve immediate problems only, the organization strives for a balance between present and future needs.

If training is providing a skill forecast to be in short supply, wage levels can be adjusted simultaneously to prevent turnover. A forecasted surplus of older workers with obsolete skills can result in programs to encourage earlier retirement. Careful selection can result in persons with characteristics to meet current needs and with potential for adjusting to anticipated job changes during their careers.

SUMMARY   Quantitative forecasting of human resource needs involves several components. It begins with an assessment of current resources. Losses based on terminations, deaths, retirements, and promotions and transfers must be estimated. The number of positions which will not be replaced must be accounted for. And finally there must be an estimate of needs based on growth.

Current talent should be inventoried on any base which is useful for the organization. Terminations, deaths, promotions, and transfers can be estimated by using historical data. Retirements can be determined from records showing those at the mandatory retirement age and by a survey of those planning early retirement. Unit managers can be surveyed to determine positions not being replaced. Growth estimates can be made by finding variables which correlate with the number of personnel.

Qualitative human resource planning is determining which characteristics in the individual will be related to successful performance in the future. This process cannot be done empirically. It must be done on a judgmental basis. This helps the organization obtain people who will meet requirements not just for today's jobs but for those in the future as well.

Labor force analysis is important from both the supply and demand sides. The labor force consists of persons employed and those persons not employed but available for and seeking employment. Forecasts of local labor markets are becoming more common and are of great assistance in organizational planning. The demand side for labor can be determined from economic forecasts and the hiring plans of individual organizations.

A program of continual monitoring of all personnel indicators is important. This includes such things as turnover, absenteeism, productivity, and grievances. This helps the organization develop an integrated personnel program. The integrated personnel program which ties together all the functional personnel areas and which strives for a balance between present and future needs is the ultimate objective in human resource planning.

SELECTED REFERENCES

BURACK, ELMER H., *Strategies for Manpower Planning and Programming*. Morristown, N.J.: General Learning Press, 1972.

BURACK, ELMER H. and JAMES W. WALKER, *Manpower Planning and Programming*. Boston: Allyn and Bacon, 1972.

FOLTMAN, FELECIAN F., *Manpower Information for Effective Management*. Ithaca, N.Y.: New York State School of Labor and Industrial Relations, 1973.

MINER, JOHN B., *The Human Constraint: The Coming Shortage of Managerial Talent*. Washington, D.C.: BNA Books, 1974.

TOMESKI, E. A. and H. LAZARUS, *People-Oriented Computer Systems: The Computer in Crisis*. New York: Van Nostrand Reinhold, 1975.

U.S. DEPT. OF LABOR, *Employment and Training Report of the President*. Washington, D.C.: U.S. Government Printing Office, 1977.

ORGANIZATION STAFFING LEVELS

◁══ IDEAS TO BE FOUND ══▷
IN THIS CHAPTER

• Work measurement and staffing levels
• Using comparative data internally
• Comparisons with other organizations
• The budgeting process
• Dealing with labor organizations

A difficult problem to resolve in personnel management is the number of persons to employ. Labor costs in the form of wages, salaries, and fringe benefits are a principal component in the cost structure of any organization. If more persons are employed than necessary, then costs become excessive; if fewer persons are employed than needed, then the quantity and quality of the organization's output is impaired. Thus, the organization is continually striving to operate with just the right number of people.

The problem is complicated by the different groups which have a stake in the decision, yet whose interests may not run parallel with those of the organization. The workers, for example, have a direct interest in the number of employees since this can affect the amount of work they are required to do. If they are represented by a labor organization, it has a similar interest in protecting the rights of its members.

But workers and labor organizations are not the only concern. Subordinate managers have their own special interests which may not be compatible with organizational goals. Most managers assume they could do a better job if allotted more staff. Status is also measured by the number of people under one's supervision. Thus, in most organizations there is continual pressure from subordinate managers to add workers.

Operating with just the right number of people is an elusive goal. It is part of the eternal question of what constitutes a fair day's work on the part of the employee. Since this matter has highly subjective elements, it cannot be answered with scientific precision. Thus, the organization is forced to pursue a goal critical for its survival but extremely difficult to measure. This chapter looks at the process.

WORK MEASUREMENT

Because determining the number of people needed is so subjective, there have been attempts to bring some rationality to the process. One of the principal ways for doing this is called *work measurement*. Work measurement is used to develop production standards. These have their main use in wage and incentive plans, but they are also helpful in determining personnel levels.

The most widely known of the work measurement techniques is that involving use of the stopwatch. Familiarly known by the somewhat dated term of *time and motion study*, this process goes back many years to the era of scientific management. It is associated with such pioneering industrial engineers as Frederick Taylor and the Gilbreaths.

The process involves observations of a worker performing a job, after which the job is broken down into tasks and elements. The elements are timed with allowance for fatigue, material shortages, and machine downtime. Then production standards are derived, along with improved work methods. The process allows for variations in worker abilities.

A variation of this approach is *work sampling*. Rather than following one worker at a time through an entire cycle, random observations are taken of a large number of workers performing the same task. Standards are formulated from these random observations.

Production standards give the expected output per worker for a given time period. The organization determines the number of workers needed by dividing total output desired by the expected output per worker. If output falls below desired levels, the organization knows whether the deficiency is caused by too few workers or too little output from those working.

Work measurement has many subjective elements. Much of it is judgmental, though this is masked by the seeming precision of the stopwatch. Nonetheless, it does represent a methodology capable of giving reasonably consistent results.

There are limitations to the type of work measurement programs described. They have found their greatest use in manufacturing operations where there are large numbers of highly standardized jobs which are characterized by repetitive and routine operations. While there have been attempts to use such methods in clerical, technical, and professional occupations, the results have been mixed. Jobs which are not of a routine, repetitive nature do not lend themselves to work measurement techniques.

Work measurement also has the drawback of creating resentment among the work force. This is not inevitable, but workers usually view work measurement as a means for management to get more work for less pay. It is very common for workers to distort their performance when being observed so as to throw off work measurement calculations.

USING COMPARATIVE DATA

A very helpful method for determining whether personnel levels are set properly is by the use of comparative data. Comparisons can be done internally to see how levels have changed over time. Or the organization can use external data sources and compare itself to organizations in the same industry. Large organizations with numerous plants or offices find it useful to compare the different units.

In making comparisons over time any significant changes that have occurred should be accounted for. If comparisons are being made with external organizations, they should be as similar as possible. The same is true for comparisons of units within the same organization. Otherwise differences that appear may be legitimate and not an indication of a staffing problem.

Internal Comparisons Over Time

Table 4-1 gives comparative sales figures for Capital Electronics over a period of six years. As shown in the table, sales per employee for Capital Electronics have declined to $28,000 in the current year from a high of $30,000 six years ago. If inflation were a significant factor during this period, the decline would be even greater.

There may be legitimate reasons for the decline. Perhaps the product mix has changed to more labor intensive products. New technology may

Table 4-1
Sales per Employee for Capital Electronics

	Number of Employees	Sales	Sales per Employee
Base Year	1900	$51,000,000	$27,000
Base Plus 2 Years	2315	70,000,000	30,000
Base Plus 4 Years	2540	74,000,000	29,000
Current Year (Base Plus 6 Years)	2755	77,000,000	28,000

have been introduced which required time for more efficient utilization. Perhaps the company has begun adding and training new workers in antici- pation of a big contract scheduled to begin in the near future. But in the absence of significant changes which can be accounted for, the organization would want to take a close look to see if it is overstaffed in relation to the present volume of business.

Comparisons as shown in Table 4-1 are a starting point to alert the organization that problems may be arising. More detailed breakdowns are helpful in enabling the organization to analyze problem areas. Table 4-2 shows a classification scheme for Municipal Hospital. As shown in the table, in a six-year period there has been a considerable expansion in the adminis- trative and supervisory staff at the expense of both the non-medical profes- sional and hourly groups. The administrative group now represents 16 per- cent of the total employees as compared with 10 percent six years earlier.

It is possible that this represents a plan on the part of the hospital directors and top administrators. Perhaps in earlier years the administrative and supervisory ranks were severely understaffed and key employees were lost as a result of being overworked. Perhaps changes in technology or more governmental regulations or insurance requirements have required closer supervision of the workers. But, again, in the absence of factors to account for such a rise, the directors would want to examine staffing procedures closely to see if somehow it has permitted itself to become top heavy with costly and unneeded administrative staff.

It is also possible in examining Table 4-2 to raise questions about the non-medical professional category. Perhaps the relative decline in this area is seriously hampering patient care. Or perhaps it represents a better bal- ance than before. Regardless, this type of analysis enables management to make more reasoned staffing decisions.

It should be noted that the categories shown in Table 4-2 are only suggestive. Some organizations might find it useful to break their work force down by department or function. It can be done by occupation or by skill

Table 4-2
Employee Classifications for Municipal Hospital

	Administrative and Supervisory	Medical	Non-Medical Professional	Hourly
Base Year	10%	18%	31%	41%
Base Plus 2 Years	12	18	29	41
Base Plus 4 Years	15	19	29	37
Current Year (Base Plus 6 Years)	16	19	28	37

level. The possibilities are limited only by the cost of acquiring such information in relation to its benefit to the organization.

**Comparisons with
Other Organizations**

Comparisons that are done internally are obviously useful only up to a certain point. Data from similar organizations provides perspective on how an organization compares with others in its field. Table 4-3 shows how Municipal Hospital compares with five similar hospitals. The data is typical of that which might be supplied by a professional or trade association.

From Table 4-3 we see that Municipal Hospital may be overstaffed with administrators; of the six hospitals, Municipal has the highest percentage of administrators and supervisors. As stated before there may be sound reasons for this. But this type of external comparison in conjunction with the internal comparison gives the directors and top administrators the basis for a possible revision of the personnel distribution.

Table 4-3
Employee Classification Comparisons among
Hospitals between 450–500 Beds

	Administrative and Supervisory	Medical	Non-Medical Professional	Hourly
Hospital A	12%	20%	28%	40%
Hospital B	11	18	27	44
Hospital C	10	23	30	37
Hospital D*	16	19	28	37
Hospital E	13	21	27	39
Hospital F	12	18	30	40

*Municipal Hospital.

**Comparisons among
Decentralized Units**

Personnel level comparisons are facilitated when an organization has decentralized units which are standardized. Government agencies, merchandising concerns, restaurant chains, and motel chains are good examples. A big advantage is that reporting can be standardized as well as made mandatory. Table 4-4 offers an example of such data from a merchandising company with stores in several cities.

By examining data such as that in Table 4-4, management can determine how personnel utilization compares among the units. The Detroit store is generating the least total sales per employee; its warehouse and accounts receivable operations also show up poorly. But in invoice processing it appears at the top among the five units.

Table 4-4
Unit Comparisons for Midwestern Merchandising Company*

	Total Sales per Employee	Invoices Processed per Financial Employee	Tons Delivered per Warehouse Employee	Credit Sales per Accounts Receivable Employee
Indianapolis	$33,000	41,234	1,104	$173,000
Dayton	37,000	38,729	1,800	201,000
Detroit	29,000	44,500	990	168,000
Toledo	38,000	26,700	1,500	149,000
Columbus	39,000	39,500	1,300	188,000

*Full-time employees plus part-time employees converted to full-time equivalents.

A note of caution is important at this point to avoid over-interpreting the kind of data presented in Table 4-4. These are productivity indices. Such data are *indicative only* and must be interpreted carefully. For example, the low tons delivered per warehouse employee at the Detroit location may not reflect excessive personnel levels. Rather it may reflect poor equipment such as old delivery trucks which frequently break down. Thus, it is possible that Detroit may have the best personnel utilization considering the poor equipment they have to use.

This cautionary note applies to the whole area of comparative data as discussed in this section. The data in such tables should never be taken in isolation from everything else. The *number* of employees, for example, completely omits the *cost* of these employees. This is extremely significant for determining profit levels in profit-seeking organizations. Thus, sales per employee is a valuable indicator only when looked at in conjunction with such things as labor costs, net profits, and return on investment.

Thus, comparative data as a means of determining whether optimum staffing levels exist is a valuable tool. But when interpreted in isolation from all other factors, it can be misleading.

Sources of Comparative Data

For large organizations with numerous decentralized units, the problems of obtaining good comparative data are greatly reduced. The organization can determine what information it would like to have, arrange to secure it as part of its management information system, standardize it for reporting purposes, and hold units accountable for deviations.

For the small organization or the large organization without comparable units, the problem is more difficult but not impossible. (And even the decentralized organization should make external comparisons.) One of the best sources of data in these circumstances are the surveys published by professional and trade associations. There are hundreds of such national, regional, and local associations. One of the most valuable services they perform is the collection of such data.

Data is typically obtained on a voluntary basis. Problems of accuracy and standardization do exist. Sampling error can exist because reporting is not mandatory. Nonetheless, such sources provide valuable aids for the organization in comparing its staffing levels with similar organizations.

Government surveys provide another valuable source. Industry surveys are published in a variety of government publications and provide benchmarks for comparison. This is true not just of the federal government but of state governments also. Practically all states have economic units and university research bureaus which produce surveys of this type.

THE BUDGETING PROCESS

Regardless of the sources or methods by which the organization derives standards for determining the number of employees needed, actual decisions regarding staffing levels are most commonly made as part of the budgeting process. The small organization may exist as a single budgetary unit. More typical is the larger organization which has numerous budgetary units throughout. Individual budgetary units are found at the lowest level. At succeedingly higher levels these individual budgetary units join together to form other budgetary units until there is one master budget for the entire organization.

These budgetary units are the means by which the organization allocates resources. Resources are always scarce in relation to the claims made against them. Physical resources such as existing plant and equipment must be used for some purposes and not others. Human resources such as engineers must be assigned to some projects and not others. Available dollars must be distributed on some basis for capital investment, new machinery, office space rentals, new product development, salary increases, and new additions to staff. Thus, authorizations for personnel levels become part of the process by which all resources are allocated.

Budget conferences and budget procedures vary widely. Some organizations have highly structured procedures with the various sub-units required to submit detailed statements of goals and operating plans. Performance data are scrutinized carefully, including the effectiveness with which personnel are being utilized. Estimates of resources needed must be backed up by supporting data.

For very large organizations this budgeting process extends from the top to the lowest budgetary units. In large business corporations, headquarters may require each operating division and subsidiary to submit a detailed operating plan. These plans are approved and expenditures authorized. A similar process is then gone through with the operating divisions and subsidiaries conducting their own internal budget conferences.

In other organizations the process may be highly informal. It may be just a routine procedure where the budget from the preceding year forms the basis for the new budget with only minor modifications. Thus, tradition in these types of organizations plays a big part in determining personnel levels as well as other expenditures.

Staffing levels reflect not only some presumably rational process based on work measurement or comparative data, but also a process whereby succeedingly lower levels in the organization seek to assert their claims against competing claims. Thus, when stripped to essentials, personnel levels ultimately reflect a bargaining process among units and between levels in the organization. This is an internal bargaining process among the organization's managers and should not be confused with collective bargaining.

Final decisions regarding staffing authorizations are made as part of this internal bargaining process. Thus, personnel levels in the final analysis are controlled by what is essentially a political process. This does not mean the procedure is necessarily unsound. Nor is it ever completely avoidable. To the extent that the organization has accurate measures of how well it is utilizing its human resources, and has the willingness to make decisions based on these measures, there is greater likelihood that purely political factors will become subordinate.

LABOR ORGANIZATIONS AND STAFFING LEVELS

The organization that must deal with one or more labor organizations confronts special problems. The labor organization has a strong vested interest in both the number of workers employed and the pace at which they work. Disputes over both have long been a source of tension between labor and management. So called "featherbedding" whereby the union requires more workers than management feels are necessary is a perennial issue.

The major impact of a labor organization is to take away management's flexibility. The labor organization insists that questions relating to the number of workers and to work standards become part of the bargaining process. This does not mean that personnel levels and work standards are explicitly written into the contract. But even on an implicit basis the issue exists in practically all labor–management relationships.

Work standards pose some of the most vexing problems in labor–management relations. They are the causes of many grievances and are troublesome for arbitrators. The determination of work standards has so many subjective elements that third parties are often hard pressed to resolve such disputes without appearing to be arbitrary.

Decisions on the part of organizations to reduce personnel levels are also a source of friction between the parties. All such questions ultimately must be resolved in terms of whether such actions are permitted under the terms of the labor contract. Management will cite its prerogatives in this area. Often contracts are written so that management can change personnel levels in the event of significant changes in technology or work methods. Often the issue becomes whether a significant change has taken place or whether management acted in an arbitrary fashion.

The issue of work standards and personnel levels is not an easy one to resolve. It is symbolic of the clash between parties with highly conflicting interests. It is an ever-present issue even without a labor organization. But the labor organization adds an extra dimension of conflict with which the organization must contend.

SUMMARY

The problem of the number of persons needed by the organization is a vexing one in personnel administration. It is part of the eternal problem of what constitutes a fair day's work on the part of the employee. Such determinations are critical if the organization is to survive and prosper. Personnel costs are among the most significant in practically all organizations.

Various forms of work measurement using the stopwatch are one means for establishing the number of workers needed. Work measurement has been found to be best suited for production-type jobs which are repetitive and highly standardized.

The use of comparative data is another means for determining whether personnel levels are at the optimum. By comparing its own performance over time and by comparing itself to similar organizations in its field, an organization can see if its personnel utilization is satisfactory. Such data has to be interpreted with caution since using such information in isolation from all other factors may be misleading.

The labor organization adds a special element in determining personnel levels. The labor organization is concerned with the number of workers used and the pace at which they work. Reductions in personnel are a common point of contention between labor and management. Questions of work standards are some of the most difficult arbitrators are asked to resolve in disputes between the parties.

Personnel levels are ultimately decided as part of the budgeting process which allocates resources to the various units within the organization. Thus personnel levels are not only subject to control by some presumably rational means. They also become part of the organization's internal bargaining process.

SELECTED REFERENCES

DUBIN, ROBERT, *Human Relations in Administration, with Readings*, 4th ed. Englewood Cliffs, N.J.: Prentice-Hall, 1974.

MAYER, RAYMOND R., *Production and Operations Management*, 3rd ed. New York: McGraw-Hill, 1975.

MUNDEL, MARVIN E., *Motion and Time Study; Principles and Practices*, 4th ed. Englewood Cliffs, N.J.: Prentice-Hall, 1970.

NIEBEL, BENJAMIN W., *Motion and Time Study*, 5th ed. Homewood, Ill.: Richard D. Irwin, 1972.

SLOANE, ARTHUR A. and FRED WITNEY, *Labor Relations*, 3rd ed. Englewood Cliffs, N.J.: Prentice-Hall, 1977.

STARR, MARTIN K., *Production Management: Systems and Synthesis*, 2nd ed. Englewood Cliffs, N.J.: Prentice-Hall, 1972.

PART 3

RECRUITMENT AND SELECTION

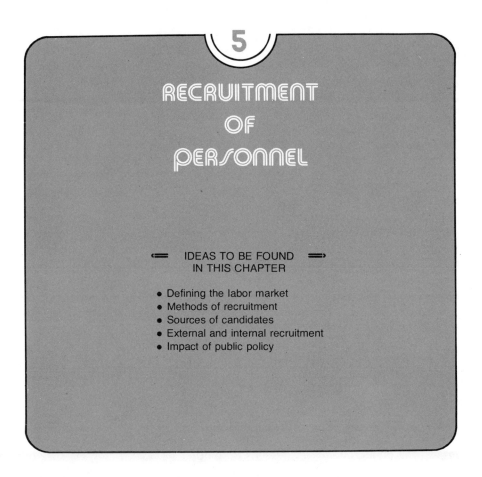

5

RECRUITMENT
OF
PERSONNEL

⟸ IDEAS TO BE FOUND ⟹
IN THIS CHAPTER

- Defining the labor market
- Methods of recruitment
- Sources of candidates
- External and internal recruitment
- Impact of public policy

Two conditions must exist for selection to occur, (1) the organization must have a candidate whom it is willing to employ, and (2) the candidate must be willing to accept an employment offer. Recruitment is the process of finding applicants who meet both of these conditions.

The process begins when the organization determines its quantitative and qualitative needs for personnel. Next the duties and responsibilities of the job to be filled have to be described. Then the characteristics desired in the potential job holders must be specified. Recruiting itself can start when the organization knows the type person it is seeking.

There is another strategy which organizations adopt (often without realizing it). This is to recruit and screen numerous candidates without a clear idea of the type person best suited for the job. Through a process of elimination the organization decides upon the type individual likely to prove effective. This approach is wasteful and inefficient. It also raises an ethical question of whether persons recruited under these conditions have been dealt with in good faith.

Recruitment can pose difficulties. But it is one of the less complex of the personnel functions. If the organization has planned properly, recruitment is usually routine. Most problems arise when labor markets are tight or because a unique and specialized skill is being sought.

DEFINING THE LABOR MARKET

The first step in actual recruiting is determining the relevant labor market. The labor market is more than a set of geographical boundaries. It refers to all the characteristics which define sources of applicants for particular jobs.

For example, an organization might have entry level clerical positions which require no skill, pay the minimum wage, and have limited advancement opportunities. It defines the characteristics of persons being sought as follows: (1) high-school graduate, (2) dropout acceptable if reason for quitting satisfactory (such as economic hardship), (3) high-school record with no discipline or attendance problems, (4) no experience (since the jobs pay so little) and (5) live within a ten-mile radius (since the salaries are not attractive enough to justify a long commute).

These characteristics become the relevant labor market. All high-school graduates or acceptable dropouts with no experience and with satisfactory high school attendance and discipline records who live within a ten-mile radius are potential candidates for these positions.

For beginning engineers, the same organization would define the labor market quite differently. It might be new engineering graduates from colleges in the northeast. Possibly it is defined this way because the jobs are not interesting enough to attract persons from other locales. Or the expense of recruiting may be too great. Another organization might have units all over the country with opportunities for promotion and transfer. It might define the labor market as engineering graduates from any college in the country.

Many factors determine the relevant labor market. The type of job is the most critical. The size of the organization and its reputation play a part. Education, certification, and licensing requirements are other factors. The willingness of people to relocate and to commute are important. The expense the organization is willing to bear in recruiting also plays a part.

The relevant labor market for a given job determines recruiting strategies and methods. Recruiting methods must cover a wide range of possibilities. Sometimes the organization seeks workers who are uneducated, untrained, and readily available. Another time it may be looking for Ph.Ds in nuclear physics who are in short supply.

METHODS AND SOURCES

Effective recruiting requires imagination and creativity. In recruiting, the organization incurs two risks. One is listing job requirements so broadly that the organization goes through a time-consuming process of screening numerous candidates who are unqualified. The other is to list requirements so stringently that qualified persons are discouraged from applying. Effective recruiting involves a compromise between these two positions.

Experience is a good example. If the organization lists a minimum of three years experience as essential, it obviously restricts possibilities to persons with that qualification. If in fact it would be willing to accept other characteristics in lieu of experience, then it has closed off a source of recruits who might be quite acceptable.

Employment Office

One of the most common methods for medium to large-size organizations to use for recruitment is an on-site employment office. This means that the organization encourages drop-in traffic where people apply for jobs without direct solicitation. During periods of labor surplus, many organizations find they can fill most of their operative positions in this manner. This is especially true if the organization is a highly visible one in the community.

The usual method in these circumstances is to have the potential employee fill out an application or preliminary application. This is put through a screening process by a pre-employment interviewer to determine if there is a possible job within the organization. If such a possibility exists, the prospect is referred to someone in the employment department for more intensive interviewing and investigation.

The employment office is a relatively inexpensive means by which the organization can recruit a pool of applicants. It is not without some cost, however, for the physical space alone is worth something to the organization. And the big expense is the personnel cost involved with having to pay trained persons to perform this function on a daily basis. Nonetheless, for many organizations this still remains one of the least costly methods for obtaining a steady supply of persons for the many positions the organization is trying to fill.

Newspapers

Newspapers are one of the most common and effective means for obtaining suitable candidates for many kinds of jobs. Most newspapers are restricted geographically. When advertising for certain positions it generally must be assumed that only persons within the distribution range of the particular newspaper will be reached. A metropolitan hospital would undoubtedly find that an advertisement in a daily newspaper reaches qualified applicants for a medical technician's position.

Newspapers are effective because people are accustomed to seeking employment through newspaper advertisements. Their major disadvantage is that the advertisements found in newspapers tend to reach only those who are actively in the job market. In other words the person must be actually seeking a position.

Persons currently employed who are satisfied with their jobs may not see the advertisements that are placed in the classified sections where most employment advertising is located. These individuals must be attracted by other methods. The same is true for persons not currently in the labor force.

Employment Agencies

Private employment agencies vary widely in what they have to offer organizations seeking job applicants. There is a wide range in the quality of the service offered. Many are highly professional and screen applicants thoroughly with the employer's qualifications understood and utilized. Many others are just the opposite. They flood the market with job applicants of dubious credentials with the expectation that some will be placed.

Private employment agencies vary in the arrangements for fees. For lower level jobs the fees are usually paid by the applicant. For higher level or hard to fill jobs often the organization will pay the fee. For the professionally run agency this fee is in return for a quality service of locating qualified applicants that the organization feels unable to locate on its own.

Operating in another realm entirely are the executive search agencies. Again the quality varies widely. The very best do not themselves obtain their pool of applicants by advertising or accepting resumes from persons seeking positions. They operate by seeking persons currently employed who typically are not in the job market.

There are a number of reasons organizations use private agencies of various types. One is that they may wish to preserve some degree of anonymity and confidentiality. While today this may conflict with equal employment opportunity laws, it does have some advantage for the organization. It can result from special situations such as wishing to avoid internal conflict by letting employees know a high placed executive is due for dismissal.

United States Employment Service

The United States Employment Service under the Department of Labor operates employment offices around the country. This program came out of the depression years of the 1930s when the government was seeking ways to reduce unemployment. Historically the U.S. Employment Service has placed people in relatively low level jobs. In recent years it has attempted to upgrade its service by also finding employment for persons at professional, technical, and managerial levels.

There is a major advantage to using the U.S. Employment Service. Their services are offered without charge to either the organization or the applicant. With the private agencies one of the parties must absorb the cost.

The major disadvantage to the employment service is a basic conflict in its mission. From the employer's point of view it is useful to the extent it provides qualified applicants. Therefore, the employer expects the employment service to screen out the marginal or unqualified job seeker.

But from a social point of view, it is just these people that the government wants to assist in finding jobs. In attempting to reach this goal, the employment service runs the risk of alienating employers since there is nothing compulsory about using the services it provides. The employment service must compete in the market just like the private agency.

This is a very difficult dilemma to resolve. Efforts in recent years by employers to hire disadvantaged persons may be resolving this to some extent. Regardless, the employment service is a possible source of job applicants without charge that organizations should not overlook.

Present Employees

A fruitful source of applicants is from persons currently employed by the organization. Present employees who are satisfied with their own employment will recommend the organization to people they know. This can be a very productive and inexpensive way for the organization to obtain applicants from which to make selection.

One difficulty of a public relations or employee relations nature is that sometimes referrals must be turned down because they do not meet the organization's standards. This can result in bad feeling on the part of the employee who did the referring unless the situation is handled with diplomacy by the personnel department.

Professional Associations

Another productive source, especially for professional positions, are the professional associations. These associations facilitate placement for their members. In so doing they help organizations hire needed people. Recruitment occurs through contacts made at the national conventions which usually take place annually. Some groups also have regional meetings. Most journals published by professional associations contain advertisements for positions that are available, and accept advertisements from persons seeking positions.

The number of such professional associations is in the thousands. Engineers, scientists, nurses, purchasing agents, accountants, and attorneys are just some of the groups which have professional associations. They are especially useful when seeking persons with skills of a highly specialized nature.

College Recruitment

College recruitment has become such an accepted method for organizations to obtain managerial and professional prospects that it is practically a complete specialty in and of itself. It began on a large scale after World War II when college enrollments soared and the economy expanded. It has flourished ever since. Many colleges and universities have developed very sophisticated programs for placing their graduates.

Many kinds of jobs are filled by college recruiting. For the organization the college degree represents a form of screening. Possessors of the degree are presumed to have demonstrated certain abilities and qualities by having graduated. These might be found by other means, but only with more risk and uncertainty.

Typically only large organizations such as the country's industrial corporations have utilized college recruiting extensively. Smaller employers have often been shut out of the process since their needs are limited and sporadic. And with demand high for available candidates in past years, the colleges and universities have had little need for expanding their lists of recruiting organizations.

In this respect college recruiting may be in for some major changes. In the 1980s there is likely to be an excess of college graduates for the available jobs. It is likely that college placement bureaus will be seeking out employers who have not used this service in the past. This should include a greater number of small employers than previously.

There is a case to be made that many organizations have overemphasized the need for college trained people for many of their openings. Persons overqualified create as many problems as those who are underqualified. This is especially true where advancement prospects are limited.

Nonetheless, from all indications the marriage between employer and higher education seems to have been one of mutual benefit. For this reason alone it is likely that college recruiting will remain a mainstay of the recruiting efforts for professional and managerial personnel.

Miscellaneous

In addition there are other sources for recruiting applicants. Organizations visit high schools in order to attract high-school graduates. Many organizations have special summer intern programs for college students, hoping these students will then join the organization after graduation. Distributive education programs in which high school students receive academic credit for hours worked are another means for obtaining qualified persons.

Trade schools, secretarial schools, and vocational schools are sources of applicants. Sometimes organizations find they must establish their own training programs or their own educational programs in order to build a qualified pool from which to select.

INTERNAL RECRUITMENT

Recruitment thus far has been discussed from the standpoint of obtaining applicants from outside the organization. But this assumes that the organization is either hiring for entry level positions or that it is going to fill higher level positions from outside.

Many organizations have promote-from-within programs. The organization fills positions above the entry level by selecting from those already employed. This means that the organization must develop an internal recruiting program. It might seem that an internal recruiting program would not be necessary. But in large organizations with thousands of employees, the process of identifying those within the organization who are both interested in advancement and who are qualified poses just as many problems as getting someone from the outside.

Until recent years when equal employment opportunity laws were passed, internal recruitment was a secret procedure in most organizations. But with the advent of the 1964 Civil Rights Act, organizations have had to reconsider their policies. There is a beginning trend for organizations to internally advertise or post jobs that become open at higher levels. (This has long been true under most union contracts.) This provides those interested with the opportunity to offer themselves for possible consideration as opposed to leaving it entirely to management's discretion.

While this may make it more difficult for management in some ways, it also offers possibilities for improving internal recruitment procedures. It provides an additional means for identifying potential candidates. Not all who apply will prove qualified, but that is true of any recruitment program.

PUBLIC POLICY   Primary impact of public policy upon recruitment comes from Title VII of the Civil Rights Act and the executive orders mandating affirmative action programs. Jobs cannot be advertised as being for one sex or the other unless there is a bona fide occupational qualification related to sex. Any suggestions for preference based on race, religion, national origin, or ethnic background are also prohibited.

Under affirmative action mandates it is no defense for employers to say that females and minorities have not applied for jobs. Overt programs of seeking out members of groups targeted under Title VII are required. This means advertising in newspapers that reach minority audiences, recruiting at predominantly female and minority colleges and high schools, specifying equal opportunity employment policies in advertisements, contacting professional and civic groups representing minorities and females, making appropriate announcements on radio and TV programs, and performing other recruiting activities that demonstrate a genuine attempt to broaden the base of qualified applicants.

In some cases, especially under court imposed consent orders for hiring females and minorities, organizations have to keep records of the numbers of females and minorities who apply for jobs. These are then compared to the number actually hired. This becomes part of the total evidence available for determining whether a case for illegal discrimination can be made.

SUMMARY Recruitment is the process of finding suitable applicants from which the organization selects to fill its jobs. It begins with planning for the quantitative and qualitative needs of the organization. Descriptions of job duties and responsibilities must be developed along with specifications of the individuals desired.

Relevant labor markets must be defined. This refers to the characteristics desired in the person to be hired. Many factors affect the relevant labor market including the type of job, the nature of the organization, certification and licensing requirements, and the willingness of people to relocate and commute.

There are many methods and sources of applicants. These include newspaper advertisements, in-house employment offices, private employment agencies, the U.S. Employment Service, college placement bureaus, professional associations, recommendations of present employees, and internal recruitment from those already employed.

Public policy has affected recruiting through the Civil Rights Act and the executive orders mandating affirmative action programs. Organizations must engage in overt programs of seeking out female and minority applicants. It is no defense to say that females and minorities have not applied for jobs if the organization has taken no overt steps to attract them. This includes advertising in newspapers that reach minority audiences, recruiting at predominantly minority and female colleges and high schools, and contacting appropriate civic and professional groups.

SELECTED REFERENCES

FAMULARO, JOSEPH J., *Handbook of Modern Personnel Administration*. New York, McGraw-Hill, 1972.

HUMANIC DESIGNS DIVISION, *How to Eliminate Discriminatory Practices—A Guide to EEO Compliance*. New York: AMACOM, 1975.

JACKSON, MATTHEW, *Recruiting, Interviewing, and Selecting: A Manual for Line Managers*. New York: McGraw-Hill, 1973.

MINER, JOHN B. and MARY GREEN MINER, *Personnel and Industrial Relations*, 3rd ed. New York: Macmillan, 1977.

SAYLES, LEONARD R. and GEORGE STRAUSS, *Managing Human Resources*. Englewood Cliffs, N.J.: Prentice-Hall, 1977.

YODER, DALE and HERBERT HENEMAN, JR., eds., *Staffing Policies and Strategies*. Washington, D.C.: Bureau of National Affairs, 1974.

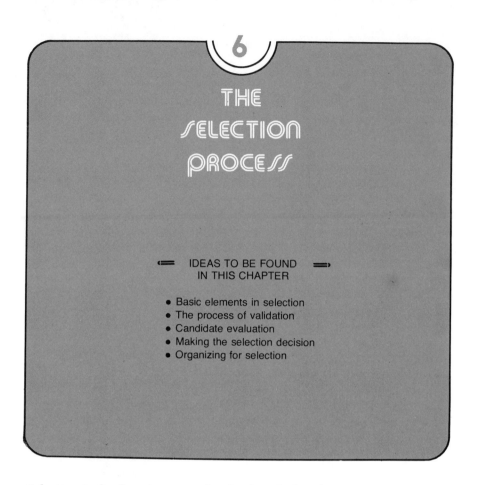

6

THE
SELECTION
PROCESS

◁═ IDEAS TO BE FOUND ═▷
IN THIS CHAPTER

● Basic elements in selection
● The process of validation
● Candidate evaluation
● Making the selection decision
● Organizing for selection

Selection is the function most closely identified with personnel administration. Even the smallest organization must engage in the process by which people are hired and put to work.

A good selection procedure is one which identifies persons who will contribute effectively to the organization. It also identifies those whose contribution is likely to be negative. The organization that selects the best talent obviously has an edge on competing organizations.

Having good talent is never enough, of course. There are examples too numerous to recount of weaker talent triumphing over superior talent because of motivation, organization, teamwork, and all the other factors which spell organizational success. Nonetheless, obtaining workers whose skills and abilities can contribute to organizational goals is a critical step for any organization.

The selection process is not equally important across all levels. Jobs can be ranked on a hierarchy in terms of their impact upon organizational success. This usually corresponds closely to rank on the organization chart. But this is not always the case. The organization may have twenty unit managers who outrank the director of research. But having twenty dilutes the impact of any one. The research director, on the other hand, may be the only manager primarily concerned with research programs which may mean the difference between long-run success and failure.

In former years selection was one area of employee relations relatively free from outside influence. The right of the organization to apply its own standards in selection was largely taken for granted. Legal influences in recent years have completely eroded that doctrine.

Because legislation and judicial decisions have had so much impact, it is easy to assume that selection can best be understood by examining the legal issues. Actually just the opposite is true. The legal doctrines now being applied cannot themselves be understood and interpreted without a clear understanding of how selection works.

On the surface, selection appears to be a fairly simple process. But in reality it raises complex issues without even considering the question of discrimination. To simply speak of obtaining good talent is one thing. To define exactly what that means and then identify it is something quite different. This chapter examines the selection process without considering the legal issues. The area of public policy is taken up in the next chapter.

BASIC ELEMENTS IN SELECTION

There are five basic elements in selection which must be linked together (see Figure 6-1).

First the *organizational goals* must be spelled out. From this stems the process of *job design* by which appropriate duties and responsibilities are outlined in a job description. For each job the *job success criterion* must be determined, meaning what constitutes successful performance. From this comes the *job specification*, the particular skills, characteristics, and traits desired in the individual selected for the job. The last step is utilizing the appropriate *selection instruments* for measuring the characteristics in the individual. Each of these is examined in turn.

Organizational Goals

The first step in the staffing process begins with a determination of the organization's mission and goals. It is impossible to design jobs until there is a clear idea of why the organization exists. What need in society does it fulfill? What are the basic products or services that it offers? How is this changing over time?

The process of actually designing jobs begins with this step. In most organizations after their founding this represents an evolutionary process that occurs on a gradual basis. For this reason it is easy to overlook as the first step in hiring. But in fact hiring cannot occur until the organization has a

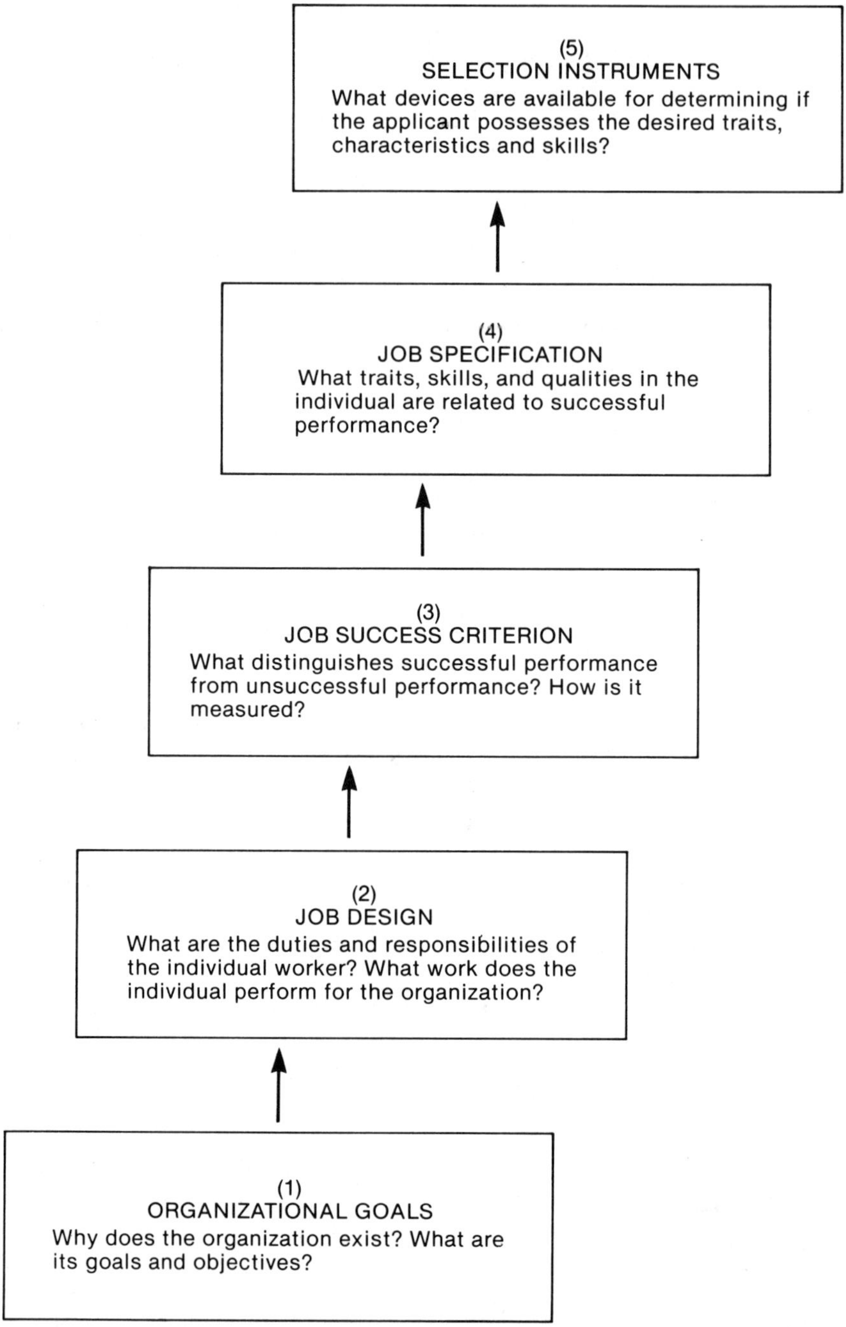

Figure 6-1
Basic Elements in Selection

The figure contains the following boxes connected by upward-pointing arrows from bottom to top:

(5)
SELECTION INSTRUMENTS
What devices are available for determining if the applicant possesses the desired traits, characteristics and skills?

(4)
JOB SPECIFICATION
What traits, skills, and qualities in the individual are related to successful performance?

(3)
JOB SUCCESS CRITERION
What distinguishes successful performance from unsuccessful performance? How is it measured?

(2)
JOB DESIGN
What are the duties and responsibilities of the individual worker? What work does the individual perform for the organization?

(1)
ORGANIZATIONAL GOALS
Why does the organization exist? What are its goals and objectives?

clear idea of how the activities to be performed by employees fit into the overall mission and purpose.

It is also important to chart organizational mission and goals as these change over time. As was emphasized in Chapter 3 on human resource planning, these changes must be reflected in the duties people perform. Otherwise there will be serious distortions between what the organization is trying to accomplish and what employees are actually doing.

Job Design   Once the organization's mission and goals have been established, the next step is to decide upon the tasks and duties to be performed by persons who are employed. These will ultimately be written down as the *job description*.

Job design is part of a broader process known as organization design. This is the process by which functions and operations are grouped in such fashion that the organization functions as a cohesive unit. Appropriate assignments of authority and responsibility are also made.

Job design occurs as part of this process. The term "job" is a very common one in our society. Its meaning when used in the selection process is more complex than its everyday usage would suggest. Figure 6-2 is a graphic representation of this.

An *element* is one particular action performed by an individual in carrying out assigned duties. An element is the insertion of paper into a typewriter by a secretary. A *task* is a group of related elements. All of the elements from inserting paper to actually typing to removing the paper comprise the task of typing letters. A *position* is the collection of tasks performed by one individual. Typing letters, greeting visitors, answering phones, keeping budget figures current would be some of the tasks performed by a person with the position of secretary. *There is one position for every individual in the organization.*

A job is a grouping of similarly related positions. Persons who have positions performing the tasks such as typing, answering phones, and greeting visitors would be grouped together under the common label of secretary. *Unless every position is completely unique, there is not one job for every individual in the organization.* This is true despite common usage of the term.

A job in hiring terminology is an abstract term derived by categorizing positions which have many similarities. But, and this is a key point so often overlooked, it also means that many dissimilarities must be included also. The organization may have a job classification listed as filing clerk. Perhaps it has one hundred filing clerk positions. All the individuals having this job will basically be doing the same thing. But if some work in accounts receivable, and some in accounts payable, and some in the supply office, then it is very likely that there will be variations in the actual duties performed. This may

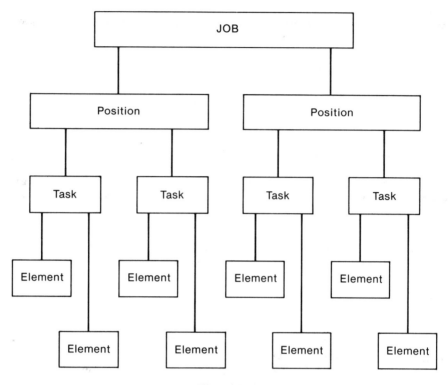

Figure 6-2
Components of a Job

be just as true for two people with the same job title who work in the same department.

This point is stressed to illustrate how misleading a job title alone can be. In constructing the traits and characteristics to be used in hiring, it is convenient and necessary to have job classifications so that the system does not become unwieldy. If the organization employs 10,000 people, it would be cumbersome and costly to have a separate listing of duties and responsibilities for each. By categorizing the positions into broader job classes, it is easier to develop a workable number of job descriptions and job specifications.

When the hiring process is underway, it is important to take into account the sometimes subtle differences that exist among positions which have the same job title. This becomes one of the responsibilities of the personnel department which normally does the initial screening of prospective employees. It also helps illustrate the difficulty of developing a universal set of applicable specifications for a classification as broad as "executive" or "salesperson." The variations within the category are simply too great.

Job Success Criterion   The job success criterion has been touched on in an earlier chapter. It raises the crucial issue: what is it that distinguishes successful performance from unsuccessful performance? It would seem that this should be the simplest part of the hiring process. In actuality it is one of the most difficult.

Take as an example a salesperson selling cosmetics from door-to-door. How does one measure successful performance in this case? It is obvious that a volume of sales at some prescribed level would be a critical factor. Selling cosmetics is what the person was hired for. But how about the salesperson who has a high volume of sales but who obtains little repeat business (perhaps because of high pressure tactics that people resent after succumbing to the original sales presentation)? Assuming the company wants to build a satisfied clientele, the factor of repeat business must be taken into consideration.

Continuing, there is the salesperson with high volume, good repeat sales, but whose reports and orders are done so carelessly that valuable time must be spent by others straightening them out. This is probably not as important as good sales volume, but it would have to be given some consideration. This is particularly true if the costs of the errors start to equal or exceed the profit made from the individual's sales.

Then going one step further, there is the person who has high sales volume, good repeat business, good reports, but whose unethical behavior towards other salespersons is creating a serious problem. Perhaps the individual moves into territories that are assigned to someone else or is taking away sales from others in violation of company rules. How should this be judged?

This should give some idea of the complexities involved in distinguishing successful performance in just one job that is fairly routine compared to many. Consider the social worker in a welfare office. What constitutes successful performance? Is it handling large numbers of cases? Might it be locating needy persons in the community and providing them with available services of which they are unaware? Or is it discouraging persons from accepting help in every way possible so as to conserve taxpayer dollars?

The problem is especially acute for staff, professional, and managerial jobs. Precise standards of good and poor performance are extremely difficult to formulate. And different individuals have differing standards as to what kind of job outcomes are good or bad. Behavior such as taking away sales from other salespersons might be viewed harshly by some who place a premium on ethical behavior. Others might view it positively as a sign that the individual lets nothing stand in the way of getting a job done. Many would react with horror to the idea of a social worker seeking out persons who need assistance. Others would consider this a necessity for properly performing the job.

Yet, and this is the point, *until agreement is reached as to what it is that distinguishes good performance from poor performance, it is not possible to have a rational selection system.* Selecting "good" talent means more than anything else that there is agreement as to what kind of performance from the individual is beneficial to the organization. Once this is established, it is possible to begin determining the kinds of traits, skills, and abilities best related to that performance.

The job success criterion should be established by supervisors and managers who impinge on the job in some way. This includes those who may have lateral or tangential relationships. The success criterion may be expressed in a number of ways depending on the job. It may be done by listing specific job behaviors, both positive and negative, or in terms of specific organizational outcomes such as sales volume or units produced. Regardless, managers must decide on behaviors and outcomes that constitute successful and unsuccessful performance. They must also decide on behaviors and outcomes that have no relevance to performance. And, finally, there must be an understanding by all parties of behaviors and outcomes on which agreement cannot be reached.

Job Specifications

After the job success criterion has been established, it is then necessary to determine what qualities in the individual should be sought when making the selection decision. These characteristics, skills, and traits are known as the *job specification*. The job specification is developed from both the job description and the job success criterion.

The qualities that are desired in the individual can be expressed in a number of ways. It might be some level of education such as high-school graduate or two years of college. Some specific training might be required such as completion of an accredited program in pharmacy. Experience might be listed such as a minimum of two years experience as an automobile mechanic. Certain skills might be wanted such as manual dexterity which can be specified by referring to a test for this ability. Personality traits such as pleasant speaking voice or ability to work without supervision can be required.

The assumption is that the *traits, skills, and characteristics required in the job specification bear a positive relationship to job performance as expressed in the job success criterion.* This is the key point in selection that much of the legal controversy deals with. Many selection procedures in the years past have been justly criticized for establishing job specifications that had no relation to job performance. Organizations would put in such requirements as high-school diploma with no evidence that high-school graduates performed better on the job than those who had not graduated from high school.

Another common weakness of job specifications is that they are often ambiguous or vague. Terms such as "dynamic personality," "self-starter," and "aggressive" are almost meaningless and of little value in selection. They are too imprecise. It is doubtful than any two people have exactly the same thing in mind when using such terms.

Job specifications become useful for selection as they become more specific. Expressing them in behavioral terms is a good practice. Instead of "good speaking ability" a specification such as "must be capable of making oral presentations of technical material so that it can be clearly understood by non-technical audiences" gives a more precise guideline for selection.

Selection Instruments   The selection process assumes that more than one candidate will be available for each position. This is largely a function of recruitment (discussed in the previous chapter). Job specifications are evaluated through selection instruments such as application forms, interviews, tests, reference checks, and physical examinations. The function of selection instruments is to increase predictive ability of how the individual will perform on the job.

The key issue with selection instruments is whether they help achieve that goal. Does the particular device being used actually measure the particular trait or skill it purports to measure? Many times they don't. Determining the relevance of selection instruments is a function of validation, which is discussed next.

THE PROCESS OF VALIDATION   In non-technical terms, *validation* is the process of establishing legitimate relationships among the various elements in selection. It is the extent to which a relationship that is either said or implied to exist does in fact actually exist. If a high-school diploma is required on the job specification, does the organization know that high-school graduates in fact perform better on the job than persons who have not completed high school? Do persons who receive high ratings on employment interviews for such things as "initiative" actually demonstrate more of this quality on the job than those who receive low ratings? And then is this quality actually related in some demonstrable or logical way to job success? These are the kinds of questions and relationships validation is concerned with.

Despite the fact that only in recent years has it been brought to popular attention by the courts, validation has been around for a long time. It is an essential undertaking if hiring procedures are to be productive (as well as in compliance with the law). It is the aspect of selection that has been of most concern to the government agencies concerned with discrimination.

75

It is perhaps a sad commentary on management in general and personnel management in particular that it took legislation and judicial decisions to awaken organizations to the critical importance of validation. Aside from questions of discrimination, no organization can be sure its selection procedures are serving any worthwhile purpose without validating them.

Validation is a complex process. It usually requires the services of an industrial psychologist or someone with special training in psychometric techniques. The use of statistical methods such as correlational analysis and multiple regression is an integral part of the process. Nonetheless, an understanding of basic validation concepts is not difficult and is essential for understanding personnel selection.

Linking the Components in Selection

Validation can best be illustrated by relating it to three of the selection elements discussed in the previous section. One is the job success criterion, those factors which distinguish successful from unsuccessful performance. The second is the job specification, those qualities in the individual associated with either successful or unsuccessful performance. And the last is the selection instruments such as tests used to measure an item on the specification.

Figure 6-3 offers an illustration of the process. The example is that of an insurance salesperson whose principal function is selling accident insurance policies which have a term of one year and are renewable annually. The illustration is not meant to be complete, but it does show typical items which might be used for the success criterion and for the specification. It also shows possible selection instruments. For purposes of illustration, the example shows how items may be stated either positively or negatively.

With reference to Figure 6-3, one set of linkages that must be established is that of the selection instruments to the job specification. Does the application blank accurately measure job experience or is it subject to distortions by the applicant? Would a reference check with former employers prove more trustworthy? Or are both subject to possible distortion? Does the Selling Aptitude Test actually measure the ability to sell?

The next set of linkages is in many ways the more critical. This is the linkage between the job specification and the job success criterion. Do persons without selling experience actually perform more poorly on the job than those with selling experience? Do persons who score below 65 on the Selling Aptitude Test perform less effectively than persons who score 65 or better? Is there a relationship between having or not having a high-school diploma and actually performing on the job? These are the questions which validation attempts to answer.

There are various validation methods for demonstrating these linkages or relationships. Different sources classify them in different ways. One help-

UNSUCCESSFUL PERFORMANCE	JOB SUCCESS CRITERION	SUCCESSFUL PERFORMANCE
— Volume of sales less than $100,000 first 12 months or less than $250,000 (cumulative) first 24 months. — Renewals less than 65 percent. — Orders, reports, paperwork inaccurate, illegible and not on time.		— Volume of sales in excess of $100,000 first 12 months and in excess of $250,000 (cumulative) first 24 months. — Renewals 65 percent or more. — Orders, reports and paperwork accurate, legible and timely.
UNSUCCESSFUL PERFORMER	JOB SPECIFICATION	SUCCESSFUL PERFORMER
— Less than six months experience in sales work. — Below 65 score on Selling Aptitude Test. — Less than high school education.		— Six months or more experience in sales work. — Score of 65 or better on Selling Aptitude Test. — High school graduate or better.
	SELECTION INSTRUMENTS	
— Application blank. — Reference checks with previous employers. — Selling Aptitude Test. — High school diploma or transcript.		— Application blank. — Reference checks with previous employers. — Selling Aptitude Test. — High school diploma or transcript.

Figure 6-3
Example of Validation Process

ful way to think of validation methods is to classify them as either (1) *empirical (or criterion related) validity* or (2) *rational validity*. There are additional subclassifications under each.

**Empirical
(or Criterion Related)
Validity**

The best type of validation evidence that can be obtained is through *predictive* validity, one of the two empirical (or criterion related) methods. It is the most scientific. If done properly it provides the most incontrovertible evidence that valid relationships exist.

Predictive validity involves determination of traits or characteristics that the organization thinks will be associated with successful performance. For example, from Figure 6-3 it might be high-school diploma and a high score on the Selling Aptitude Test. *Then persons are hired without considering these dimensions in the hiring decision.* Persons with and without high-school diplomas and persons with both low and high scores on the Selling Aptitude Test are selected for employment. After a reasonable length of time on the job, the organization checks to see if there are significant differences in the job performance of the two groups. If there is a significant difference in the job performance and there are no contaminating factors, then the organization can be more than reasonably safe in assuming that it has established a valid relationship.

The big drawback to predictive methods is the time and expense involved. The organization must in effect gamble by hiring persons it feels have a high probability of not being successful. They are also not feasible in small organizations where the number of persons on any one job is not enough to constitute a large enough sample to conduct such a study. And even large organizations have numerous unique positions such as director of research which do not afford a large enough sample to make a predictive study feasible. And it often takes years to conduct a predictive study and obtain conclusive results (especially true of managerial positions). But where predictive validity can be used, it offers the best possible proof of valid relationships.

The second type of empirical validation is *concurrent* validity. In concurrent methods the present work force is divided into categories of high performers and low performers. Attempts are then made to find significant differences between the two groups. If the present work force shows that high-school graduates consistently outperform dropouts then this standard can be used in hiring people. Or a test can be administered to the present work force, and if high performers score significantly higher than low performers, then the test can be used as a standard in hiring new persons.

The big advantage of concurrent methods is that they avoid the time, expense, and risk involved in predictive validity. The organization does not have to wait for results over long periods of time. It also does not have to take persons it feels have little chance of succeeding.

The big drawback to concurrent validity is that there is no way of knowing with certainty whether the characteristics found to be related to successful performance are a result of experience on the job or whether these are characteristics independent of job experience. For example, if high performers in the organization score higher on a test than low performers, it is possible that experience within the organization of being a successful performer may have influenced the kinds of responses given on the test. The responses might have been different before the individuals joined the organization.

Thus, the organization is dealing with an internal population which may be significantly different from the general population from which future workers must be chosen. But in situations where predictive validity is too costly or is not feasible for other reasons, concurrent validity provides an acceptable means for validating predictor items. Its limitations, though, must be kept in mind.

Rational Validity

In contrast to empirical methods of validation, there are a group of validation methods which involve more judgment and which are more subjective. These are classified as rational methods. The two best known of these are content and construct validity, and while there are technical differences, they have certain basic attributes in common.

Rational methods involve having persons knowledgeable about the job establish what might be called a logical or rational relationship between a job specification and the job itself. The most common example is that of a job which requires enough typing so that it can be accepted logically that a typing test is a reasonable requirement for selection. This would be content validity. Or it might involve a more theoretical construct such as spatial ability, which can be logically related to certain types of jobs. This would be an example of construct validity.

Rational methods are considered less acceptable than empirical methods, but are used in circumstances where empirical methods are not practical or feasible. They are particularly valuable in small organizations where the number of persons ever hired for any position is quite small or in large organizations for jobs for which only a few positions exist. In these situations rational methods are about the only ones the organization can utilize.

Contaminating Factors in Validation

In validating any selection model, there are a number of contaminating or biasing factors which must be guarded against. These contaminating factors are not unique to selection validation alone but can appear whenever the scientific method is used. If the data are not kept free from contamination, it is not possible to draw correct inferences or conclusions.

A very common error is that of the *self-fulfilling prophecy*. The self-fulfilling prophecy is whether or not everyone being tested has an equal chance for success. To phrase it another way, does the organization incorporate factors into its testing program that make certain results inevitable while not permitting others?

An example would be an organization that is convinced that a high-school diploma is necessary for successful performance. Perhaps a tight labor market forces them to hire without regard to educational attainment. Without realizing it, the organization favors those who have high-school diplomas. It provides better training. Supervisors unconsciously give cues that they expect poor performance from those who have not graduated from high school. When promotions are made, the high-school record is taken into consideration.

Later when the organization does a study, it finds that high-school graduates have outperformed dropouts. But the conclusion that high-school graduates are better performers could not be drawn. The organization has fulfilled its own prophecy by providing high-school graduates with greater opportunities. It is possible that high-school graduates *are* better performers. But the conclusion could not be validly drawn from the evidence because both groups did not have an equal chance at success.

Another common error is that of *distortions in the sample*. An organization might be testing two groups, those with low college grades and those with high college grades. The assumption in any comparison of this type is that the groups will vary only on the dimension being tested. If the organization has applied different standards to the groups, then the comparison will not be valid. The differences may be based on some extraneous variable.

By way of illustration assume the organization picked its people with high grades primarily from engineering and selected those with low grades primarily from liberal arts. If those with high grades later prove more successful, it may be due to their engineering training rather than the grades they received. Valid conclusions could not be drawn about the relationship between grades and success.

Additionally, statistical tests play an important part in validation studies. They must be carefully chosen and appropriate for the conditions of the study. Some are useful under some conditions and not under others. Sample sizes must also be adequate for the particular test being used.

Continuing Checks on Validation — It is also extremely important that continuing checks be made on the validation process once relationships have been established. A common mistake is to assume that a valid relationship once established will hold indefinitely. For the relationship to hold, the assumption is that all factors associated with the job have shown no change. A change in one or more of the myriad factors associated with the job such as technology, job design, supervisory methods, or organization goals can change the items associated with success. Thus, validation must be a continuing and ongoing process to insure currency.

Generalization of *Validation Studies* Another common error in using validation studies is to assume that a valid relationship found in one organization will be just as applicable in other organizations. Valid relationships established in one organization can be generalized to other organizations *only to the extent the organizations are identical in all significant components that impinge upon the relationships being established.* For instance, piloting an aircraft involves the same skills whether one flies for Delta Airlines or Pan American; however, it is less clear that this would be true of sales work.

It is impossible to establish exact guidelines as to when studies can be generalized. If different studies in different organizations of the same job consistently produce the same results, then it obviously becomes safer to generalize the results. All too often, however, organizations have relied upon psychological tests and other selection instruments solely on the basis that they appeared to work in other organizations. Guidelines for validation established by the Equal Employment Opportunity Commission have been emphatic on the need for organizations to conduct their own validation studies and not attempt to use studies from other organizations or other jobs without clear evidence that job similarities are so great that validation results are applicable.

EVALUATING CANDIDATES Candidates for selection are evaluated through use of various selection instruments already referred to. The most common ones are discussed below.

Application Forms The application form dates back to the earliest days of personnel administration. It gathers together much information which the organization finds useful, such as work experience and educational background. It also collects personal data needed for personnel records.

Recent legal developments have restricted the kinds of information which can be requested. Information that relates to age, religion, national origin, or ethnic background is prohibited. Information such as marital status and number of children cannot be asked of one sex and not the other. It also cannot be used for hiring if it discriminates between the sexes. Some states limit or prohibit questions about criminal records.

From the organization's point of view the central question is whether such restrictions will limit the organization's ability to select good workers. It is probably true that such restrictions curtail the organization's ability to select workers it would *like* to have. The organization may wish to avoid hiring women with young children. *But whether this will result in hiring persons who perform less effectively on the job is another question entirely.*

There is little evidence to support application forms actually resulting in the selection of superior workers unless used in controlled situations where data is correlated with job performance. When validated properly the application form can help predict performance on the job.

Interview
The interview has long been the most widely used selection device. The idea of selecting someone for a position without actually having a face to face talk, particularly for jobs beyond the entry level, would undoubtedly be anathema for most organizations.

The main charge leveled against the interview is that it is not a valid measure of items on the job specification. Even if the assumption is made that the job specification is validly related to the job success criterion, critics have charged that the interview does not measure the things it is supposed to be measuring. What is charged is that the interview tends to reflect far more the biases of the individual doing the interviewing. Hiring decisions are said to be made more on the basis of making a good impression during the interview than on one's ability to actually perform on the job.

The interview has been written about extensively and validation studies have been conducted. Much of the literature has been proscriptive in nature, dealing with what questions to ask to elicit traits such as "motivation" and "ability to work with others." The bulk of this literature ignores the question of proof that these questions are actually measuring anything at all, much less whether they help predict job performance.

The validation studies have produced mixed results. Under some conditions where interviewers have been trained and use a standardized interview format, reliability has been increased. This means different interviewers will agree about the same candidate. It is less clear that this increases predictive ability of how the individual will perform on the job.

This interview serves other purposes besides predicting job performance. It serves as a recruiting device, giving the interviewer the chance to sell the organization as a desirable place to work. There is no better method for permitting the prospective employee to ask questions about the organization and the role he or she might play in it. It also helps screen people for organizational maintenance purposes as opposed to strict productivity. This means that the interviewer judges whether the individual will fit the organization and be acceptable to present employees. This is a controversial use. It obviously raises the question of illegal discrimination.

Reference Checks   Reference checks are another tool for selection. They are used mostly to obtain information from former employers. College and high school instructors are also contacted by some organizations. Personal references are sometimes asked for. In years past records from police files, credit bureau reports, and reports of private investigative agencies have been used, the latter especially for high level jobs.

Recent legislation and court decisions pertaining to privacy have placed restrictions on such information. Persons suspecting they have been refused employment because of information contained in credit reports have the right to request access to such information and have it corrected if wrong. This undoubtedly means that information from this source will be more limited in the future.

The current climate of litigation also discourages the furnishing of negative information. Organizations have always been somewhat reluctant to put negative information in writing and written reference requests have probably always been of limited value. Regardless of limitations, the best reference still comes from contact either in person or over the phone.

Aside from any legal considerations, the problem with reference information has always been its predictive value. There has been little research on whether negative or positive reference data correlates with job performance. The employee discharged for dishonesty may have learned his or her lesson. Hiring someone with a spotless record is no guarantee of honesty in the future.

Reference checking has value besides that of making the original selection decision. It can also serve a useful purpose in helping placement of the individual. Former employers and teachers can sometimes supply information about aptitudes and abilities that aid the acquiring organization to better utilize the individual's talents.

Physical Examinations   Physical examinations have long been standard in organizations of any size. Physical examinations are used to disqualify persons from being hired because of physical limitations. From the organization's point of view the physical examination helps avoid excessive medical costs resulting from injury or illness on the job. It also helps the potential employee avoid work that may result in crippling type injuries.

With new requirements coming out under the Occupational Safety and Health Act, it is likely that the physical examination will assume more importance in the future. If OSHA places more severe penalties on employers for injuries or illnesses suffered by workers on the job, it is possible that employers may place even higher restrictions than at present on permitting workers who give evidence of some medical history from obtaining employment. This could result in a serious social problem.

Tests No class of selection instruments has created the controversy as has the use of tests. Even the term has become so emotionally laden that definitions are important at the outset. The term "tests" is often used to denote a particular class of written instruments which supposedly measure personality traits. They are often referred to as psychological tests.

There are actually a wide variety of tests employed by organizations, including general aptitude and skill tests. Typing and shorthand tests for prospective employees have been used for decades with little controversy.

Going one step further, *any* selection criterion used, whether it be college grades or physical endurance or visual ability, is a form of test that the applicant must pass before being hired. Having these characteristics measured is part of the testing procedure the prospective employee must go through.

By their nature the personality or psychological tests have come under the most severe attack, largely because of their seemingly impersonal nature and their lack of what is called "face validity." This means that it is hard to establish a relationship between such tests and job performance that seems plausible to the applicant. There are literally hundreds of different kinds of tests available which are supposed to measure a variety of attributes. They range from perhaps the best known, the Wonderlic, a short paper and pencil test of intelligence, to esoteric instruments that require hours to complete.

All tests are supposed to measure some quality in the individual. The assumption is that a certain score on the test will be associated with a certain level of performance on the job. The test score can then be used as an input to help predict performance and thus aid the selection decision.

The charge made against the use of tests, and that means all selection criteria, but especially written tests, is not that such tests automatically discriminate, *but that they were and are being used without any attempt to determine if an actual relationship exists between the test score and job performance.* In other words, few organizations were making any effort to see if the tests were valid.

Aside from the social question of illegal discrimination, there is a strong case to be made that use of such tests without any attempt to determine their effectiveness is dysfunctional for the organization. It is paying for a procedure with no knowledge of whether it is making a positive contribution.

Another current controversy around psychological tests is whether they are culturally biased. This is the issue of *differential validity*. Do minority groups score lower on such tests because of genuine differences or because the tests are slanted in favor of the majority culture? Opinion on this issue is far from unanimous among psychologists. Regardless, some organizations have conducted separate test validation studies for minorities and females.

Psychological tests have decreased in use since the Civil Rights Act was enacted. This does not mean that such tests have been made illegal. What it does mean is that organizations must be better prepared to show valid relationships between test results and job performance.

When used properly, and this means by using sound validation procedures, tests can aid in the selection decision. They have been shown to help increase predictive accuracy of job performance in many jobs. What the organization must decide is whether the expense of using such tests correctly justifies the benefit they produce.

Polygraph Examinations Another controversial selection instrument is the polygraph, more familiarly known by the somewhat misleading designation of "lie detector." By measuring physiological responses to a pattern of inquiries, the polygraph is supposed to provide information as to whether the respondent is telling the truth or engaging in evasion or outright deception.

Organizations highly vulnerable to employee theft use polygraph tests to screen employees before hiring. They use the polygraph to detect persons who have criminal records they are trying to conceal or who have engaged in theft or other kinds of criminal behavior for which no arrest was made.

Two major objections exist to the use of polygraph examinations. One is the question of validity and reliability—meaning do they measure what they are supposed to measure and do they do it with consistency. Many investigations claim to show that persons guilty of fabrication often go undetected while innocent parties are often unfairly accused of lying, particularly if they are nervous and upset about facing the examination. Part of the problem is that great skill is required in administering and interpreting such tests, and they are often administered by persons who are not qualified.

The other major objection rests on ethical considerations concerning constitutional guarantees of freedom against self-incrimination and the broader issue of the right to privacy. This is particularly sensitive when examinations delve into such areas as homosexual behavior and sexual preferences that are difficult to directly relate to job performance.

Several states have enacted outright bans on the use of polygraph tests and their use in the activities of the federal government has been been restricted in recent years. But many employers feel it is an important weapon in the battle against employee theft. For this reason, the polygraph will probably continue to be used unless completely outlawed.

MAKING THE SELECTION DECISION

It is not always realized that successful validation studies do not automatically make the final selection decision. What they do is increase predictive ability. This means the validation of items on the job specification increases the probability of making a correct decision and decreases the probability of making a wrong decision. But no matter how effective validation is, success is never guaranteed. There are still risks every time a selection decision is made.

The risks referred to are known in statistics as the alpha and beta risks. In hypothesis testing they are the risks of rejecting as false a hypothesis that is true and accepting as true a hypothesis that is false. In hiring terms it is: (1) the risk of offering employment to someone who will not be successful (accepting a bad prospect), or (2) not making an employment offer to someone who would have been successful if given the opportunity (rejecting a good prospect).

Table 6-1 is an example of a validation study relating academic standing to job performance. Assuming the study is sound with no data contamination, it shows clearly that the higher the academic standing, the greater the likelihood of success on the job. Therefore, the basic question is, where should the organization draw the line in deciding who should receive offers of employment?

The organization must consider that restricting hiring to those from the top third of the class eliminates the 180 candidates from the middle and bottom thirds (75 + 105) who have less chance of being successful. But it also eliminates the 120 candidates (75 + 45) who would have been successful if given the opportunity (rejecting a good prospect). And even the top third of the class involves a 30 percent chance that the candidate will not be successful (accepting a bad prospect).

Every selection decision involves one or both of these risks. They are inversely related and can never be eliminated simultaneously. Minimizing the risk of one maximizes the risk of the other. By selecting only those with high class standing, the organization minimizes the risk of accepting candidates who will not be successful but maximizes the risk of rejecting good candidates (the 120 prospects who would have been successful if given the opportunity). By taking persons without regard to academic standing the organization minimizes the risk of rejecting potentially good applicants but

Table 6-1
Example of Validation Results

	Unsuccessful		Successful		Total	
	Number	*Percentage*	*Number*	*Percentage*	*Number*	*Percentage*
Top Third of Class	45	30	105	70	150	100
Middle Third of Class	75	50	75	50	150	100
Bottom Third of Class	105	70	45	30	150	100

maximizes the risk of accepting potentially unsuccessful candidates. *These two risks are inversely related and are always present in every selection decision.*

Balancing the Costs

How then does the organization make its selection decisions? How does it decide which risk to maximize and which to minimize? (This assumes it has done validation studies and knows what the risks are.)

It does this by balancing two sets of costs: (1) the costs of rejecting a good prospect (who would have been successful if given the opportunity) compared to (2) the costs of accepting a bad prospect (who is not successful even though given the opportunity).

These costs can be conceptualized even though the actual dollars involved may be difficult to compute. The costs of accepting a bad prospect are fairly obvious and include such things as training that is wasted, poor quality of product or service offered, morale costs because competent employees have to cover for the individual, opportunity costs involved in having positions filled by incompetent persons instead of competent persons, and damage to the reputation of the organization.

Some of the costs of rejecting a good prospect include extra screening and recruiting costs, the costs of unfilled jobs if enough suitable candidates cannot be found, the opportunity costs of losing someone who would have been productive, and the costs if the individual successfully works for a competitor.

These costs vary in every situation and in every job. Commercial airlines establish very high selection standards for jet pilots because the costs of accepting a bad applicant are so great. Training costs are heavy. Monetary damages from accidents can be severe, not to mention loss of life. The commercial airline willingly turns away many potentially good pilots in order to avoid as completely as possible ever taking someone who will not succeed. The same would even be more true in selecting astronauts.

On the other hand, the same airline will be far less selective in choosing custodians. The costs of accepting a bad custodian are relatively low and the recruiting and screening costs of rejecting good applicants are relatively high. Accepting a bad custodian is far less threatening to the organization. And conducting the same type of high standard screening process as is used for pilots would be prohibitively expensive.

Thus the organization must consider many factors in developing the relative costs of accepting the bad versus rejecting the good. These include such things as the type of job, how critical it is to fill it without delay, what steps competitors are taking, the consequences of job errors, and one of the biggest factors of all—the condition of the labor market.

During times of a tight labor market with few workers in relation to jobs, organizations have to be less choosy and thereby lower their selection criteria—i.e., thus minimizing the risk of rejecting potentially good prospects but accepting a higher percentage of candidates who will probably not be successful. During times of a loose labor market with plenty of workers in relation to jobs, organizations can raise their selection standards and thereby increase the risk of rejecting potentially good workers but decrease the risks of accepting potentially unsuccessful prospects.

But, and this is absolutely crucial, all this assumes that the organization through the process of validation has accurately calculated what the risks are and which job specifications are associated with successful performance. The point cannot be made too many times. During loose labor markets, organizations assume they are raising hiring standards by doing such things as refusing employment to those without high-school diplomas, insisting upon high grades, or demanding high performance on written tests. But unless the organization has conducted validation studies (or uses studies by others which are legitimately applicable to its own jobs), it has no way of knowing with certainty what factors contribute to success. It therefore has no way of being certain which selection criteria raise standards and which lower standards.

ORGANIZING FOR SELECTION

The selection process illustrates the personnel staff department performing in its service capacity. Most organizations centralize the recruiting and screening function in the personnel department. This avoids costly duplication and avoids having operating managers spend valuable time interacting with numerous candidates who offer no possibilities for employment.

The employment activity is one of the central functions of a personnel department. Typically staff employment specialists work with operating managers to determine unit needs and requirements. Recruiting proceeds from this as discussed in the previous chapter.

One of the most important jobs the personnel department is faced with is the initial screening of applicants for employment. For reasons of both public relations and legal requirements, the organization wants to make sure that everyone who applies for a job receives proper screening. At the same time the organization does not want to spend a great deal of costly time on persons who are obviously not suited for employment. This may be on the basis of qualifications presented for the jobs available or the fact that openings do not currently exist.

Pre-employment screening has become an extremely sensitive area in recent years. In years past, it was often used as a means for quickly eliminating from consideration groups now protected by law such as females and minorities. Nonetheless, screening has a legitimate role to play if it is not used for purposes of violating the antidiscrimination statutes. For highly visible organizations who receive much "drop-in" traffic in their employment offices, some kind of screening is absolutely essential.

Expressed this way the screening process may sound somewhat negative—that its purpose is to avoid legal and public relations repercussions. This is not the case at all. Pre-employment screening is a very positive device. Done with skill it enables the organization to uncover useful talents and abilities in applicants of which the applicants themselves may be totally unaware. The clerk typist with superfluous typing skills in a particular labor market may have excellent employment qualifications in terms of industry, reliability, and intelligence that can be readily applied in other areas through skillful insight by a screening specialist.

It is common practice for employment departments to place their most junior and inexperienced persons in the pre-employment screening jobs. For the reasons suggested above, it may well be that this function should be covered by more experienced individuals. At the very least it should be supervised closely by someone qualified.

If individuals survive the initial screening, they are usually subjected to more intensive investigation by other employment specialists. If this further screening is passed, then persons are referred to operating managers as eligible candidates.

A common practice, and probably a good one, is for the using manager to make the final selection decision. This is considered important for preserving managerial autonomy. It upholds the concept that with accountability for results should go the authority for making selection decisions which will have an important impact upon the results obtained.

Naturally, operating managers do not have the latitude they once enjoyed. In order to meet equal employment opportunity requirements, it is often necessary for staff personnel departments to assume greater control than was formerly the case.

SUMMARY   There are five basic elements in the selection process. First is the determination of organizational goals and mission, the reason for the organization's existence. Second is the process of job design, the grouping together of tasks and activities to be performed by the workers. Third is the job success criterion, those behaviors or outcomes that distinguish successful performance from unsuccessful performance. Fourth is the job specification, the traits and characteristics desired in the individual to be hired. Last are the selection instruments, those devices used for measuring items on the job specification.

Validation is the process of linking together various elements in selection. It consists of establishing relationships among the job success criterion, the job specification, and the selection instruments. There are two basic kinds of validation: empirical (or criterion related), and rational.

Predictive and concurrent are two types of empirical validity. In predictive validity, applicants are tested for various predictor items. They are then hired without regard to their scores or ranking. After a reasonable period to demonstrate job performance, comparisons are made to establish relationships. In concurrent validity, predictor items are tested on the present work force and then applied to future job seekers.

Rational validity is establishing relationships on the basis of logical or rational reasoning. It involves no data collection. Construct and content are two types of rational validity.

In evaluating candidates for selection, various selection instruments are used. These include the interview, application form, tests, reference checks, polygraph examinations, and physical examinations. None has been demonstrated to offer consistently high correlations with later job performance. Of all the selection devices the interview has been the most widely used. Few organizations have done validation studies on the selection interview. Its value as a predictive device can be improved by proper validation. The same is true for tests of all types.

Validation studies do not automatically make the selection decision. Perfect predictor items do not exist. Every selection decision involves two inversely related risks. These are the risks of accepting someone for employment who does not prove successful and rejecting someone who would have been successful if given the opportunity. The organization makes its selection decisions by balancing the costs between these risks.

Organizations usually centralize the recruiting and screening functions in the staff personnel department. Pre-employment screening represents a compromise between giving everyone adequate consideration and not spending excessive time on persons obviously unqualified for employment. Final selection decisions are usually made by the operating or using manager.

SELECTED REFERENCES

HAMNER, W. CLAY and FRANK L. SCHMIDT, eds., *Contemporary Problems in Personnel.* rev. ed. Chicago: St. Clair Press, 1977.

MCCORMICK, ERNEST and JOSEPH TIFFIN, *Industrial Psychology*, 6th ed. Englewood Cliffs, N.J.: Prentice-Hall, 1974.

MILLER, KENNETH M., ed., *Psychological Testing in Personnel Assessment.* New York: Halstead Press, 1975.

SCHNEIDER, BENJAMIN, *Staffing Organizations*. Pacific Palisades, Calif.: Goodyear Publishing Co., 1976.

SIEGEL, LAWRENCE and IRVING M. LANE, *Psychology in Industrial Organizations*, 3rd ed. Homewood, Ill.: Richard D. Irwin, 1974.

YODER, DALE and HERBERT G. HENEMAN, JR., eds., *Staffing Policies and Strategies*. Washington, D.C.: BNA, Inc., 1974.

PUBLIC POLICY AND PERSONNEL SELECTION

7

⟸ IDEAS TO BE FOUND ⟹
IN THIS CHAPTER

- Development of public policy
- Principal laws and executive orders
- Leading judicial decisions shaping policy
- Affirmative action programs
- Systematic discrimination and its effects

In recent years government efforts to eradicate discrimination have affected practically all aspects of the employment relationship. The selection process, though, has been the target for most of these efforts. The previous chapter looked at selection without considering the legal aspects. This chapter examines public policy and its impact.

**DEVELOPMENT
OF PUBLIC POLICY
AGAINST DISCRIMINATION**

Modern efforts to end employment discrimination began toward the end of World War I.[1] At that time the U.S. Department of Labor established a Division of Negro Economics to improve race relations. The New Deal programs to aid the unemployed in the 1930s were supposed to be implemented without regard to race, creed, or color.

[1]U.S. Department of Labor, *Growth of Labor Law in the United States*. Washington, D.C.: U.S. Government Printing Office, 1967, pp. 221–249.

In 1940 the Civil Service Act was amended so that employment in the civil service without regard to race or religion became the official policy of the Civil Service Commission. This was followed in 1941 by an executive order from President Franklin D. Roosevelt establishing the Fair Employment Practice Committee. It was charged with ending discriminatory practices in companies holding defense contracts which were involved in federal vocational and training programs.

State legislation prior to World War II was largely limited to civil service, teaching, public works, and defense industries. Only about one-third of the states had such laws and enforcement was limited. It was only in 1945 that public policy began to deal with discrimination in private employment. In that year the state of New York enacted the first fair employment practice act to apply to private employers.

Concern with discriminatory practices became more pronounced during the years following World War II. But it was not until the 1960s that the federal government took direct action to deal with discrimination in anything besides government employment.

LEGISLATION AND EXECUTIVE ORDERS

Equal Pay Act of 1963   The Equal Pay Act was passed in 1963 and became effective in 1964. The Equal Pay Act amended the Fair Labor Standards (Wage–Hour) Act. Its primary purpose was to eliminate differences in compensation based on sex. It came about as a result of numerous investigations showing that females doing the same work as males were often paid less.

The act is administered by the Wage–Hour Division of the Department of Labor. Its major provisions are found in Section 6 (d):

> No employer having employees subject to any provisions of this section shall discriminate, within any establishment in which such employees are employed, between employees on the basis of sex by paying wages to employees in such establishments at a rate less than the rate at which he pays wages to employees of the opposite sex in such establishment for equal work on jobs the performance of which requires equal skill, effort, and responsibility, and which are performed under similar working conditions, except where such payment is made pursuant to (i) a seniority system; (ii) a merit system; (iii) a system which measures earnings by quantity or quality of production; or (iv) a differential based on any other factor other than sex: Provided that an employer who is paying a wage differential in violation of this subsection shall not, in order to

comply with the provisions of this subsection, reduce the wage rate of any employee.

Civil Rights Act of 1964

The Civil Rights Act of 1964 was a major step in dealing with problems of discrimination in employment. While the entire act deals with many areas and aspects of civil rights, the parts pertaining to employment are found in Title VII, and in particular Section 703(a) which says:

It shall be an unlawful employment practice for an employer—

1. to fail or refuse to hire or to discharge any individual, or otherwise to discriminate against any individual with respect to his compensation, terms, conditions, or privileges of employment, because of such individual's race, color, religion, sex or national origin; or
2. to limit, segregate, or classify his employees in any way which would deprive or tend to deprive any individual of employment opportunities or otherwise adversely affect his status as an employee, because of such individual's race, color, religion, sex, or national origin.

Title VII was originally sponsored as a measure to deal with the employment problems of minority groups, especially blacks. Almost by accident, and some feel in an attempt to have the bill defeated, sex discrimination was added as an amendment to the categories of race, color, religion and national origin. At first it received lukewarm support, even from some of the staunch supporters of women's rights. They were afraid the controversy and uncertainty that would be associated with sex discrimination might damage efforts to achieve equal employment opportunities for minorities.

But support for eliminating sex discrimination grew. And the bill in its final form was passed with sex discrimination prominently mentioned along with the other four.

The act established the Equal Employment Opportunity Commission (EEOC). This regulatory body was charged with investigating and resolving complaints of discrimination, and later with prosecuting violations of Title VII where necessary. Employment discrimination refers to much more than just the initial hiring. The "terms, conditions or privileges of employment" covers selection, promotion, transfers, demotions, management development—in short the entire range of personnel activities. It has thus involved the government directly in the employer–employee relationship to an extent not seen before. It has also provided impetus for many states to update or enact their own equal employment opportunity statutes.

Age Discrimination in Employment Act of 1967

The Age Discrimination in Employment Act as originally passed in 1967 dealt with discrimination against individuals "who are at least forty years of age but less than sixty-five years of age." With respect to individuals in this age group, an employer was not permitted:

1. to fail or refuse to hire or to discharge any individual or otherwise discriminate against any individual with respect to his compensation, terms, conditions, or privileges of employment, because of such individual's age;
2. to limit, segregate, or classify his employees in any way which would deprive or tend to deprive any individual of employment opportunities or otherwise adversely affect his status as an employee, because of such individual's age; or
3. to reduce the wage rate of any employee in order to comply with this Act.

The act did provide that it was not unlawful for an employer to take actions "where age is a bona fide occupational qualification reasonably necessary to the normal operation of the particular business."

In April, 1978, President Jimmy Carter signed into law an amendment to this act prohibiting discrimination up to age 70. The effect of this is to prohibit mandatory retirement for most persons except those Federal employees who are exempt from the provision. The act became effective in January, 1979, though tenured college teachers will not be covered before July 1, 1982. Mandatory retirement at age 65 is still permissible for executives who are entitled to an immediate, nonforfeitable retirement benefit (excluding Social Security) of at least $27,000.

Equal Employment Act of 1972

One of the widespread criticisms of the 1964 Act was that the EEOC had no enforcement powers. Unlike its somewhat equivalent body in labor–management relations, the National Labor Relations Board, the EEOC as originally constituted could resolve discrimination disputes only by mediation and conciliation. It thus depended upon voluntary compliance on the part of employers.

The Equal Employment Act of 1972 changed this. It provided the EEOC with powers to bring suit in the courts when conciliatory efforts proved unsuccessful. It also brought employees of state governments under the provisions of the 1964 act.

Vocational Rehabilitation
Act of 1973

Physically handicapped persons are covered under the Vocational Rehabilitation Act of 1973. It is administered by an interagency committee composed of representatives from the Civil Service Commission, Administration of Veterans' Affairs, the Department of Labor and the Department of Health, Education and Welfare.

The act has various provisions to assist the hiring, placement and advancement of handicapped persons. It also provides for affirmative action programs for all executive branches of the federal government and for all federal contractors who have contracts in excess of $2,500. Additionally, it states that no program receiving federal financial assistance may discriminate against handicapped persons. Handicapped persons who feel their rights have been violated may file complaints with the Department of Labor.

Veterans' Readjustment Act
of 1974

The Veterans' Readjustment Act is designed to maximize employment and advancement opportunities for veterans and disabled veterans of the Vietnam War. It requires affirmative action programs to employ veterans and disabled veterans on the part of agencies within the executive branch and for government contractors who hold federal contracts in excess of $10,000. It is administered by the Veterans' Employment Service of the Department of Labor.

Executive Orders
Regarding Discrimination

In addition to legislative enactments, the federal government has also taken steps to end employment discrimination through a series of executive orders. These are orders issued under powers granted the chief executive to provide rules for private companies doing business with federal agencies.

The most important of these is Executive Order 11246 issued by President Lyndon B. Johnson in 1965. It was amended by Executive Order 11375 issued in the same year. These orders delegate to the Secretary of Labor broad responsibilities for implementing and enforcing equal employment opportunity measures by federal contractors and subcontractors. They also mandated affirmative action programs for covered organizations.

These orders also established another important enforcement agency, the Office of Federal Contract Compliance (OFCC). The OFCC has established compliance agencies within other federal agencies such as the Treasury Department and the Department of Defense. It has given them jurisdiction over industries appropriate to their function. While in many ways the OFCC has overlapping jurisdiction and responsibility with the EEOC, the agencies as established were independent of each other.

Executive Order 11478 (1969) reaffirmed policies of nondiscrimination on the part of federal agencies. In effect it applied the provisions of the two executive orders of 1965 to agencies of the federal government. It also established procedures for the Civil Service Commission to implement and enforce the order.

Executive Order 11141 (1964) establishes a policy for federal contractors and subcontractors barring discrimination based on age. Executive Order 11701 (1974) covers returning veterans and requires the listing of job openings for veterans of the Vietnam War. Executive Order 11914 (1974) deals with discrimination against handicapped persons by federal contractors and subcontractors.

State Legislation

In addition to federal laws and executive orders, there is a whole body of state legislation pertaining to discrimination in employment. *Title VII of the Civil Rights Act does not supplant state law.* Rather it encourages the states to pass legislation of their own that covers discrimination, both for organizations under federal law and for organizations not engaged in interstate commerce and thereby exempt from federal law.

Over thirty states today have antidiscrimination legislation which provides for administrative hearings on alleged violations and then judicial enforcement. Some states go beyond federal law in the rigor of their requirements for fair employment practices. The Civil Rights Act requires the EEOC to defer to state agencies for a reasonable length of time when violations have been charged.

JUDICIAL DECISIONS AND THEIR IMPACT

The courts have had significant impact in shaping public policy towards employment discrimination. The newness of the area has resulted in many court decisions which are unclear and seemingly contradictory. Nonetheless, some patterns are already beginning to emerge.

A major case in this area is that of *Griggs v. Duke Power Company* decided by the U.S. Supreme Court in 1971.[2] It was a landmark decision, setting the tone for many of the antidiscrimination cases which followed.

In this case black employees for Duke Power Company headquartered in Durham, North Carolina, were largely limited to jobs as common laborers. To qualify for higher level positions, the company required a high-school diploma or equivalent and satisfactory scores on the Wonderlic Personnel and Bennett Mechanical Aptitude Tests. Whites met these requirements in

[2]*Griggs v. Duke Power Co.*, 401 U.S. 424 (1971).

far greater proportions than did blacks. The result was to limit blacks largely to the lower level jobs.

Suit was filed under Title VII of the Civil Rights Act. Both the trial and appellate court found for the defendant (Duke Power Co.). The courts ruled that illegal discrimination had not occurred since the tests including the high-school equivalency examinations had been applied to both groups equally and there was no evidence the company intended to discriminate against blacks.

The Supreme Court also noted there was no proof of intent to discriminate. By a unanimous vote, however, it overturned both lower courts. The Court noted:

> Nothing in the Act precludes the use of testing or measuring procedures: obviously they are useful. What Congress has forbidden is giving these devices and mechanisms controlling force *unless they are demonstrably a reasonable measure of job performance.* Congress has not commanded that the less qualified be preferred over the better qualified simply because of minority origins. Far from disparaging job qualifications as such, Congress has made such qualifications the controlling factor, so that race, religion, nationality and sex become irrelevant. What Congress has commanded is that *any tests used must measure the person for the job and not the person in the abstract.* (Emphasis added.)

Thus, the Court put the burden on the employer to show that requirements for employment are related to job performance. The burden is *not* on the job applicant to show that such requirements are not job related. The Court also ruled in effect that it is the *consequence* of employment actions *not the intent* which shall be the governing factor in discrimination cases.

Decisions since *Griggs* have both reaffirmed some of the principles set down in that case as well as narrowed them considerably. In *McDonnell Douglas Corp. v. Green* (1973) a black employee was fired for blocking access to the plant during a labor dispute.[3] The company refused to rehire him. The Supreme Court upheld the company in a discrimination charge. It accepted the company's argument that the reason for not hiring was job related and thus justified.

In 1975 the Supreme Court decided *Albemarle Paper Co. v. Moody.*[4] In this case the principal issue was what constituted evidence of nondiscrimination on the employer's part. The Court rejected the company's proposition that quick validation studies were adequate to refute a discrimi-

[3]*McDonnell Douglas Corp. v. Green,* 411 U.S. 792 (1973).
[4]*Albemarle Paper Co. v. Moody,* 422 U.S. 405 (1975).

nation charge. The Court appeared to rely on EEOC testing guidelines of 1970 which were quite rigorous in their requirements for validation. This case placed considerable burden on the employer with respect to validation evidence that would be acceptable to prove discrimination had not occurred.

Washington v. Davis was decided a few months after *Albemarle.*[5] In this case black applicants for police officer positions in the District of Columbia claimed that an aptitude test screened out blacks disproportionately. The appeals court in reversing a district judge upheld the plaintiffs saying the test measured performance in a training program and not actual job performance. The Supreme Court reversed, saying that job relatedness could be shown by different methods, thus seemingly retrenching somewhat from *Albemarle.* The Court also decided the case under the Constitution and not Title VII, thus raising some questions about its applicability to Title VII cases. The Court said under the Constitution *intent* to discriminate would be an important factor.

It is interesting to note that the Supreme Court was not unanimous in these three cases following *Griggs.* Strong dissents were filed in each of the cases indicating disagreement among the justices. The Court was obviously having difficulty with the complex issues raised by employment discrimination.

More recent cases seem to be narrowing the definition of illegal discrimination.[6] In 1976 in *General Electric Co. v. Gilbert* the Court overturned the conclusions of six federal appeals courts in ruling that Title VII does not require employers to include pregnancies in disability plans.[7] It seemed to modify the ruling in *Griggs* that it was the effect of seemingly neutral employment policies which should be looked at in deciding whether illegal discrimination had occurred. The Court said it was not women being discriminated against; rather, it was "pregnant persons" as opposed to "non-pregnant persons" and this was not prohibited by Title VII.

In a 1977 case, that of *Trans World Airlines v. Hardison,* the Court rendered a more restrictive interpretation of Title VII's prohibition against religious discrimination.[8] It said in a 7–2 vote that employers are not required to violate a seniority system or incur additional expenses to permit an employee to observe a Saturday Sabbath.

In another 1977 case, *Teamsters v. United States,* the Supreme Court ruled that even though a seniority system perpetuates an employer's previ-

---

[5]*Washington v. Davis,* 426 U.S. (1976).

[6]See Gregory J. Mounts, "Labor and the Supreme Court: Significant Decisions of 1976–77," *Monthly Labor Review* (January, 1978), 12–17.

[7]*General Electric Co. v. Gilbert,* 45 U.S.L.W. 4031 (U.S. December 7, 1976).

[8]*Trans World Airlines v. Hardison,* 45 U.S.L.W. 4672 (U.S. June 16, 1977).

ous discriminatory practices, it is not unlawful if it was not designed with discriminatory intent.[9] It said that Title VII protects legitimate seniority systems enacted prior to the Civil Rights Act even though they lock in the effects of currently illegal employment discrimination. Other cases have also protected the employer against charges of discrimination which occurred prior to the 1964 act.

Employment discrimination is a relatively new area in public policy. The courts are slowly developing a body of precedent in this area. It will undoubtedly require many years and many more decisions before a reasonably coherent and consistent policy develops.

Other important court decisions have dealt with questions raised by affirmative action which is discussed in the next section.

AFFIRMATIVE ACTION PROGRAMS

Affirmative action programs require organizations to not only end discriminatory practices but to take positive steps to insure that females and minorities are represented at all levels of the organization's work force in some acceptable proportion. In effect they impose upon organizations the obligation to give preferential hiring to these groups. Some affirmative action programs have come about as a result of judicial action resulting in consent decrees. Many large corporations such as American Telephone & Telegraph have agreed to affirmative action programs through the consent decree.

Title VII itself does not specifically say anything about affirmative action. The key provision for affirmative action is found in Executive Order 11426 which says:

> The contractor will not discriminate against any employee or applicant for employment because of race, color, religion, sex, or national origin. The contractor will take affirmative action to ensure that applicants are employed, and that employees are treated during employment without regard to their race, color, religion, sex, or national origin. Such action shall include, but not be limited to the following: employment, upgrading, demotion or transfer, recruitment or recruitment advertising; layoff or termination; rates of pay or other forms of compensation; and selection for training; including apprenticeship. The contractor agrees to post in conspicuous places, available to employees and applicants for employment, notices to be provided by the contracting officer setting forth the provisions of this nondiscrimination clause.

Many difficult questions are raised by such programs. One sensitive

[9]*Teamsters v. United States*, 45 U.S.L. W. 4506 (U.S. May 31, 1977).

issue is the question of numerical goals or targets. In order for organizations to demonstrate progress towards achieving equal employment opportunities for females and minorities, some kind of measurement is necessary. But measurement of necessity implies some type of numerical figure or "score." Numerical targets or goals are noxious to many in our society. They seem no different than quotas which have been used for decades to *exclude* minority groups from equal participation. Many attempts have been made by government officials to draw a distinction between numerical goals and quotas, but the distinction has not always been apparent.

Another disturbing question is whether organizations should lower standards to meet affirmative action requirements. In many cases this is a false issue because "lowering" hiring standards has meant not being able to impose desired qualifications as opposed to standards which are demonstrably related to job performance.

But the question is a genuine one where organizations can show that certain groups consistently do not perform as well. Or where a court order insists upon a certain percentage of females and minorities by a certain date without permitting the organization adequate time to hire and train them. In strict interpretation of the law, discrimination should not be made in favor of any group if it means selecting unqualified persons. But agency guidelines and court decrees have not been completely free from ambiguity on this point.

And probably the most sensitive and troublesome issue of all is so-called "reverse discrimination." It is one thing to base selection upon merit without regard to race, religion and the other categories. But affirmative action appears to go a step beyond this and in effect requires remedies for the effects of *past* discrimination. Thus a program for advancing certain numbers of females and minorities means that equally qualified white males may be denied opportunities to which they feel equally entitled. How should their rights be accounted for?

It will undoubtedly be many, many years before the courts have provided anything approaching a definitive answer to this extremely difficult problem. Affirmative action represents equally compelling rights in direct confrontation in which compromise is almost impossible. In 1976 the Supreme Court in *McDonald v. Santa Fe Trail Transportation Co.* ruled in a case involving two whites and a black accused of stealing.[10] The white workers were discharged and the black was not. The white employees brought suit on the basis of reverse discrimination. The Court ruled that the company erred and that whites were equally entitled to protection against racial discrimination under Title VII. The 1977 *Teamsters v. United States* case, already referred to, upholding a seniority system where there was no intent to

---

[10]*McDonald v. Santa Fe Trail Transportation Co.*, 427 U.S. (1976).

discriminate indicates that the judiciary is concerned that attempts to remedy past discrimination do not abridge the rights of persons not included among the target groups in the Civil Rights Act.

On June 28, 1978, the U.S. Supreme Court handed down a long-awaited decision in a much-publicized case, *The Regents of the University of California v. Allan Bakke*. This case involved the University of California at Davis Medical School which had reserved a specific number of admissions to medical school for disadvantaged persons. Allan Bakke, a white male who had been denied admission, sued claiming he was more qualified than some of the disadvantaged persons admitted. By a narrow margin of 5–4, the Court voted that Allan Bakke should be admitted to Davis Medical School. At the same time, however, the Court also ruled by a 5–4 margin, with Justice Lewis F. Powell providing the swing vote, that race could be used as a factor in medical school admissions provided it was not done in a rigid, quota-like manner as at the Davis Medical School. The latter vote seemingly endorsed in a general way the basic concepts of affirmative action programs.

It is important to note that the Bakke case did not involve a question of employment, and the Court made clear its decision did not touch upon the employment issue. Therefore this decision did not do much to clarify programs of affirmative action for employers, except by inferring what the Court might do in a similar case dealing with employment and not university admissions.

On July 3, 1978, the U.S. Supreme Court refused to review a 1973 consent decree that required American Telephone and Telegraph to hire more blacks and women. The company had agreed to set employment goals for race, sex, and ethnic groups, and, if necessary, to pass over senior workers in favor of "under-represented" groups to achieve these goals. This program was challenged by three unions—the Communications Workers of America, the International Brotherhood of Electrical Workers, and the Alliance of Independent Telephone Unions—who charged that the agreement violated seniority rights won in collective bargaining. The Court's refusal to review two lower court verdicts upholding the company program did not set a national legal precedent, but it suggested that affirmative action programs in employment may be viewed differently by the Court from the university admissions procedure involved in the Bakke case.

Numerous cases in the court system which involve reverse discrimination and affirmative action in employment will be reaching the Supreme Court in the years ahead. The badly split Court in the Bakke case (six justices wrote separate opinions) is indicative of the difficulty involved in establishing clear guidelines in this complex area. As already indicated, it is undoubtedly going to require many years and many court tests to evolve a coherent policy.

SYSTEMIC DISCRIMINATION

One confusing issue in employment discrimination is the nature of the discrimination government policy is attempting to eradicate. Overt discrimination is clearly against the law. This is a policy of deliberately reducing employment opportunities for members of groups singled out by the Civil Rights Act.

There is another type of discrimination which is more subtle and difficult to detect. This is **unintentional discrimination**, when seemingly innocent employment practices result in adverse impact upon the protected groups. The term for this is *systemic discrimination*.

Systemic discrimination is illustrated by an employer who, without any intent to disregard the law, imposes a height requirement of 5'6" for security personnel. The result is discrimination against females because there are fewer females than males who meet this height requirement. Thus this seemingly innocent requirement results in adverse impact upon females.

Another example is the employer who requires a high–school diploma for employment. Probably without realizing it this employer has possibly engaged in illegal discrimination against blacks and persons over forty. There are proportionately fewer blacks than whites with high-school diplomas and education and age are inversely related. Persons over forty are less likely to have been graduated from high school than are younger persons.

It is this type of subtle discrimination that enforcement agencies and courts have been most concerned with. Based on the *Griggs* decision, the question of whether this is illegal discrimination revolves around whether the height requirement or the requirement of a high–school education are related to successful performance on the job.

The effect of efforts to end systemic discrimination has been to force employers to examine every aspect of their employment process to make sure that seemingly innocent practices are not having adverse impact. There is a strong case to be made that this is a healthy trend for improving the total effectiveness of personnel programs aside from the social objectives being sought. Imposing requirements which are not related to job performance reduces the potential labor market from which selection can be made. This means organizations may be denying employment to persons who have the potential for being good workers and making a contribution to the organization.

SUMMARY

In recent years government efforts to end discrimination in employment have had significant impact upon the employment function. The Civil Rights Act of 1964 prohibiting discrimination based on race, color, religion, sex, or national origin is the principal measure in this area. Other legislation includes the Equal Pay Act, the Age Discrimination Act, the Equal Employment Opportunity Act of 1972, the Vocational Rehabilitation Act, and the Veterans' Readjustment Act. Several executive orders have also been issued dealing with discrimination by government contractors and subcontractors as well as federal agencies. Over thirty states also have equal employment opportunity statutes.

Numerous judicial decisions have shaped public policy. The landmark decision was *Griggs v. Duke Power Company.* This 1971 decision said it was the consequences of employment actions and not the intent that determined whether illegal discrimination had taken place. The Court also said that organizations must show a relationship between hiring criteria and job performance if groups mentioned in the Civil Rights Act are affected adversely. Subsequent decisions by the Supreme Court have both reaffirmed and modified considerably the stand taken in *Griggs.*

Affirmative action programs require organizations to take overt steps to end discrimination. This means either active programs of recruitment or actual numerical targets for hiring or promoting certain percentages of females and minorities according to a timetable. Affirmative action programs raise the difficult question of reverse discrimination. This concerns the rights of those not protected by the Civil Rights Act. In 1977 the Supreme Court heard arguments in the *Bakke* case dealing with a white male denied admission to a University of California medical school that has a program for admitting minorities.

The major kind of discrimination which has been of concern to government regulatory agencies is systemic discrimination. This is discrimination which results from seemingly neutral employment policies. A height requirement, for example, tends to discriminate against females because males are taller on the average. Following the *Griggs* doctrine the question of illegal discrimination then rests on the issue of whether or not the hiring standard is related to job performance.

SELECTED REFERENCES

COMMITTEE ON THE OFFICE OF ATTORNEY GENERAL, *Equal Employment Opportunity: An Overview of Legal Issues.* Raleigh, N. C.: The Committee on the Office of Attorney General of the National Association of Attorneys General Foundation, 1976.

GLAZER, NATHAN, *Affirmative Discrimination, Ethnic Inequality and Public Policy.* New York: Basic Books, 1975.

HAUSMAN, LEONARD J., ORLEY ASHENFELTER; BAYARD RUSTIN; RICHARD F. SCHUBERT; DONALD SLAIMAN, eds., *Equal Rights and Industrial Relations.* Madison, Wisc.: Industrial Relations Research Association, 1977.

LEVINE, MARVIN, *What Business Needs to Know About Equal Employment Opportunity Requirements.* Reston, Va.: Reston, 1977.

MINER, MARY GREEN AND JOHN B. MINER, *Policy Issues in Contemporary Personnel and Industrial Relations.* New York: Macmillan, 1977.

WALLACE, PHYLLIS A., ed., *Equal Employment Opportunity and the A.T. & T. Case.* Cambridge, Mass.: MIT Press, 1976.

PART 4

DEVELOPMENT AND APPRAISAL

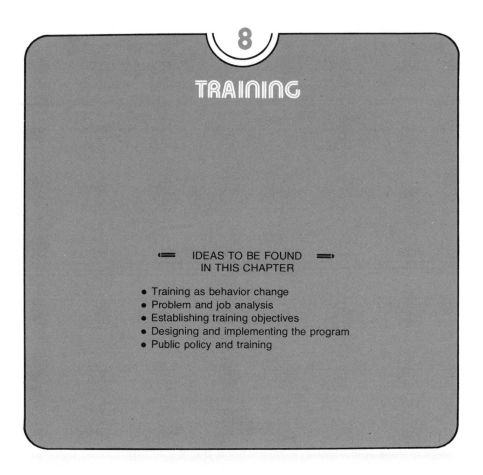

8

TRAINING

◄═══ IDEAS TO BE FOUND ═══►
IN THIS CHAPTER

- Training as behavior change
- Problem and job analysis
- Establishing training objectives
- Designing and implementing the program
- Public policy and training

There are two principal methods for insuring that the organization's members have the desired traits, skills, and abilities. The first is through selection, which grants access only to those thought to have the desired qualities.

Selection is far from a perfect process. Of necessity it is almost always a compromise. Candidates rarely offer a perfect match for the job specifications. Strength in some areas must compensate for deficiencies in others. In times of tight labor markets, standards may have to be lowered. And, most important, organizations constantly face pressure for change—the kind of change that requires workers who possess different qualities from those currently employed.

The second method for matching organizational needs with worker characteristics is the process of behavior modification. It is usually known by the simpler term of training and development.

It is a popular convention to think of training as dealing primarily with operative personnel, and development with managers and executives. It is important to keep in mind that while there are differences between the two processes, there is also considerable overlap. This chapter focuses on training of operative personnel.

TRAINING AS BEHAVIOR CHANGE Training is often thought of as something which occurs in a classroom or in an on-the-job encounter between someone who is teaching and someone who is being taught. It implies that something is being done by one person to another. In terms of modern learning theory, this view is greatly oversimplified as well as inaccurate.

Training is more appropriately thought of as something which occurs as part of the learning process. Learning itself cannot be observed but must be inferred from behavior. Thus, learning is defined as behavior change, the change in behavior that results from experience. Training, then, can be defined the same way—behavior change.

There is an implication which flows from this view. Training becomes not a matter of someone doing something to someone else; rather, focus is on the individual being trained who controls whether or not behavior change will occur. It also implies that training is not confined to those specific encounters we associate with teaching. Rather, training in the form of behavior change is occurring all the time.

The learning theory that has greatest applicability to the organizational setting is encompassed under the term *operant* or *instrumental conditioning*. It is also known as reinforcement theory. One form of conditioning (now known as classical) was first demonstrated experimentally by the Russian psychologist Ivan Pavlov in his experiments with dogs salivating at the sound of a bell. The concepts of operant conditioning were developed and refined by such American psychologists as E. L. Thorndike and B. F. Skinner.[1]

Operant conditioning is based upon the *law of effect*. This behavior principle says that behavior which is rewarded (reinforced) tends to be repeated. Behavior which is not rewarded or which is punished tends not to be repeated.

While much of the experimental work in operant conditioning has taken place with animals, experimental work with humans suggests that it is not just animal behavior which is responsive to reward–punishment contingencies. Humans, too, respond in similar fashion.

Thus, whether or not the organization has a formal or planned training program is almost irrelevant to the continual process of behavior change which occurs on an informal or unplanned basis. Every time a decision is made to grant or withhold a wage increase, some kind of behavior is being reinforced. When organization members discover that Smith has been promoted instead of Jones, Wilson, or Adams, they learn that Smith's behavior is more appropriate for promotion than the other three. (This is true even though management's reasons for promoting Smith may be totally different

---

[1]For an excellent discussion of these concepts see Fred Luthans and Robert Kreitner, *Organizational Behavior Modification.* Glenview, Ill.: Scott Foresman, 1975.

from what employees think they are.) The military officer who accepts reports from subordinates that are obviously inflated just to make the unit look good is training people, whether this is realized or not—training them that achieving results is less important than appearing to achieve results.

Through this informal training process, which is omnipresent and unavoidable, organization members are constantly receiving clues as to appropriate and inappropriate behavior. Often these clues are below the threshold of conscious recognition. Thus, while the organization may go to great expense and effort to conduct formal training programs, these may not have nearly the impact of the informal training.

Since behavior change is always occurring, it is extremely important that the organization be as much aware as possible of how employees perceive the reward–punishment contingencies. And it is essential not only that formal training be designed with operant conditioning concepts in mind, but that it is tied back into the organization's reinforcement structure. Training persons to utilize a new technique and then permitting supervisors to continue rewarding the old behavior (and *not* rewarding or even penalizing the new behavior) is a sure way to nullify the impact of formal training.

THE FORMAL TRAINING PROCESS

Formal training is what most people have in mind when they refer to training in organizations. Formal training consists of those planned programs which are specifically designed to impart new skills, abilities, and attitudes. They may consist of highly structured classroom teaching efforts. Or they may be simple verbal instructions at the job site between the supervisor and the new employee. But they have a common element. Regardless of the degree of structure, they are planned efforts at behavior change.

There are a number of elements or steps which are involved in formal training. Figure 8-1 shows these elements in sequential fashion. But with the exception of the first two, problem analysis and job analysis, it is not essential that the exact order be followed. And some of the steps can occur concurrently. But it is probably true that no training program should be undertaken without a thorough problem analysis and job analysis as a beginning point.

Defining the Problem

Training always implies a dissatisfaction with the status quo. There must be a deficiency either present or foreseen to make training necessary. Thus, the first step in the training process is to define precisely what the problem or deficiency is. *The next step is to make absolutely certain that a training deficiency is either the cause or one of the causes of the deficiency or problem.* Without this step, it is possible to design and implement a training

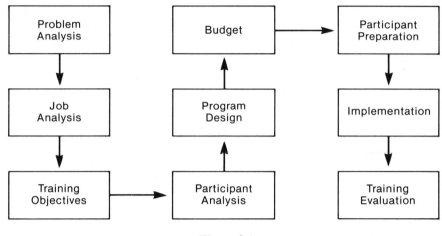

Figure 8-1
Elements in Training

program as the solution to a problem that is not related to a training deficiency! This is the most common mistake in training and probably accounts for more wasted resources in this area than all other factors combined. An example will make this clear.

A department store finds that excessive errors are occurring in customer charge accounts. This is traced to erroneous information being placed on charge slips by sales personnel. A training program in how to record and ring up charge slips is designed and implemented. All sales personnel take part. At the end of the training, they demonstrate their proficiency in handling credit transactions.

A month after the training has been completed, it is noticed that the same errors are occurring. Further investigation reveals that the problem is not a lack of skill on the part of the sales personnel. Rather, it is carelessness resulting from indifference and even antipathy towards their jobs. The sales personnel know how to do the job correctly. But they are not motivated to do it correctly. The reason for this is traced to hostile feelings toward management because of a misunderstanding over some bonuses the sales personnel thought management was withholding.

It should be obvious that a program of skill training is not going to resolve the problem as newly defined. It is possible, of course, that some type of training may be utilized as part of the solution. Perhaps training in constructive ways to handle unresolved grievances in the future might be of some use. But the major point remains the same and need not be belabored. The first step in any kind of training program is to make certain that a training deficiency of some kind is involved. Otherwise, the organization may have a problem and a solution—but unfortunately no relationship between the two.

Analyzing the Job   Closely related to problem analysis is an analysis of the job being performed by those under consideration for training. Sometimes the steps are so closely related that it is not easy to make a clear distinction between the two.

On occasion, the organization faces a situation that does not stem from a specifically defined problem such as the errors made in the preceding example. Rather, a thorough analysis indicates that upgrading the work force offers the possibility of an improvement in operations.

Under these circumstances the job analysis step is closely related to problem analysis. And, it should occur even when there is a specific problem. In job analysis, the job is examined thoroughly to determine which behaviors are associated with successful performance and which behaviors are associated with unsuccessful performance. It is the job success criterion once again. Without knowing precisely which behaviors are contributing positively to the organization and which behaviors are having a negative or neutral impact, it is not possible to design a sound training program.

After job analysis occurs, it is possible, even likely, that the organization will discover that some of the behaviors associated with good performance cannot be developed through training. It may also find that some of the undesirable behaviors cannot be eliminated through training. This information is important so that time and resources are not wasted in fruitless efforts.

An example clarifies this. A chain of fast food shops specializing in hamburgers does a study to determine what factors are associated with successful performance of counter personnel who take and assemble orders. This stems from analysis that the chain could offer faster service of better quality through improvements in the performance of counter personnel. The chain finds the following factors distinguish the best performing counter persons from the poorest:

1. They make change accurately and quickly.
2. While waiting for one part of an order to be cooked, they assemble other orders without getting them confused.
3. They prepare orders at a speed level significantly faster than the poorest workers.
4. They withstand stress better. They do not become flustered and disorganized during periods of rush business.
5. They exhibit higher energy levels. They work a full shift without tiring and losing speed and efficiency.

The analysis shows that the majority of counter persons acquire the first three characteristics as a result of experience on the job. Some learn faster than others and attain higher levels of proficiency. The analysis also shows that items 4 and 5 do not change as a result of experience or time on the job.

As a result of its job analysis, the organization decides to improve worker performance on the first three items by instituting a week-long training program for all new hires. Since experience on the job does not seem to affect the ability to withstand stress or energy level, the organization decides to obtain these qualities not by training but through selection.

Defining the problem and job analysis, then, are two critical beginning steps in the design of training programs. Failure to undertake these steps often results in training by imitation. This means that an organization undertakes training because others are doing it and are reporting that it has proved effective for them. The assumption is that it will probably do our organization some good as well.

It is always possible that training undertaken in this way might have some benefit. It is based on the assumption that training is not likely to do much harm and just might do some good. This may or may not be valid, but it is hardly the approach to recommend to organizations which want to make sure that all functions, including training, are providing benefit commensurate with cost.

Developing Training Objectives

Once problem and job analysis have taken place, it is desirable to develop training objectives. Much has been written on this subject. There is a wealth of literature on managing by objectives and on applying the concept to the instructional arena.[2]

Establishing specific training objectives provides the organization with the basis for proper program design and evaluation. Training objectives are positively stated solutions to the problems outlined in the problem and job analysis. They provide the means for measuring what has been accomplished and establishing performance standards for determining the level of accomplishment. Here is an objective for training fire-fighting personnel:

The objective of the training program is to improve the skills of fire fighting personnel.

This objective is poor because it is much too general. A better objective would be the following:

[2]For a concise and well written statement on educational objectives see Robert F. Mager, *Preparing Instructional Objectives*. Belmont, Calif.: Fearon Publishers, 1969.

Given the ten most commonly encountered situations at residential fires, the fire fighter will demonstrate his or her ability to take proper action to protect both lives and property in all ten situations.

This more specific objective provides the means for properly designing the training program as well as for evaluating it.

Analyzing
the Participants

Before any serious attempts at program design get underway, a comprehensive analysis of the training participants should be made. In many ways the participants dictate the kind of training that is most likely to be effective. Many factors must be considered. What is the educational level of the group? Are they high-school graduates or less? Are they college graduates? Will there be a wide range of educational backgrounds? Are their backgrounds largely in technical areas or nontechnical? Have they been exposed to formal training before? Are they likely to feel threatened by training? Have previous training experiences left them cynical about the process? Or have previous experiences aroused their enthusiasm for more?

Answers to these kinds of questions need to be gone over thoroughly. Individuals respond quite differently to training. Most college graduates will adjust readily to classroom situations, while similar activities may be very threatening to those without college degrees. Persons with technical backgrounds can be presumed to have familiarity with certain information that will be completely strange to those with nontechnical backgrounds. All these factors must be weighed.

Designing
the Program

Program design refers to the actual training itself. It is the contact point for bringing the trainee together with those experiences which are supposed to modify behavior in some planned way. Serious attempts at program design should not be made until the previous steps have taken place. Otherwise the training experience may be unrelated to the organization's needs and to the needs and capacities of the participants.

There are two major categories in designing training programs, *on-the-job* instruction and *off-the-job* instruction. On-the-job training takes place while the worker is actually performing or observing the work at the job site. Practically all jobs involve some type of on-the-job training.

Off-the-job instruction refers to classroom or similar type training activities which take place away from the job site itself. It may take place during normal working hours when the worker is being paid for the time. The category refers to the physical location of the training.

There are advantages and disadvantages to both approaches. On-the-job training can be directly related to behaviors required on the job, thus the problem of transferring knowledge to the job itself is minimized. On the other hand, there are many things which are difficult to teach at the work site because of distractions and the nature of the material. For example, teaching workers how to operate data processing equipment can be effectively done at the work place with the machines themselves. But discussions of how to handle difficult customers would be inappropriate if the customers were in a position to overhear what was being said. For this reason off-the-job instruction is utilized for many types of training. It offers more flexibility in utilizing various training techniques. In most cases a combination of the two makes for the best approach.

It should be noted that off-the-job training is typically not performed by the supervisor. Thus it is important that the supervisor reinforce what has been learned away from the job; otherwise the training will not be effective.

There are many other questions which must be dealt with in program design. Should the training take place for short periods spread over a long time span, or should it take place for longer periods over a shorter time span? (That is, would one sixty-minute training period a week for eight weeks be preferable to two sixty-minute training periods a week for four weeks?). Would outside instructors be more effective than in-house trainers, or would some combination be best? If off-the-job instruction is utilized, should it be on the organization's premises or at some outside location? What types of training methods will be most effective?

Unfortunately, while it is not difficult to conceptualize many of the questions which must be dealt with, it is difficult to arrive at hard and fast answers. Despite much research into the educational process, it is still very much an art and not a science.

The realities which exist in all training situations necessitate a compromise between the ideal and the possible. For example, a program is being set up to train operating personnel in handling a new computer system. Learning would be enhanced by a concentrated three-day program away from the job. But the nature of the computer operation, which involves around-the-clock manning including weekends, does not make this feasible. Thus, a compromise must be reached. Workers can be spared for three hours on a rotating basis during their shifts and the training can be spread over a longer time frame. This is less desirable from a pedagogical point of view, but it is a necessary compromise dictated by the circumstances.

On-the-job training offers fewer teaching possibilities then does off-the-job instruction. It typically consists of demonstrations by the instructor accompanied by verbal explanations. The learner then performs the task under direct observation and, after satisfying the instructor, is put on his or her own. Frequent follow-up is necessary to answer questions and to make sure the trainee continues to perform properly. It sounds simple, but adequate preparation and planning along the lines already discussed is essential for maximum effectiveness.

Off-the-job instruction permits the entire range of pedagogical techniques. While it has become fashionable in recent years to deride and denigrate it, the *lecture* (or lecture and discussion) is still the backbone of most classroom instruction. Comparisons with other forms of instruction are usually made on the basis of the "traditional, dull, dry" lecture compared to some "dynamic, exciting" new pedagogical technique.

The fact remains that in the hands of an enthusiastic, competent instructor, the lecture can be both stimulating and informative, and has proven to be an effective learning device. Some of the newer and supposedly more dynamic methods can be dull and uninspiring when developed poorly or implemented inappropriately. And even when they elicit an enthusiastic response from participants, their effectiveness in the actual learning process can be questioned.

But with this implied caveat, it is true that there are newer methods of instruction which can add much to a training program, both in increasing learning and in the positive response of participants. Indeed, one advantage of the lecture is its flexibility, which permits its ready adaptation and use with other teaching methods.

Among the newer teaching methods ("new" is used in a relative sense, since some of these have been around for a long time) is the *case* and its variations including the *in-basket exercise* and the *incident process*. These are simulations of organizational situations which involve the learner directly in analysis and decision making. A common premise in the case and its variations is that there are no right or wrong answers. The assumption is that the analytical process involved in reaching a decision and defending it promote learning that has direct application on the job. Cases can easily be combined with lecture materials to provide a stimulus when participants have been in a passive listening role for a long time.

The *role-play* is another type of simulation which requires the participant to assume and act a role of some type. In police training it might require one police officer to assume the role of arresting agent and another to assume the role of a harassed minority person. Everyone in a group can be involved in the role playing or only a few can do it while the others observe. The role-play is especially effective at dealing with affective or feeling kinds of change as opposed to cognitive or intellectual changes.

Programmed learning has become popular in recent years. This is self-instruction based on the concepts of operant conditioning with immediate reinforcement for correct responses. While programmed instruction has not proved to be the educational panacea it was originally touted to be, it can still be an effective learning tool. A programmed learning exercise is expensive and time consuming to develop. It is thus best used for instruction with large numbers of people where the subject matter is expected to stay constant for a long enough period to amortize the investment. An example would be teaching the fundamentals of electricity to appliance repair people.

Business games, both computerized and noncomputerized, have also become popular in recent years. As a training technique, they have found their greatest application in management development rather than the training of operative personnel. They usually involve group decision making and management skills in a broad sense.

In addition to the above, when one considers the use of *audio-visual techniques* such as movies, 35mm slides, overhead transparencies, and closed circuit television, the possibilities in program design become almost limitless. Each of the different methods have their advocates and their detractors. No research has ever demonstrated that one type is superior to others in all situations.

As already stated, teaching and learning are still very much in the realm of art and not science. Techniques that are comfortable and effective for some will prove entirely ineffective for others and vice versa. Thus, in the final analysis, program design will always involve judgment, intuition, and an inevitable amount of trial and error.

Developing the Budget

Training, especially formal training, is costly for the organization. There are direct costs including instructor fees, rental for facilities, meals and lodging, printed materials, travel expenses, and numerous other miscellaneous expenses. There are also indirect costs involving the wages and salaries of participants who are away from their regular jobs. These costs, while indirect, involve considerable amounts of money. Thus a budget must be part of the training process.

There are two basic approaches to follow with regard to budgets. One is to determine what is likely to be available from the organizational sources which must approve such expenditures and develop the program around this amount. The other is to design the program without regard to cost and then retrench as necessary.

While there is no firm rule to follow in this situation, there is much to be said for following the latter approach. With something approaching the ideal in mind during the design stage, it is more likely that all options will be given consideration. Modifications can be made if costs are too high, with the most essential elements retained.

Designing the program on the assumption of a limited budget may result in neglecting desirable elements which would be approved if the advantages were shown. As indicated, there is no firm rule to govern every situation, and there will be many occasions when it is made clear prior to the planning stage that only so much money is available and no more will be forthcoming.

Orienting the Participants

Participant orientation is an important and often neglected step in formal training. Workers are frequently sent to training programs with no idea of what to expect or why they were selected. As a result, participants may suffer from high anxiety levels or become indifferent and apathetic. Without orientation, the training is likely to be far less effective than it might be.

Persons selected for formal training should be thoroughly and comprehensively briefed prior to commencing the program. This is especially true for off-the-job training. Participants should know exactly why they were selected, what the objectives of the training are, and what they can expect to occur during the training period.

This briefing can be by letter, by direct contact in a meeting or individual conference, or by telephone. Someone in a position of authority should be available to answer participants' questions and thereby reduce anxiety.

Another reason for preliminary briefing is its strong motivating effect on the participants. It is also desirable to plan training programs so that participants can see their personal goals realized, as well as those of the organization. This too can have a strong motivating effect.

Implementing the Program

All the analysis and planning for training go for naught if nothing ever happens. Thus, the training program must be implemented after final approval has been obtained. Implementation involves arranging for instructors, obtaining materials, securing facilities, notifying participants, running pilots if deemed desirable—in other words thoroughly following through on all the details that can spell the difference between success and failure.

Evaluating the Outcome

Evaluation is essential for determining whether the training should be continued in its present form or whether it should be modified or even discarded entirely. Basically, the organization wants to know if it is receiving benefits from the training that are commensurate with the costs.

If training were performed in an ideal world, it would be possible to calculate both its monetary costs and its monetary benefits and by simple subtraction to determine its monetary contribution to the organization. This would be a form of return on investment calculation and would be extremely useful. Unfortunately, the real world places a barrier to this process.

Training costs are relatively easy to determine, both direct and indirect. The difficulty is in placing a monetary value on the benefits. Attempts have been made in this direction, but training benefits involve so many intangibles that it is extremely difficult to compute actual dollars of value with any degree of accuracy.

Regardless, it is still highly desirable to evaluate the training within the limitations imposed. Training evaluation involves use of a validation model as shown in Figure 8-2.

As the figure shows there are two links in the validation process. The first link is referred to as *internal validation*.[3] Internal validation attempts to find out if learning has occurred. Is there some measurable behavior change which can be attributed to the training?

Most training validation studies have dealt with this link. While it is a link not always utilized in organizational training programs, it is relatively simple to develop for most situations. Ideally, it involves both a pre-test to determine the performance level prior to training and a follow-up test to determine how much learning has taken place as a result of the training.

The second link is referred to as *external validation* and is in many ways more critical than the first. It also poses far more conceptual and methodological problems. External validation asks whether organizational goals are enhanced because of the learning or behavioral change that the training has produced. This is a link that is extremely hard to validate empirically.

The reasons for this are not too difficult to discern. For many kinds of training, it is not always easy to detect whether the new skills are being utilized. Even when this is obvious and easily measured, it is difficult to relate changes in organizational results directly to the training. This is a common problem in social science research and involves the fact that there are so many contaminating variables which must be accounted for. For example, telephone installers may receive training in customer courtesy and a test may show measurable changes in behavior on the job. But does this lead to higher profits for the organization? This is much more difficult to determine since profits and other organizational results are always a function of a myriad of factors.

While the second or external validation link is very difficult to validate empirically, it is crucial to conceptualize it during program design. It is easy when designing training programs to become so intoxicated with learning

[3]John P. Campbell, *et. al.*, *Managerial Behavior, Performance and Effectiveness*. New York: McGraw-Hill, 1970, Chapter 12.

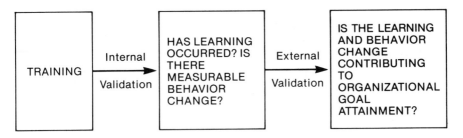

Figure 8-2
Training Validation

itself, that it is easy to forget that ultimately training must justify itself in terms of organizational goal enhancement. Keeping this in mind aids in designing an effective training program. It is likely, though, that it will always be difficult to attribute such things as profits and return on investment directly to the training.

ORGANIZING FOR TRAINING

Most organizations of any size have the responsibility for training divided between the line managers and the staff training department. Most management concepts suggest that the prime responsibility for training rests with the immediate supervisor. It is the immediate supervisor who is accountable for everything in his or her section. Therefore, in this sense, training of personnel becomes part of this overall responsibility.

At the same time the staff training department also has an important function. This goes back to the divided responsibility between staff personnel departments and the line organization discussed in chapter one. If every line department, unit, or section had to provide its own training, this could result in unnecessary and wasteful duplication. Therefore, for certain kinds of training and especially that which cuts across department lines, it is important to centralize this function. Greater expertise can also be obtained through specialization. The result, though, is that there can be conflict between line and staff.

Conflict between staff training and the line organization comes about as a result of staff training operating in its control capacity. This control role means that in addition to providing advisory and service functions, staff training also has the responsibility for making sure that line managers are doing an adequate job of training their personnel. There may be numerous cases when lax supervision results in employees who are working or performing at a substandard level. It is staff training's job to spot these situations and take corrective action. Obviously this can often result in a conflict.

Too much emphasis upon the conflict element, however, can obscure the fact that most successful training programs represent a shared and compatible responsibility between the staff training specialists and the operating supervisors. The staff department, in addition to providing expertise, can handle much of the detail work that the individual operating manager simply does not have time for. More important than questions of who is in charge of the training is that the fundamentals of sound training design are followed throughout the organization.

PUBLIC POLICY AND TRAINING

The training area does not pose the kinds of public policy issues that are found in selection. Antidiscrimination legislation is concerned with training only in an indirect way. Title VII of the Civil Rights Act deals with employment in the broadest sense. This means that employers must not discriminate in any aspect of the employment relationship which would thus include training. But the training function itself has not been the arena for the major legal battles over discrimination. Training, though, just like selection, must be made available without regard to race, color, religion, sex, or national origin.

Comprehensive Employment and Training Act

One of the two principal legislative enactments in the training area is the federal government's 1973 *Comprehensive Employment and Training Act* (CETA). This legislation is a revised and amended version of the original *Manpower Development and Training Act* of 1962. The Comprehensive Employment and Training Act deals with the social issues of unemployment and underemployment, but it still has impact upon the personnel function in organizations.

CETA is primarily concerned with the economically disadvantaged and is designed to provide a system of federal, state, and local programs to make this group economically self-sufficient. To this end, it provides a variety of manpower services including training for both the unemployed and underemployed. The act is divided into six titles.

> Title I provides authorization for such things as skill training, remedial education, testing, counseling, and job placement. It also provides job training with private and public employers as well as auxiliary services such as child care assistance and health services.
>
> Title II deals with transitional public service employment. It provides this kind of employment during periods of high unemployment, defined in the act as six and one-half percent or above for three consecutive months.
>
> In Title III the Secretary of Labor is given the right to provide

manpower services to those segments of the population which are especially needy. This includes seasonal farm workers, Indians, ex-offenders, and similar groups. It also authorizes the Secretary to engage in auxiliary services such as providing labor market information and computerized job placement to assist these groups.

The Job Corps is established by Title IV within the Department of Labor. This furnishes residential and nonresidential manpower services for low income, disadvantaged young males and females.

Title V establishes a National Commission for Manpower Policy. It also directs the Secretary of Labor to study a number of issues including such things as the impact of energy requirements on manpower needs.

Title VI deals with a number of general provisions. It prohibits discrimination in any of the programs offered and has regulations governing work and training performed under auspices of the act. It provides financial assistance for employers providing training for workers at the entry level or re-training for workers whose skills have become obsolete. Tax credits are also provided for wages paid to welfare recipients under the federal Work Incentive Program.

Apprenticeship Training

Legislation establishing apprenticeship programs is the other major public policy matter affecting the training function. This program dates back to 1937 when Congress passed the National Apprenticeship Act. The Act is administered by the Bureau of Apprenticeship and Training in the U.S. Department of Labor. It assists industry in the development, expansion, and improvement of apprenticeship programs for training skilled workers.

In addition to federal legislation, twenty-nine states have established apprenticeship agencies which work closely with the national apprenticeship system. Standards have been developed for apprenticeable occupations which must involve manual, mechanical, or technical skills. Such occupations as cement mason and dairy-products maker are examples of the kinds of trades which are included in the apprenticeship programs.

SUMMARY

Training, better thought of as behavior modification, is one of two ways for insuring that the organization has workers with the requisite skills and abilities (the other being selection). Informal training is the process by which behavior is continually being modified by the reinforcements and rewards which are an inevitable part of organizational life. Operant or instrumental conditioning are the terms which describe this on-going phenomenon.

Formal training, which consists of planned efforts at behavior change, is what most people have in mind when they think of training. There are key elements in the process of designing effective training programs. Problem analysis and job analysis are essential beginning points for determining if a training deficiency exists and to determine which behaviors are associated with successful performance and which with unsuccessful performance.

After these steps come the development of training objectives, an analysis of the participants in the training, program design, determination of a budget, orienting the participants, implementation of the program, and finally, training evaluation.

Program design may be either on-the-job training or off-the-job training. Both have advantages and disadvantages. In most cases, a combination of the two methods will prove most satisfactory. For off-the-job training the organization has a variety of training methods from which to select, including cases and related simulations, the traditional lecture and discussion, role-playing, programmed instruction, business games, and teaching aids in the form of audio-visual materials.

Training evaluation consists of internal and external validation. Internal validation deals with the question of what did the participants learn from the training. External validation is concerned with the relationship of the learning to the enhancement of organizational goals.

Most organizations of any size have training as a shared responsibility between the staff training department and the operating or line supervisor. Major legislation in the training area is the *Comprehensive Employment and Training Act* (CETA) and the *National Apprenticeship Act.* CETA provides training and employment opportunities for disadvantaged persons, and the apprenticeship program is designed to increase the nation's supply of skilled workers.

SELECTED REFERENCES

CAMPBELL, JOHN P., MARVIN D. DUNNETTE; EDWARD E. LAWLER, III; KARL E. WEICK, JR., *Managerial Behavior, Performance and Effectiveness.* New York: McGraw-Hill, 1970.

FAMULARO, JOSEPH, ed., *Handbook of Modern Personnel Administration.* New York: McGraw-Hill, 1972.

GOLDSTEIN, I. L., *Training: Program Development and Evaluation.* Monterey, Calif.: Brooks/Cole, 1974.

ODIORNE, GEORGE S., *Training by Objectives.* New York: Macmillan, 1970.

OTTO, CALVIN P. and ROLLIN O. GLASER, *The Management of Training.* Reading, Mass.: Addison Wesley, 1970.

U.S. DEPT. OF LABOR, *The National Apprenticeship Program.* Washington, D.C.: U.S. Government Printing Office, 1972.

MANAGEMENT DEVELOPMENT AND CAREER PLANNING

⇐ IDEAS TO BE FOUND ⇒
IN THIS CHAPTER

- Organizing the development function
- Managerial job analysis
- Managerial selection and assessment centers
- Career planning
- Objectives and activities for developing managers

Management development insures the organization of having a future supply of persons trained and prepared to assume managerial responsibilities. It exists in all organizations because work experience alone provides some preparation for being a manager.

But this is not the personnel function called management development. Neither is management training management development even though the two terms are often used interchangeably. Management training refers to activities which impart particular skills. Management development is a broader concept. It includes all the personnel functions involved in forecasting, recruiting, selecting, promoting, counseling, training, and compensating those with management potential.

Management development has traditionally been characterized by certain implicit assumptions and by certain operating methods. First, it was assumed a direct correspondence existed between the organization's needs and wishes and those of the individual. Second, the process of managerial succession was highly secret. Only a select few were privy to information about managerial vacancies and promotion procedures. Third, self-nomination for management consideration was practically nonexistent. Fourth, management's wishes were supreme; the *in loco parentis* doctrine of the education system was transferred to the world of work.

It would be an exaggeration to say that this way of operating has completely disappeared. But it has certainly eroded in recent years. Today there is greater realization that not all persons viewed as having management potential have identical personal and career goals. Equal employment legislation has spurred challenges to management autonomy in determining who should be considered for higher level jobs. Secret systems are giving way to more open systems. And today's better educated work force is insisting upon more input into decisions affecting their careers and lives.

The result has been a recent emphasis upon something that goes by the name of career planning (or career development). It is part of the management development process and probably has as many meanings as there are organizations with such programs. But one common feature is that career planning attempts to balance and combine the needs of the organization with the needs and aspirations of the individual.

Much recent literature seems to suggest that management development and career planning are separate and distinct entities. Conceptually they are, but pragmatically they are so closely intertwined that operationally it is difficult to separate the two. Career planning will be treated here as part of the broader process called management development.

Sound management development programs are involved with all persons in the supervisory and managerial categories. They do not concentrate upon any single group, such as recruits fresh from college. Thus, "management trainee" can refer to newly hired college graduates as well as to vice presidents with thirty years experience. Obviously, a development program suitable for one cf these groups will be quite different from that for the other.

One effective way to accomodate such differences is to establish various development categories or "management tracks" as they are often called. Some managers will have reached their potential and development will consist of activities to remain current and effective in their present jobs. Those on a promotion track will be prepared for future assignments as well.

ORGANIZING THE DEVELOPMENT FUNCTION

A major responsibility for management development must be carried by the immediate superior of the individual being developed. The subordinate must also show initiative instead of relying strictly upon the organization. But leaving the responsibility for development solely in the hands of the superior and subordinate creates a risk. Some will be capable and conscientious. Others will be less capable and conscientious. Under these conditions development becomes a very uneven process.

Management development, therefore, is most effectively carried out as a shared responsibility between the individual, the immediate supervisor, and a centralized staff department. This staff department, typically part of the personnel function, has responsibility for planning and implementing the overall management development program. It also has responsibility for designing long- and short-range development plans for each individual and for monitoring and evaluating progress. Much of the actual work will be carried out by the immediate superior, but this will be done in conjunction with the staff department.

Reinforcement is important in making sure the immediate superior does the job properly. Operating managers are told that development of subordinates is one of their responsibilities, but good performance in this area is not rewarded, nor is poor performance penalized. Unless this function is built into the organization's reward structure, it is not likely to receive the attention it deserves.

Direct access to top management is extremely important to the management development function. It is not something that can be implemented effectively in the abstract. There is no universal management development program. Development must be tailored to the specific needs of the organization, based on its future plans. If as part of its strategic plan the organization is planning to phase out certain operations and expand others, then the development program must be tailored accordingly.

ANALYZING THE MANAGERIAL JOB

Management development ideally begins with a thorough analysis of the managerial jobs within the organization. This is to determine what characteristics are associated with managerial success and which are neutral or are linked to poor performance. The organization may find certain characteristics common to most of its management positions while others may be associated only with management jobs of a particular type.

A definitive list of traits universally applicable to all management jobs has yet to be found. Some are more common than others. But there is reason to believe the traits associated with successfully managing a hospital maternity ward might be different from those associated with managing a research division for an electronics company.

Organizations can undertake this process by analyzing the reasons why certain managers receive regular promotions and others do not. Many managers are retained because their performance is satisfactory and others are dismissed for unsatisfactory performance. Bonuses are given to some and withheld from others. Assuming the organization has engaged in some type of rational process for these actions, an analysis of why these actions were taken can provide valuable clues to developing a list of traits and abilities.

An excellent look at this process is provided by work done at American Telephone and Telegraph in a longitudinal study of management progress.[1] In their analysis researchers at AT&T found approximately twenty-five traits associated with managerial success within the Bell System.[2] Some examples are:

1. Oral and written communication skills (ability to present a report orally and in writing).
2. Human relations skills (ability to lead a group to accomplish a task without arousing hostility).
3. Behavior flexibility (ability to modify behavior to reach a goal).
4. Inner work standards (desire to do a good job even though superiors will accept less).
5. Social objectivity (freedom from prejudices against racial and ethnic groups).
6. Resistance to stress (to what extent will this person's work performance stand up in the face of personal stress).

These are some examples from one organization; the list might well vary for other organizations. And no one individual is likely to possess all the desired traits. Some traits will be deemed essential while others can be compensated for in other ways. And there is no reason to believe one particular set of characteristics will be good for all time. For instance, looking at the AT&T list, it would seem social objectivity is undoubtedly far more important today than ten or twenty years ago.

The next step is to make some assessment of which traits and characteristics can be modified by a development program and which can not. The latter will have to be obtained through the selection process. For example, the organization might decide that oral and written communications skills are definitely subject to modification and can be included in a development program. It may also decide that a characteristic like resistance to stress is unlikely to be changed. (It may be that nothing short of psychotherapy will alter resistance to stress.) Other characteristics will fall in between these extremes.

To sum up, after deciding which traits and characteristics are as-

[1]Douglas W. Bray, Richard J. Campbell, and Donald L. Grant, *Formative Years in Business—A Long-Term AT&T Study of Managerial Lives.* New York: John Wiley & Sons, 1974.

[2]*Ibid.*, pp. 18–20.

sociated with success, management development must assess the probabilities that desired characteristics are modifiable.

IDENTIFYING AND SELECTING MANAGERS

Regular selection procedures are followed for bringing persons with management potential into the organization. But managerial selection also involves another dimension not encountered when hiring for entry-level positions. This is the internal selection process to identify and select managers from those already with the organization.

Internal selection poses special problems and places additional burdens on the organization. This is especially true for organizations with large numbers of employees scattered in many different locations. The problem is compounded if foreign locations are also included. Keeping track of this vast reservoir of people in some systematic fashion is a prime responsibility of the management development department. In recent years, computerized systems have been developed to help deal with this problem.

The central issue in managerial selection, though, remains that of prediction. Which individuals from among the many available are most likely to be successful when moving up to higher level responsibilities? Promotion from within does not solve this problem. Successful performance at one level is no guarantee of successful performance in a job of greater responsibility.

The problem is given added dimension at the managerial level because the decision is more critical. As a general rule, the greater the degree of responsibility involved, the greater is the cost of making a bad decision. It sometimes takes years for organizations to recover from a poor choice of chief executive.

Historically, organizations have relied upon the judgmental methods associated with selection techniques in general. Attempts have been made to increase the probability of success by the use of tests and other psychometric instruments. Where validated, such methods have proved helpful.

In an effort to bring more objectivity to the process and to increase predictive ability, researchers in recent years have developed a new approach to managerial selection. This is the assessment center, which was developed by Douglas Bray and his associates at the American Telephone and Telegraph Company. Because it represents one of the most promising approaches seen in recent years, it will be examined in some detail.

THE ASSESSMENT CENTER

The assessment center is a type of laboratory where persons being considered for managerial careers are sent for evaluation. The typical evaluation lasts from two to five days. Candidates undergo a series of written tests, in-basket exercises, simulations, projective tests, leaderless group exercises, oral examinations, biographical question-naires, and other experiential-type exercises.

The purpose of the battery is to provide ratings on a number of dimensions associated with effective managerial performance. Each candidate receives a composite score, which provides an overall rating of management potential. Included in the evaluations are self- and peer-ratings, as well as evaluations by trained observers.

The observers, or "assessors" as they are called, are usually managers from the same organization as the candidate. They receive special training before serving as assessors at the assessment center. Many organizations feel a prime benefit from the assessment center, in addition to evaluating potential candidates, is the training in evaluating and appraising that managers receive in their roles as assessors.

Assessment centers are now used by a number of companies, as well as by government agencies. They are based on the concept, by no means universally accepted, that the majority of managerial traits are determined by genetic and environmental forces that are largely completed by young adulthood. Thus, the assessment center concept places heavy emphasis upon selection in producing qualified managers. Development is not ignored, but it is subordinate to selection.

The assessment center was given a great boost by the initial validation study performed by its developers. Several hundred Bell System candidates were put through a battery of assessment center exercises. Predictions were then made as to the likelihood of further managerial advancement. The predictions were then sealed for eight years while the subjects continued their careers. After eight years, the original predictions were compared to managerial progress. High correlations were found between the original predictions and actual progress in the company.

Other studies since then have tended to confirm these findings. The later studies have been criticized, though, because in the majority of cases the predictions were not hidden from those making the promotion decisions. Thus, they cannot be considered unbiased.

The assessment center has far greater predictive ability than other techniques of managerial selection. Judgments of management potential based on supervisory ratings, the most common alternative, have not proved effective in predicting managerial success. A major advantage of the center is that it minimizes the personal bias inherent in judgmental approaches. Thus, it provides one answer for managerial selection that is in keeping with the requirements of the Civil Rights Act.

While emphasis is upon selection, assessment centers also make a contribution to development. Each candidate receives a score on the numerous dimensions being measured, which provides valuable information for focusing development efforts.

But assessment centers raise many difficult questions. Their cost is high and the number of candidates attending is limited. What is the effect on the morale of those who are not selected or who score low? Do they become organizational pariahs? How do you avoid problems associated with the "crown prince or princess" syndrome of those who have scored well? Since correlations are high but far from perfect, how does the system deal with cases where predictions are clearly inaccurate?

These problems are not insurmountable, but they do suggest caution. The assessment center appears to be one of the more promising managerial selection methods. Not everyone is meant to be a manager, and if assessment centers help place people in jobs commensurate with their aptitudes, they are making a contribution to the individual as well as the organization.

Organizations that obtain the best results from assessment centers appear to be those which utilize them, but do not rely on them exclusively for making promotion decisions. Thus far, the centers have not been found to be discriminatory by the courts. While it is still too early to give them an unqualified endorsement, they do offer encouragement for those looking for more objective ways to select managers.

ANALYZING CANDIDATES

Periodically each person on the management track should have a thorough analysis and evaluation of strengths and weaknesses. Once a year would seem too often, but the period should probably not be less than once every three years. This assessment is for the purpose of tailoring a development program appropriate to the individual's needs.

This assessment is much more than the annual performance review. It involves a total look at the candidate, and should comprise educational background, information from performance reviews, ratings by superiors and even peers, psychological profiles, and, by no means least, honest self-evaluation. Assessment center evaluations can aid in this process.

This kind of analysis takes place in conjunction with the managerial job analysis. The individual is not being developed in a vacuum, rather development must take place in conjunction with the kind of jobs and career he or she is preparing for.

A typical personal analysis might note weaknesses in the individual's ability to make presentations before groups. Oral communication skills need attention since this will be a regular part of future duties if advancement continues. Another problem might be a tendency to become rattled under pressure. Ways to cope with this could be discussed. A strength might be that the individual appears to have great capacity to persevere in a task. This strength could be built on as the individual prepares for future assignments.

Such an assessment is not an evaluation review for allocating organizational rewards. Nor is it for assessing penalties for poor performance. It is strictly a developmental review designed to provide assistance for better job performance, thereby aiding the individual as well as the organization.

CAREER PLANNING Career planning is a relatively new concept in personnel administration. Stated quite simply, it is an attempt by the organization to take the individual's needs, aspirations, and preferences into account when making promotion and transfer decisions.

Historically this has not been the case. The assumption was not so much that the individual's needs should be subordinated, rather it was assumed that what was best for the organization was best for the individual. Management personnel were assumed to have a close identity with the organization. Promotions and any resultant relocations were seldom turned down.

This thinking has changed in recent years. There are many different ways that individuals can satisfy their personal aspirations in large organizations. Some will prefer continued advancement into more demanding jobs in general management; others may prefer careers in staff and supporting operations. An individual's aspirations are not constant and unchanging as was once assumed. They are likely to change over time.

For example, many persons find themselves rethinking their personal goals at certain stages of life. For both sexes, the 40s and early 50s are one such time. Often so much energy has been expended raising and educating children that little thought is given to what happens when the children have left home.

At this stage of life an individual who has spent a career in line management may recall an earlier ambition to teach. Perhaps a move into the training department can be arranged. This might be the means for restoring some lost zest, if that has become a problem.

Or the individual may find other ways to realize this ambition. Perhaps he or she can teach some evening courses at a local college or high school. The organization could cooperate by making some adjustments in the individual's office schedule. Or perhaps the individual will decide that a complete change is appropriate and will leave the organization entirely.

Under these circumstances the organization can make a significant contribution to itself and the individual through a career planning program of the type being discussed. Before severing relations entirely, a leave of absence can be arranged to let the person find out if this is just a transient whim. It may be nothing more than that. With time and counseling, the individual can return to the organization with a more realistic approach to personal goals. Perhaps certain aspects of the working relationship which have been causing a problem can be adjusted.

There are no formulas for installing career planning programs. It is more a matter of organizational philosophy than of technique. It involves periodic discussions between persons on the management track and organizational representatives concerning what the individual wants in relation to the alternatives available.

In large organizations with thousands of employees, career planning programs will not be easy. Certainly the wishes and preferences of individuals cannot always be given precedence. There will always have to be compromise. But permitting personnel a degree of input into decisions affecting their lives is becoming more and more common in enlightened organizations.

Some organizations have begun to experiment with systems similar in concept to the assessment center, which permit the individual to receive insights into motivations, aptitudes, needs, and feelings that often remain hidden. Some persons may find their needs can only be met by occupations totally unconnected with the present organization. The assumption is that in the long run both parties are better off, even if the organization loses people who are good performers.

DEVELOPING OBJECTIVES AND ACTION PLANS

Overall objectives and action plans should be established by the staff management development department for the overall program and for each managerial track. In addition, it is desirable that each managerial candidate periodically establish a set of personal development objectives and plans for meeting these objectives. This should be done in conjunction with the immediate supervisor and the staff department.

Objectives and action plans permit a systematic approach to development. They encourage better coordination since development is affected by what the immediate supervisor does, the activities provided by the organization, and the things the candidate must do on his or her own. They are based in part on the managerial job analysis and the candidate assessment already discussed.

For example, an engineer in a manufacturing firm with aspirations for management might establish the following objective:

OBJECTIVE

Improve skill in making oral presentations of technical material that can easily be understood by nontechnical audiences.

Action Plan

1. For general improvement in public speaking, enroll in non-credit public speaking course offered in the evening division of the local university.
2. For particular emphasis upon oral presentations of technical material, attend three-day workshop on this topic offered by the leading engineering society.
3. Additionally, attend as a nonparticipating observer for the next year the division's presentations to top management at the quarterly budget and progress reviews.

A police officer in a metropolitan area with plans for continuing advancement into higher level positions might establish an objective like the following:

OBJECTIVE

Improve skills at handling crowds of an aggressive, hostile nature so as to reduce the chances of riot and to hold property damage and personal injuries to a minimum.

Action Plan

1. During July attend the two-week FBI riot control school offered in Washington, D.C.
2. Participate in the department's training simulations in crowd control held every two months.
3. When current duties permit, join the department's riot control squad as observer during actual or potential riots during the following year.

This is the kind of systematic approach that is likely to achieve tangible development results. There is no special number of development objectives each individual should have. Obviously all development cannot occur in one period, and objectives can be long range as well as short range.

ACTIVITIES FOR DEVELOPING MANAGERS

Development On-the-Job Job rotation has been the primary traditional means for developing managers. This remains true today and will probably always be the case. Experience is still the best teacher.

But to speak of job rotation as the primary development tool require⁻

qualification. Job rotation in some random, unplanned fashion is not what is meant. An individual can spend years in a variety of jobs. But if those jobs have little relation to the skills that will eventually be needed to achieve one's long-term career goals, much time can be wasted.

More systematic planning of development activities has resulted in something called *career pathing.* Career pathing is job rotation, but rotation in a planned, orderly sequence. With career pathing the organization reviews the usual job steps required for advancement to determine if all are necessary. Are any important areas of knowledge being neglected? Career pathing requires a thorough understanding of the managerial jobs at higher levels so that the kinds of work exposure necessary to attain those higher levels can be determined accurately.

Career pathing has come about because of pressures related to affirmative action to prepare females and minorities for management. This has caused organizations to closely examine their career progression lines. If the organization is expected to have a certain number of females and minorities in management jobs by a certain date, then it is imperative that on-the-job training not be extended unnecessarily.

But career pathing makes sense for more than simply meeting affirmative action goals. Just exactly what previous job exposures really enhance performance in higher level positions? Career pathing concepts help provide an answer.

Rotation among jobs needs to be tied closely to the individual's objectives for development. Some supervisors are better trainers than others. Some delegate little to their subordinates and job rotation can result in hard work but little opportunity for acquiring decision making and other skills. By specifying precisely what skills the individual is to acquire as a result of performing in a certain job, it is easier to maintain control of learning.

There are other miscellaneous ways organizations have for imparting skills on the job. Coaching by superiors is a largely informal method that will always be important. Some organizations establish special boards and committees for junior executives to give them practice at tasks performed by higher level executives. Acting as an understudy to a high level executive without actually assuming responsibilities may have some merit. Again, if these kinds of activities are planned for by the staff management development department as part of the overall program, they can add to development.

Development Off-the-Job

Development activities off-the-job are limited only by the imagination and the budget. Training programs come in great variety today. These can be developed as part of the in-house training effort. Or the organization can take advantage of the plethora of training programs offered by colleges and universities, consulting firms, private individuals, and professional and trade groups.

Courses vary from "fundamentals of management" for new supervisors to "strategic planning" for senior executives. Management by objectives, leadership concepts, marketing for nonmarketing managers, team building, transactional analysis for workers and managers, operations management, computerized information systems, cost accounting, complying with equal employment opportunity laws—these are just a sampling of the topics available. It is difficult today to find a topic for which a training program has not been prepared. Modes of presentation also vary widely from standard lecture and discussion to programmed learning modules combining workbooks, 35mm slides, and cassette tapes.

The principles involved in planning good training programs are crucial in utilizing these kinds of activities. Some of these programs are highly specialized and deal with tightly defined areas. Others, especially the various university and business school programs, are broad gauge and are supposed to up-grade the manager in a more general way.

Individual study, night courses at college, professional meetings, interaction at conventions—all of these offer possibilities for development and growth. What is important is initiative on the part of the individual and the organization. Off-the-job development, in particular, shifts more of the burden to the individual. Here is where the individual can assume responsibility for his or her career in a very direct way. By enterprise and effort that takes place away from the work site, the individual can maintain and enhance those skills and abilities needed for managerial growth.

MONITORING AND EVALUATING THE DEVELOPMENT PROGRAM

For a development program to be successful, continual monitoring and evaluation is essential. This is true for the overall program. It is especially important for each individual on the management tracks. Organizations go to enormous expense to recruit highly qualified candidates with great potential. But the candidates can become bogged down in what they see as dead-end jobs; they can encounter supervisors who provide little guidance and direction. Monitoring is needed to make sure development is meeting the expectations of both the individual and the organization.

Monitoring and evaluation is one of the principal functions of the staff management development department. It requires a delicate touch at times if operating supervisors feel their authority is being usurped. But unless this function is centralized, it is not likely to be performed.

Monitoring includes letting individuals know when they are perceived as having reached as high in the organization as they are likely to go. While such honesty can be difficult, it permits the individual to make informed decisions regarding his or her career. It also raises the opportunity for lateral moves to prevent stagnation.

Evaluation of the management development program poses the same problems as does training. The validation model is the same. The organization wants to be sure that learning has occurred. Has behavior change happened as planned? It then wants to be sure that the behavior change or learning is related to organizational goals. Some of this can be done formally through pre-tests and post-tests. And some evaluation will always involve subjective judgments.

PUBLIC POLICY AND MANAGEMENT DEVELOPMENT

The same legislation governing selection applies to management development. Equal opportunities for management training and promotion must be given without regard to race, religion, age, sex, or national origin.

The Civil Rights Act of 1964 is the basic legislation in this area. The most difficult area for management to cope with relates to affirmative action programs. This important area is still being tested in the courts. Providing opportunities for females and minorities under decrees that require meeting numerical goals opens the organization to charges of reverse discrimination. Organizations will have to struggle with this difficult problem until clearer guidelines are provided by the enforcement agencies and the courts.

What is certain is that regardless of numerical goals and timetables, organizations have a legal obligation to provide access to management positions for females and minorities. This means that management development programs must be greatly widened. Organizations correctly insist that only qualified persons should become managers. This places additional burdens on organizations to examine their traditional selection procedures and devise imaginative development programs for qualified females and minority group members.

SUMMARY

Management development insures that the organization has persons prepared to assume managerial responsibilities. It should be a shared responsibility between the candidate, the immediate supervisor, and the staff department. The first task in management development is analyzing the managerial job to ascertain the traits and qualities associated with successful performance.

Managerial selection involves both an internal and an external process.

The assessment center shows signs of being a valuable tool in managerial selection. At the center managerial skills and traits are measured in a laboratory setting. Assessment centers assume that obtaining effective managers is more dependent upon selection than development.

Each candidate on the management track should have a periodic analysis of strengths and weaknesses. The development program is then tailored individually, based on this analysis. A relatively new process in development is career planning. This permits the individual to have inputs into his or her career choice.

Objectives and action plans are important parts of the development process. Activities for developing managers can be on the job and off the job. Job rotation is still the primary on-the-job development technique. Career pathing is a systematic approach to job rotation to insure that the jobs held contribute to the individual's growth. Off-the-job development activities can involve everything from university executive programs to individual reading.

Continuous monitoring and evaluation of the development program is essential. This is largely a staff personnel function. Management development is affected by the Civil Rights Act. Access to management positions must be given to females and minorities without resulting in reverse discrimination.

SELECTED REFERENCES

Bray, Douglas W., Richard J. Campbell, and Donald L. Grant, *Formative Years in Business—A Long-Term AT&T Study of Managerial Lives.* New York: John Wiley & Sons, 1974.

Hall, Douglas, *Careers in Organizations.* Santa Monica, Calif.: Goodyear, 1976.

Holland, John, *Making Vocational Choices: A Theory of Careers.* Englewood Cliffs, N.J.: Prentice-Hall, 1973.

Kaufman, Herbert, *Obsolescence and Professional Career Development.* New York: AMACOM, American Management Association, 1974.

Miner, John B., *The Human Constraint—The Coming Shortage of Managerial Talent.* Washington, D. C.: Bureau of National Affairs, 1974.

Silber, Mark B. and V. Clayton Sherman, *Managerial Performance and Promotability: The Making of an Executive.* New York: AMACOM, American Management Association, 1974.

PERFORMANCE APPRAISAL

⟸ IDEAS TO BE FOUND ⟹
IN THIS CHAPTER

- Goals in performance appraisal
- Appraisal methods
- Who performs the rating?
- Frequency and timing of appraisals
- Innovations in performance appraisal

Evaluating others is inevitable in human existence. Whether choosing a tennis partner or voting for a political candidate, it is natural and unavoidable for people to rate one another.

Organizations have two appraisal systems which exist side by side. One consists of the informal evaluations that all persons make about others; the other consists of the formal judgments which become part of the official record. Formalizing performance appraisal as an organizational function adds new dimensions to the process.

A problem frequently encountered is that the two systems do not coincide. Persons perceived by many as undeserving often receive organizational rewards. Persons perceived as meritorious often go unrecognized. For many people the official judgments they hear or think they hear have no relation to the organizational rewards they receive.

This chapter is devoted to the formal appraisal process. But the existence of the informal should be kept in mind. It is a complicating factor to the difficult and troublesome issues raised by performance appraisal. What are the purposes of performance appraisal? Who should do the appraising? How is performance to be defined? When and how often should appraisal occur?

These are just some of the issues with which the organization must grapple and which are touched on in this chapter. The perfect appraisal system does not exist. All methods have their advantages and disadvantages. Achieving one objective with appraisal often means another must be sacrificed. The organization must make choices among the many trade-offs and compromises that are inevitable in developing a workable and useful appraisal system.

DEFINING PERFORMANCE

The most important step in any appraisal system is that of defining performance. This is the job success criterion discussed at length in earlier chapters. What is it that distinguishes good performance from poor performance?

Without a clear definition of what constitutes good performance, it is not possible to have a rational appraisal system. Some methods, including conventional rating which is widely used, largely ignore this question. Ratings are given that rank the employee's performance without the rater having to specify the basis for making judgments.

Other methods have the advantage of forcing those using the system to come to grips with this issue. These systems require persons familiar with the job to systematically determine the behaviors and outcomes that relate to successful performance. This is done before any individual is actually rated or appraised.

When this approach is used, it is common to find wide disagreement among potential raters over attributes related to different levels of performance. One supervisor feels that salespersons should sacrifice sales rather than promise delivery dates which can't be met. Another feels just the opposite. Making the sale takes precedence and the consequences can be worried about later. Yet a third supervisor may vacillate between the two positions. Appraisals have little meaning unless these differences are ironed out.

SETTING GOALS

Performance appraisal serves one major goal in *evaluating past performance*. This enables the organization to allocate financial rewards such as wages, salaries, and bonuses. The evaluation function also helps assess organizational penalties such as dismissal and demotion. And information provided by evaluation also aids the promotion decision.

140

Employee development is another major goal of performance appraisal. This means improving employee performance in the future. It is based on an analysis of strengths and weaknesses revealed by past performance.

Problems arise because these goals are not always compatible. Evaluation is of necessity always a process of judgment. Few persons are comfortable either judging others or being judged. Measuring performance is a difficult task. Giving someone else an honest, candid evaluation based on that measurement can be difficult psychologically.

Evaluation forces a deity-like role on the evaluator. Defensive behavior on the part of the person being evaluated is common. This is especially true if organizational tenure, salary, wage, or promotion are at stake. This in turn can lead to defensive behavior on the part of the evaluator if the rating must be defended.

Thus, evaluation easily leads to an adversary relationship in which both parties can feel threatened. And yet the development function, to be performed effectively, requires a trusting, collaborative relationship. The evaluator must give honest assessments. Shortcomings must be pointed out. The person being developed must be candid in admitting weaknesses and areas for improvement.

Recognizing this conflict is a beginning step in its resolution. It must be consciously dealt with by the organization. Performance appraisal systems which try to accomplish both at the same time tend to encounter difficulties. It is best handled by making some separation between the appraisal which evaluates and the appraisal which is for development.

COMMON ERRORS   All performance appraisal systems are subject to certain errors, and some appraisal systems are more prone to errors than others. Errors can never be completely eliminated, it seems.

Unreal Consistency   A common error is that of ratings which show similarity where such similarity does not actually exist. A person may be rated high on all dimensions of performance based on an assessment of one or two dimensions. This is the familiar "halo" effect, also called *leniency*. Many persons who are cooperative with supervisors receive inflated ratings on other dimensions.

Variations of unreal similarity are *central tendency* and *strictness*. Central tendency is rating the individual average on all dimensions when this is not true. Strictness is giving a poor rating on all dimensions when actual variation exists.

The same errors can be applied to groups as well as individuals. In a group there may exist wide variations in performance among the members. But the supervisor may give them all high ratings (leniency), average ratings (central tendency), or rate them all poorly (strictness).

Differences Among Raters

Differences among raters in their evaluation of performance leads to errors. These differences may be a result of dissimilarities in perception. Two raters observe an employee disagreeing with a supervisor. One perceives this negatively as insubordinate behavior. The other perceives it positively as a willingness to stand up for what one believes.

Different value systems can also play a part. As already indicated, to one rater customer service is paramount even if sales volume has to be sacrificed. To another sales volume is critical even if customer service is curtailed.

Another problem is created if raters observe different aspects of behavior. One rater sees the employee on the job where the individual feels comfortable and functions effectively. The other rater may see the individual only at meetings where performance declines because of nervousness.

Lack of Motivation

Another problem is lack of motivation on the part of the rater. Rating subordinates is one of those required managerial tasks that is time consuming and not pleasant for most people. It is often put off as long as possible. Then it may be done hurriedly simply to get it over with. This is one of the reasons for unreal consistency errors.

Organizations often unwittingly encourage this kind of behavior. Supervisors are not rewarded for giving honest, comprehensive ratings to subordinates. Not only are positive rewards not received, but honest appraisals which are negative create problems with subordinates. Under these circumstances managers find the best solution is to rate everyone the same and everyone high.

Related to this is that supervisors may find that there is no relation to the rewards subordinates receive and the rating which the supervisor gave. Some persons were rated high, some medium, and some low. And yet everyone receives the same salary increase. The supervisor may also notice that promotions seem to be based on factors other than the ratings which were given. Informal judgments made by higher level managers seem more important than the formal ratings given by the supervisor. Under these circumstances also supervisors may become very lax about giving honest, comprehensive evaluations.

This is an area which needs much attention. Little investigation has been done on factors which cause supervisors to do a conscientious job in performance appraisal. One essential ingredient is the use of organizational rewards for a good job on the part of the supervisor.

METHODS OF APPRAISAL

Appraisal methods are generally of two types. One compares *people against each other*. These are usually the simplest methods. The other compares the individual against some *absolute standard*. These tend to be more complex. Some systems combine the features of both.

Straight Ranking

The simplest appraisal method is that of *straight ranking*. This is ranking all the members of a group from first to last (best to poorest). Straight ranking is usually done on some subjective global dimension of performance. It has the advantage of simplicity and of eliminating the error of consistency.

But it has drawbacks. The persons in the group may not conform to a normal distribution from high to low. All may be poor or good or average performers. It is difficult to compare one group with another. And it offers no feedback for improving performance.

Forced Distribution

A variation of straight ranking is *forced distribution*. Categories such as outstanding, above average, average, below average, and poor are established. A predetermined percentage of the group must be placed in each category. In college it is known as grading on the "curve."

Forced distribution has the advantage of eliminating leniency, central tendency, and strictness. A major drawback is that as in straight ranking the group may not conform to a normal distribution. Perhaps more or fewer than the pre-determined percentage should be rated as outstanding.

Forced distribution is also weak for development purposes. It usually relies upon a subjective definition of performance by the rater. And the basis for placing persons in the various categories is usually not specified.

Conventional (or Graphic) Scale Rating

The most popular rating system is *conventional rating*, also known as the *graphic scale*. It is easy to develop and apply and rates people against a standard. Figure 10-1 is an illustration of a typical conventional rating form.

The major advantage of conventional rating is that it is simple to develop and install. Managers can fill out the forms quickly. The rater does not

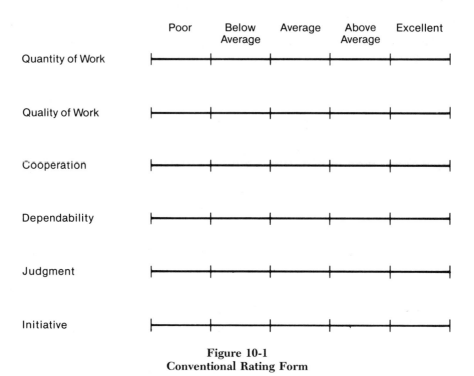

	Poor	Below Average	Average	Above Average	Excellent
Quantity of Work					
Quality of Work					
Cooperation					
Dependability					
Judgment					
Initiative					

Figure 10-1
Conventional Rating Form

have to rate people in accordance with some pre-determined percentage as in forced distribution. And it provides some information for developmental feedback.

But conventional rating is extremely vulnerable to the error of unreal consistency. The rater can easily rate an individual high, average, or low on all dimensions. And the group as a whole can easily be put in one category even though real differences exist.

Another problem is that dimensions such as "quality of work" and "dependability" are rarely defined. This permits each rater to apply his or her own definition to these nebulous terms. And another criticism is that the dimensions being rated may have little relation to actual job performance. Rather than job performance, it is easy for the rater to be influenced by personality.

Nevertheless, conventional rating is still the most popular system. The low cost, simplicity of design, and ease with which the form can be filled out will probably continue to make it widely used.

Forced Choice

Forced choice is an interesting method which usually requires development by a trained psychologist. It consists of pairs of statements which the rater must select as either most characteristics or least characteristic of the ratee. Figure 10-2 is an example.

In each of the following pairs of statements, select the one which is most characteristic of the employee.

    1-A. Always comes to work on time.
    1-B. Frequently stays late to complete work.
    2-A. Is intolerant of mistakes made by fellow workers.
    2-B. Reacts with anger to criticism.

Figure 10-2
Examples of Forced Choice Statements

The developer of the forced choice system divides the present work force into segments reflecting the quality of their job performance. Pairs of statements are developed. Supervisors are asked to apply these statements to the present work group. Some pairs of statements will discriminate between good and poor performers. These are retained. Others will not and are discarded. By this process the developer acquires pairs of statements which can then be used to rate other workers who were not part of the test group.

The forced choice method eliminates the problem of unreal consistency. The rater does not know which statements are correlated with good performance and which with poor performance. Thus, the rater cannot bias the result by personal prejudices about the individual.

This, however, is also a drawback. Raters tend to dislike systems which do not let them know if they are giving a good or poor rating. Another problem is that there is no feedback for development. These systems are also expensive to develop and maintain.

Behavioral Scales   There are several relatively new appraisal methods which focus on actual job behaviors and which compare performance against a standard. These are the *weighted check list*, the *critical incidents method*, and the *behaviorally anchored rating scales*. More than other systems they deal directly with the criterion problem of defining good performance.

In these systems persons familiar with the job develop statements that illustrate good and poor performance. Agreement is sought on such statements. Where there is disagreement statements are discarded. Figure 10-3 is an example of statements for the job of bank teller.

In the weighted check list, developers attach numerical scores which show how important each statement is towards good or poor performance. This has the effect of weighting the statements. Raters then check statements which apply to the individual. Adding up the scores provides a grand total.

Is absent from work no more than one day per month.

Drawer fails to balance at end of working day one or more times each week.

Acknowledges presence of regular customers by name from memory.

Provides assistance to new, inexperienced tellers without having to be asked.

Handles the twenty most common bank transactions accurately, without having to ask for help or refer to manual.

Keeps customers waiting while engaging in small talk with co-worker.

Figure 10-3
Examples of Behavioral Statements for Bank Teller

The critical incidents method varies this. Statements similar to those above are developed by persons familiar with the job. Through sophisticated statistical techniques such as factor analysis statements are condensed into five to ten broad categories such as customer relations. The supervisor keeps a record of examples or "incidents" of behavior which fit each of the categories.

The behaviorally anchored rating scales are developed similarly. Statements are developed and factor analysis is used to condense these into a smaller number of categories. Each category is then described by statements which range from very good performance to extremely poor performance. An example is shown in Figure 10-4.

These methods attempt to substitute systematic assessments of job performance for the subjective judgments that characterize other methods. They require raters to focus on what they mean by good and poor job

Customer Relations for Bank Teller

Acknowledges presence of regular customers by name from memory.	+3	EXCELLENT
Acknowledges customer at completion of transaction with verbal "thank you" or similar comment.	+2	
Apologizes to customer if there has been a delay in service.	+1	
Makes small talk with customer during transaction.	0	NEUTRAL
Displays signs of irritation if customer has not filled out deposit slip or other forms properly.	−1	
Frequently fails to give customer proper receipt upon completion of transaction.	−2	
Keeps customers waiting while engaging in small talk with co-worker.	−3	POOR

Figure 10-4
Statements for One Category in a Behaviorally Anchored Rating Scale

performance. They are useful for providing feedback for employee development. They help clear up misperceptions between superior and subordinate about what is expected on the job.

Their major drawback is the time and expense of development. They cannot be prepared hastily. A separate scale must be developed for each job. And they must be periodically updated as the job changes.

Direct Indices

If a direct measurement can be made of the worker's performance, then appraisal is greatly simplified. *Direct index* plans, for example, are those where so many units produced in a particular time period provide a direct measurement.

But direct indices can be used only when the worker has some tangible output which can be counted. And, most important, the worker must have complete control over the output. To the extent that factors beyond the worker's control affect results, then the measure becomes invalidated.

The nature of the direct index is such that only a small percentage of jobs qualify for its use. For most managerial jobs this is especially the case. A plant manager, for example, may have low production with a high rate of defects. But this may be the result of poor quality raw materials which were purchased by a central purchasing department, not controlled by the manager. Or defects may be caused by indifferent workers who are protected by a union contract.

But even where they cannot be relied upon exclusively, indices can still be helpful in performing appraisals. Judgment is unavoidable in determining how much is the responsibility of the individual. But indices do add tangible data about performance which is extremely helpful.

Performance Against Objectives

The use of management by objectives as an appraisal system has achieved a certain vogue in recent years. This is where persons are measured by whether agreed upon objectives have been achieved. Management by objectives is better described as a managerial system or managerial technique. But it has been recommended as an answer to the problems raised by performance appraisal.

On the surface it would seem that relating actual performance to agreed upon objectives would be an ideal method. If objectives are met or exceeded, then this is evidence of good performance. If objectives are not met, then this is evidence of poor performance.

For example, a sales manager might have the following objective:

During the current calendar year, increase the market share of steel-belted radial tires from 15 percent to 18 percent.

Assume that the market share went from 15 to 20 percent. During the critical selling period the chief competitor was on strike for two months. Is this evidence of good performance? Assume that the market share dropped from 15 to 13 percent. During the year a quarter of the tires proved to be poorly constructed and were returned as part of a recall program. Should the sales manager be penalized?

Or the manager for a department processing unemployment claims may have the following objective:

> Reduce the average time for processing unemployment applications from seventy-four hours to sixty hours during the coming six months.

Assume the time is reduced to fifty hours. Because of a pick-up in the local economy the number of applications declined during the period by one-third. This made it easy to exceed the target. Should the manager be rewarded for this? Or assume the time went to ninety hours because applications doubled as a result of a downturn in the local economy. Should the manager be penalized?

This should suggest that measuring performance against objectives is not the panacea adherents sometimes claim it to be. Performance against objectives is a useful input to the entire evaluation process. It provides helpful information for those doing the evaluating. But it does not eliminate the problem of accounting for good and bad conditions beyond the control of the individual. Judgment is also involved in determining how realistic the objectives were to begin with.

Some writers have suggested that management by objectives is better used for developmental purposes than evaluative ones.[1] When utilized properly it permits the individual to have input into his or her job requirements. Establishing objectives requires analytical skills. Planning for their attainment is excellent training. Discussing reasons for failure to reach objectives provides valuable input for improving future performance.

Essay Rating

Many appraisal systems, especially those for managers, require narrative statements from the rater describing performance. These essays often supplement rating systems already described. They typically are written in answer to such questions as "What are the employee's strong points?" and "Discuss what the employee needs to do to become promotable."

Such essay ratings are quite subjective. Thus, they may have limited value for evaluative purposes, especially if individuals are compared to one

---

[1] L. L. Cummings and Donald P. Schwab, *Performance in Organizations—Determinants and Appraisal.* Glenview, Ill.: Scott, Foresman, 1973, pp. 95–97.

another. But they do provide helpful comments for developmental use. Their main drawback is the time they require to fill out. Thus, they are best used on a limited basis so that supervisors are motivated to comment in conscientious fashion. When overdone such essays easily degenerate into meaningless platitudes.

WHO DOES THE APPRAISAL?

The immediate supervisor of the person being rated normally performs the rating. This seems to be accepted as the natural and right way to do it. The immediate superior has authority over the individual and accountability for his or her actions. And usually the immediate superior is in the best position to observe the individual's work behavior.

But in complex organizations these assumptions may not hold. Many persons have jobs where their primary working time is spent interacting with persons other than their immediate supervisor. Or the formal hierarchy is such that they are responsible to numerous superiors.

Under these circumstances there is much to be said for multiple rating systems. These provide inputs from additional supervisors in a position to observe the employee's performance. Multiple rating systems aid in giving a better look at the employee's total performance. They also provide protection in that the possible biases of one superior can be offset by others who see the individual under different circumstances.

Peer ratings are an infrequently used method of appraisal. They can be effective under very special conditions. They require a high degree of trust and cohesiveness within a work group. They are unsuitable when differential rewards are allocated to the group members. Being penalized because of a high rating given to someone else can easily affect the honesty of peer ratings.

Subordinate ratings are occasionally encountered. When used for evaluation they can be extremely threatening to supervisors. And they can be dysfunctional for the organization if supervisors become lax because they fear subordinate retaliation. And subordinates themselves can feel threatened about providing honest evaluations if they feel the supervisor will have access to them.

But subordinate ratings if done honestly may have some positive impact upon development. Supervisors may benefit from knowing how their subordinates perceive them as managers. This can lead to improved supervisory performance. But it takes a very emotionally secure person to benefit from subordinate criticism without feeling threatened and possibly vindictive.

Self-ratings can be helpful for development. They probably have little use for evaluation. There is a tendency for people to rate themselves too highly (in comparison to superior ratings), though there are many exceptions to this. But especially for candidates on the management track, honest self-evaluation can be a great help to personal growth and development.

FREQUENCY AND TIMING

The majority of organizations with appraisal systems rate their employees on a regular basis. This means either every six or twelve months. It is typically performed on a certain date, such as the anniversary date of joining the organization or a specified time period since the last promotion or transfer.

The strongest argument for regular appraisals is that control can be maintained. Supervisors can be more effectively monitored to make sure the task is done. And it reduces some uncertainty on the part of the employee who knows when to expect the appraisal.

But having an appraisal at a regular, fixed interval has limitations in terms of reinforcement theory. It does not, except by accident, relate the appraisal (the reinforcer) to the actual job behavior. Reinforcement theory suggests that for maximum effectiveness the reinforcement should follow actual behavior as closely as possible. Thus, it reduces the likelihood that reinforcement will be effective.

This line of reasoning leads to the concept of a *variable appraisal schedule*. Appraisals would be done at irregular intervals based on actual happenings on the job. From a standpoint of proper reinforcement there is much to recommend this.

For example, based on the promotion anniversary date, a department manager might be scheduled for a regular review in January. But at the end of September a major reorganization of the department is completed. The department manager has spent six months intensively engaged in this activity. A variable schedule would suggest performing the appraisal early in October when the manager's performance during the six-month period is still fresh in everyone's mind. Both evaluation and development can be enhanced by performing the review in October instead of reconstructing things in January.

The drawback to the variable schedule is the same as that which makes the regular interval so appealing. And that is a variable schedule may mean that supervisors never get around to performing the appraisal. Employees wait in vain for superiors to provide them with formal feedback on performance.

There is little evidence to suggest how frequent appraisals should be. They should not be so frequent as to place unnecessary burdens on the supervisor. And yet the intervals should not be so long as to leave employees uncertain of their standing.

Most organizations adopt policies that apply across the board to all jobs. This is probably a mistake. On some sales and production jobs where measures of performance are available weekly and even daily, formal review should take place more frequently. This enables these employees to make necessary changes quickly as problems arise. For positions where results are less tangible, appraisals can probably be made less frequently without endangering performance.

ORGANIZING FOR APPRAISAL

Among the many responsibilities that go with supervision is seeing that subordinates are appraised in accordance with organizational policy. As already stated, without some control it is easy for managers to neglect this task.

Providing this control is one of the responsibilities of the personnel department. It monitors the operating departments to make sure that appraisals are being carried out. It also evaluates the performance appraisal system itself. Is it serving the purposes for which it was designed? Do supervisors and subordinates understand how it operates? If results are not satisfactory, should the system be modified?

The monitoring function has become more important in recent years. Legislation dealing with discrimination has focused more attention on appraisal procedures and their relation to personnel actions. If a supervisor gives lenient ratings that are undeserved, this can have repercussions if the employee is later subjected to disciplinary action. Undeserved favorable appraisals can also create problems if promotion is not forthcoming at a later date. But the organization is also vulnerable if unfavorable appraisals cannot be defended.

Thus the role of the personnel department becomes more critical in standardizing and validating the appraisal process. The system itself must be evaluated and reviewed more often. Continuing checks must be made on operating managers to insure that appraisal procedures are being implemented properly. And a continual program of feedback from both supervisors and subordinates must be maintained so that problems can be spotted and corrected early.

PROVIDING FEEDBACK

It has long been axiomatic that feedback of the rating to the ratee is desirable. Development, for one thing, depends upon awareness of areas needing improvement. And it seems morally right for employees to know how they rank with their superiors.

There is a case to be made, though, for not providing feedback to the person being rated. The rationale behind this is that supervisors are inclined to be less candid in their evaluations if they have to defend them. The errors of leniency and central tendency become more pronounced under these conditions. Support for this claim is found in legal provisions permitting college students to waive their right to examine recommendations that go into their files. The assumption is that instructors will be less honest in their evaluations if they know they will be seen by the student.

To the extent this is true the organization faces a dilemma. For development purposes feedback is essential. And it must be honest feedback else the individual being rated lacks the necessary information to modify behavior. Yet providing this feedback may reduce the honesty required for both development and evaluation.

It is probably a moot question given today's social climate. Secret appraisal systems which hide information from employees are not in tune with the times. Commissions dealing with employee rights have already made recommendations that employees be permitted access to their files similar to the procedure in the educational system. Some large companies such as IBM have already inaugurated such a policy.

Thus, regardless of any effects upon rating accuracy, feedback seems essential. Suggested techniques for conducting feedback interviews tend to follow a pattern. Usually included are suggestions that the supervisor be well prepared and that he or she put the subordinate at ease.

There is no magic formula for providing feedback. It is important that the rating methods attack the criterion problem of defining good and poor performance. Both the supervisor and subordinate should have a clear understanding of what is expected in the way of performance. This itself can minimize many of the problems generated by providing feedback.

INNOVATIONS

Performance appraisal, along with selection, was among the first areas to be developed in personnel administration. For a great many years it has been an area utilizing techniques and concepts developed long ago. Only in recent times have some innovative ideas been brought to this area.

Developing Different Appraisal Systems

One of the best suggestions in recent years comes from Cummings and Schwab.[2] These investigators suggest that different groups within the organization have different needs and goals in appraisal. This leads to their recommendation for three types of appraisal

[2]*Ibid.*, pp. 118–130.

programs: the Developmental Action Program, the Maintenance Action Program, and the Remedial Action Program.

The development program is for persons on the management track. Techniques geared to development rather than evaluation are suggested since this group will consist of high performers who are being groomed for the future. Maintenance programs are for persons not seen as promotable but whose performance remains satisfactory year after year. And remedial programs are for those whose work is below standard.

Different appraisal methods and techniques can be used for the different groups. For the development program, management by objectives and other developmental tools can be most appropriate. For the maintenance program behavioral scales which define performance might be suitable. And for the remedial program precise specification of deficiencies and requirements for improvement are essential. Persons are not restricted permanently to one program but may move from one to another as circumstances change.

Splitting Performance Reviews

Another concept that has received attention in recent years is that of separating performance reviews. Reviews for evaluation and reward allocation should be split off from reviews for development. This innovation recognizes the incompatibility that exists between the two.

This approach helps minimize the defensive behavior so common when evaluation and development are combined. Defensive behavior will undoubtedly still exist during the evaluation review. But it is less likely to intrude during development if matters of reward allocation are not being considered. This enables the superior and subordinate to focus attention on one area instead of two.

Does Everyone Need Appraisal?

An innovation which has not received much attention is whether or not everyone in the organization needs to be continually appraised. The majority of employees reach a plateau at some point in their careers. Most of these will prove to be steady and dependable workers year after year. The formal performance review once or twice a year becomes highly routine. The informal process usually provides adequate positive reinforcement from superiors.

It might be helpful to give these employees the option of whether or not they wish regular performance reviews. This assumes, of course, that their work remains satisfactory. To the extent that many do not opt for regular appraisals, it would relieve supervisors of what can be an onerous chore. It would permit concentration on those who really need and desire reviews. That everyone must have a regular performance review is one of those accepted "truths" that needs to be examined.

It might seem that not having a performance review would make it difficult to allocate financial rewards. But for persons not on a promotion track such rewards tend to become standardized. Persons in each pay classification whose work is satisfactory usually receive similar pay increases. Where exceptional performance is being recognized financially, this can easily be incorporated in a special review.

PUBLIC POLICY AND APPRAISAL

As in management development, there is no actual mention of performance appraisal in legislation dealing with employer–employee relations. But performance appraisal is covered indirectly by the Civil Rights Act. This means that appraisal systems are part of the total employment process and must be utilized so that discrimination does not occur. Discrimination can be either overt or systemic, the latter meaning seemingly neutral appraisal systems which have adverse impact upon females and minorities.

The major impact of public policy is to require validation of performance appraisal systems. They must be demonstrably measuring job performance. For example an organization might be promoting a disproportionate number of males in comparison to females. Promotions might be based on appraisals which are nothing more than unsubstantiated opinions of supervisors. This is likely to be unacceptable to the appropriate regulatory agencies.

Appraisal systems must come to grips with the criterion problem of defining performance. They must then be shown to be actually measuring that performance.

SUMMARY

Performance appraisal serves two major purposes in the organization, evaluation and employee development. These two can be incompatible. Performance appraisal systems are subject to many errors including unreal consistency and differences among raters. Lack of motivation on the part of the rater also creates errors. Systems vary in their susceptibility to error.

Appraisal methods are of two types. One type compares persons against one another. The other type compares people against a standard. Within these two types are numerous methods of appraisal. Some are simple such as straight ranking. Others are more complex such as behavioral scales which attempt to establish a success criterion by defining performance be-haviors.

The immediate superior usually performs the appraisal. But other methods are possible, such as multiple ratings from numerous superiors, as well as peer and subordinate ratings. The latter work best under special circumstances. Most organizations rate their people on a regular, fixed inter-val basis. This offers the best possibilities for control. From a reinforcement standpoint, variable interval schedules have some advantages.

Staff personnel departments have a monitoring function in perfor-mance review. Providing feedback of the appraisal poses problems if honest evaluations are sought. But feedback is probably necessary given today's social climate. An innovation in performance appraisal is to use a different system for different groups in the organization. One way is to classify people as on a development, maintenance, or remedial track.

SELECTED REFERENCES

Bureau of National Affairs, *Employee Performance: Evaluation and Control*, Personnel Policies Forum Survey No. 108. Washington, D.C.: BNA, Inc., 1975.

Cummings, L. L. and Donald P. Schwab, *Performance in Organizations—Deter-minants and Appraisal*. Glenview, Ill.: Scott, Foresman, 1973.

Hamner, W. Clay and Frank L. Schmidt, *Contemporary Problems in Personnel*, rev. ed. Chicago: St. Clair Press, 1977.

Kellogg, Marian S., *What to Do about Performance Appraisal*, rev. ed. New York: AMACOM, American Management Association, 1975.

Maier, Norman R., *The Appraisal Interview: Three Basic Approaches*. La Jolla, Calif.: University Associates, 1976.

Winstanley, Nathan B., ed., *Current Readings in Performance Appraisal*. Lexington, Mass.: Xerox Publishing, 1975.

PART

5

COMPENSATION AND PRODUCTIVITY

WAGE
AND
SALARY
ADMINISTRATION

⟵ IDEAS TO BE FOUND ⟶
IN THIS CHAPTER

- Goals in wage and salary administration
- Determining the general wage level
- Establishing the internal wage structure
- Job evaluation plans
- Determining the actual wage rate

A basic transaction in an industrial society is the exchange of human physical and mental effort for money. Money is the means for obtaining the goods and services necessary for survival. It is also the means for acquiring goods and services which make life something more than simply the struggle for existence. Money has great symbolic value and its acquisition provides innumerable psychic satisfactions.

People work for a variety of reasons; they work to satisfy a variety of needs, of which those that are satisfied by money are only a part. Nonetheless, without the inducement of financial compensation, vast changes would have to occur in society to obtain the daily productive effort that is so much taken for granted.

If the effort–money exchange is a basic one in society, the organization's wage and salary program is the device for administering that exchange. There are two major considerations in this process. One is the *general (or absolute) wage level*, also referred to as the *external wage structure*. What does the organization pay in absolute dollars for its jobs and how do the wage levels for its jobs compare with those of other organizations? The other consideration is referred to as the *vertical (or relative) wage structure*, also known as the *internal wage structure*. Within the organization, how does the wage for one job compare with the wage paid for other jobs?

Ideally, the employee should be paid an amount which reflects his or her contribution to the organization. Unfortunately, this rather nebulous principle is of little value in making the concrete decisions as to exactly how much each person should receive. There is no formula that spells out with precision exactly what an individual's contribution is. Much falls within the area of subjective judgment. It is the purpose of the wage and salary program to help implement this important but abstract principle.

This chapter takes a look at some of the major issues in wage and salary administration and the methods used to resolve them. How is physical and mental effort translated into dollars and cents? What kinds of physical and mental effort are more valuable than others? Is there some logical and acceptable way for making distinctions? If the internal wage structure indicates that nurses should be paid $700 a month but a wage survey shows $800 is the minimum being paid, which rate should be used? These are some of the myriad questions raised by this complex and challenging area.

GOALS IN WAGE AND SALARY ADMINISTRATION

With a sound, well-conceived program of wage and salary administration, the organization tries to achieve these goals:

1. **Obtaining the right number of qualified persons.** The wage level must be high enough to attract workers. If the organization sets a price (wage or salary) that is too low in relation to what competing sources are offering, it will find that it is unable to hire enough employees.

2. **Retaining workers once hired.** The wage level for retaining workers is not always or even usually the same as that for hiring. Working conditions, accumulation of seniority, on-the-job social relations, and inertia can act to keep workers with the organization. Nonetheless, there is some point at which workers will not stay if the wage drops too low.

3. **Maintaining costs at a reasonable level.** The organization does not want its wage level excessively high. As organizations become larger and more complex, the number and variety of jobs grows correspondingly and unless care is taken, it is easy to slip into a posture of paying certain job classifications more than necessary. The result is obvious—excessive costs the organization does not want to bear.

4. **Inducing workers to prepare for and accept advancement.** Employees must be motivated to prepare for and assume the greater responsibilities, demands, and risks that go with higher level

jobs. Horatio Alger is so much a part of the American myth it is easy to forget how important the pricing mechanism is in inducing people to compete for advanced positions. Few assistant department heads would work to become department head if they did not anticipate receiving additional compensation.

5. **Encouraging workers to put forth greater effort.** Pay is an important motivator; however, paying people more does not guarantee they will produce more. Decades ago studies showed that workers put ceilings on their output (and earnings) rather than violate group norms. Wage and salary programs must be highly sophisticated and interrelated with other programs to encourage productive behavior.

6. **Channeling employees' efforts in directions desired by management.** Not only is greater effort desired, but it must be channeled properly. Monetary inducements are an important part of the reinforcement process. If a retail chain does not want its store managers concentrating on sales volume at the expense of profits, it must compensate for profits and not volume.

7. **Maintaining equity within the organization.** Few things are more disruptive to an organization than for employees to feel their pay is not fair in comparison to what others receive. This relates to how they view the work they perform compared to what others do. This equity factor has been extensively written about. Workers judge their paychecks not just in absolute terms but relative to others. To offset such feelings of inequity is the function of the vertical pricing structure.

8. **Observing government requirements regarding compensation.** Provision must be made to comply with laws covering compensation. To give a few examples, the minimum wage standard must be met if it is applicable;overtime pay must be computed properly; and pay differentials based solely on sex must be eliminated.

THE GENERAL WAGE LEVEL

The *general wage level* is the average of the actual dollars the organization pays for its jobs. It takes into account *all* jobs from custodian to president. Another term for the general wage level is *absolute wage level*. This is to distinguish it from pay comparisons in which jobs are ranked internally *relative* to one another. The general wage level is evaluated externally in comparison with other organizations.

As already stated, the general wage level is important for hiring and retaining workers. It is not the case that typists will join the organization at $3.15 an hour and shun jobs if they are $3.10 an hour. Nor will the organization usually become insolvent if it pays $3.15 an hour when $3.05 would be enough to attract and retain typists. But there are limits as to how different the organization can afford to be.

**Factors Affecting
the General Wage Level**   Of all the factors which determine the general wage level of the organization, the most important is the *"going rate."* This is the rate being paid for particular skills or jobs by other organizations. The going (or market) rate has always been of major importance in determining wage levels. The organization validates its wage scales (paying neither too little nor too much) by checking them against what others are paying.

Rarely is the going rate one specific amount. Usually it encompasses a range from which the organization makes its choice. Thus, the going rate implying a singular figure is something of a misnomer. It is really a *range* of rates, providing the organization with some latitude.

Another important factor in determining the general wage level is the *ability to pay*. Organizations do not have unrestricted choice in this matter. Highly profitable organizations have more discretion in establishing pay scales than those with low or non-existent profits. Organizations in the public sector are affected by their funding levels (as well as legislatively enacted wage scales).

One element in the ability to pay is the organization's labor intensiveness. Organizations vary in how much labor costs are a part of total costs. Public accounting is extremely labor intensive. Salaries and wages must be watched closely. Petroleum refining is the opposite. Low labor intensity permits some margin for error.

The *desire to pay* also affects the organization's wage level. This assumes the organization is profitable enough or funded well enough to have some discretion. Some organizations feel that desirable working conditions, organizational prestige, job security, and other factors enable them to pay less and still attract good workers. Other organizations prefer to be known as high-paying employers. This may reflect management's desire to be a leader in all aspects of its operations, including compensation of employees.

Wage levels are also determined through the process of *collective bargaining*. This process includes the factors previously mentioned, with union bargaining strength as an additional element. Procedures established by statute determine wage and salary schedules for public sector employees. As in collective bargaining, the previous factors play an important role, but the political process adds another dimension.

Since so many factors affect the general wage level, organizations arrange themselves on a continuum from high to low. Some become high-paying employers while others are in either the middle or the low range. But this represents the average wage and salary level and can be deceptive. The high-paying organization will likely have some job classifications which are in the middle or low range. And, the low paying organization may find itself with some job classifications in the high or middle category.

Determining
the Going Rate
The going rate is typically determined by a wage and salary survey. These may be simple and informal, consisting of nothing more than a few phone calls to several concerns in the local area. Or they can be vast undertakings which compare scores of jobs over a wide industrial and geographic area that may be national or even international in scope. Few organizations of any size try to price their jobs without relying to some extent on wage and salary surveys.

Regardless of the survey's scope, there are several criteria which must be met for the survey to be factual and useful. First of all is determining the relevant labor market. For the particular positions being surveyed, what other organizations compete for the same workers? Clerical positions usually involve a localized labor market. A bank in Chicago does not compete with a bank in New York for clerical help. But in hiring management trainees just out of college, the Chicago bank competes with financial institutions all over the country. It also will have some competition for these same individuals from other organizations such as manufacturing and government agencies. Thus, it has to broaden the dimensions of the labor market considerably for this group.

Jobs being compared must be similar in duties and responsibilities, otherwise comparisons may be distorted. This is why sound wage and salary surveys do not rely on job titles alone. Complete job descriptions revealing similarities and differences in work requirements are essential.

As already indicated, wages are not strictly one specific amount. Practically all organizations have ranges reflecting such factors as length of service and performance levels. These ranges must be incorporated into the wage and salary survey to give an accurate picture. The speed of progression from one wage level to another must also be considered.

Economic supplements should be calculated, since these can add as much as 30 percent or more to the base rate. This includes such common supplements as health insurance and retirement plans as well as less common items such as meal and clothing allowances. Some organizations require matching funds for pension contributions, while others pay the entire amount. All of this must be figured in.

Other aspects of the conditions of work must be included. One organization may have a thirty-eight-hour week for the same pay for which another organization requires forty hours. Paid rest breaks must be included, and the amount of time for meals is important. Other elements such as odd working schedules and night work must be part of the comparison.

A wage and salary survey to be done properly is not a simple undertaking. It takes much planning and preparation. Not all organizations are willing to share complete information about their employment conditions. Fortunately, the reciprocal need for information reduces this resistance.

163

The organization can perform its own wage and salary survey. Or it can combine with similar organizations in a joint undertaking. In addition, professional groups and trade associations periodically conduct surveys which are helpful to their member organizations. Wage surveys are also available from the U.S. Department of Labor, which does extensive work in this area. Many state agencies perform this function also.

THE VERTICAL WAGE STRUCTURE

The *vertical wage structure* is concerned with comparisons of the duties and responsibilities of jobs *within* the organization. (It is also known as the internal wage structure or the relative wage structure.) Jobs are ranked from lowest to highest and this ranking is used for assigning wages and salaries.

The vertical wage structure serves two major purposes. One is to establish a relationship between the compensation for a particular job and its contribution to the organization. The term "job" is used deliberately. It is a *job* that is being measured for its worth and *not* the individual who is performing the job. This is an important distinction to keep in mind.

The other major purpose is to establish equity within the organization. Workers compare their job duties and responsibilities with those of other employees. This leads to feelings that a fair wage is being paid or that there is inequity. No internal wage structure could hope to satisfy everyone in this respect. But the process of establishing the internal structure should offer assurance that some rational process is at work. If the organization decides that a beginning payroll clerk's job is worth more than a beginning typist's job, employees should see some reasonable system making this decision. Failure to have such a system can create great stress within the organization.

The methods and procedures for determining the worth of jobs within the organization go by the name of *job evaluation.* Unfortunately the term can be confusing because it is used in different ways. Often job evaluation is used to refer to sophisticated ranking systems which involve formal steps and some quantification.

A more useful way for thinking of job evaluation is to use the term for *any* method which ranks jobs internally. The difference is that some systems are very *formal,* using systematic step-by-step procedures. Others are quite *informal* and their methodology quite casual. Regardless, all serve the same purpose.

Formalized Job Evaluation Systems

The *point system* is the most widely used formal job evaluation method. It establishes factors such as "consequence of job error" which are used to distinguish the worth of one job

164

compared to another. These factors are assigned points or weights to establish a ranking for the job.

The first step in the point system is to divide jobs into broad categories in which the jobs are similar. Clerical jobs, warehouse jobs, and factory jobs are common classifications. This is necessary because it is difficult to compare jobs if the differences are too extreme.

Factors are then developed to measure the jobs in each broad category. For example, in clerical positions such factors as experience necessary, education required, supervisory responsibilities, and physical effort involved might be used.

These factors are then weighted by deciding how important they are to the particular classification being evaluated. For clerical positions, the amount of education required would typically be more important than physical effort since most clerical positions do not require unusual exertion. Weighting is accomplished by providing a range of points for each factor. This is shown in Table 11-1.

As the table shows, confidentiality of information handled is more important for clerical jobs in general than working conditions. Thus, it has a wider range of possible points. Determination of the number of points for each factor is assisted by establishing steps within the range. Table 11-2 shows how this is done for the factor of education and training. Verbal descriptions aid in establishing the steps or degrees within the factor.

Each job within the clerical classification is now evaluated factor by factor. Points are assigned for each factor and a final total obtained. This total is the means for ranking the job.

It would be possible to have as many job levels as there are total points. But obviously, this would make the system unwieldy and difficult to administer. To avoid this, it is customary to establish job grades which cover

Table 11-1
Point Ranges for Clerical Position Factors

	Points				
Factors	Degree 1	Degree 2	Degree 3	Degree 4	Degree 5
Experience	15	30	45	60	75
Education and Training	20	40	60	80	100
Consequence of Errors	15	30	45	60	75
Initiative	10	20	30	40	50
Confidentiality of Data	25	50	75	100	125
Working Conditions	5	10	15	20	25
Interactions with Others	10	20	30	40	50
Physical Effort	5	10	15	20	25

Note: Range of points for a factor is the lowest to highest, e.g., range of points for "Experience" is 15 to 75.

Table 11-2
Verbal Descriptions of Factor Degrees

Education and Training

Degree	Points	Level Required
1	20	Job requires little education beyond ability to read and write and perform elementary arithmetic calculations. Can be learned in two weeks or less with on-the-job instruction.
2	40	Requires high-school education including one year of typing with minimum speed of 50 words per minute and one year high-school training or equivalent operating standard office equipment. Six weeks on-the-job training.
3	60	Must have one year post-high-school education or equivalent in operating computerized office equipment. On-the-job training 3 months.
4	80	Requires two-year college certificate in bookkeeping. Six months on-the-job training. Infrequent refresher courses necessary to keep abreast of new developments.
5	100	Requires two-year college certificate in accounting. On-the-job training 9 months. Frequent refresher work necessary to keep abreast of accounting changes.

Note: Measures both the formal education required to perform job and the formal and informal training necessary. Training refers to both on-the-job and off-the-job training. Includes the necessity for continuous training to keep skills current.

a range of points. Thus, the lowest level clerical jobs might be those in the range zero to fifty points. The next level might be grade two, from fifty-one to 100 points. All jobs within each grade can be treated the same for compensation purposes.

A variation of the point system is the *factor comparison method*. In factor comparison, selection is made of key or benchmark jobs which are common throughout the organization and which the organization feels are being paid a fair rate. Examples in the clerical classification might be filing clerk, secretary, and bookkeeper. Average rates for these jobs have usually been established by wage and salary surveys.

As in the point system, the organization selects factors on which the jobs should be evaluated. Instead of assigning point ranges, job evaluators decide how much of the rate to allocate to each factor. This is shown in Table 11-3.

Given this breakdown of the key or benchmark jobs, other jobs can then be slotted in. For the job of computer operator, it might be decided on the dimension of education and training that it requires more than the secretary but not quite as much as the bookkeeper. On this dimension a rate

Table 11-3
Apportionment of Rates in Factor Comparison Method

Factors	Jobs				
	Secretary	Filing Clerk	Bookkeeper	Key Punch Operator	Typist
Experience	$.65	$.40	$.55	$.35	$.50
Education and Training	.85	.50	1.05	.60	.70
Consequence of Errors	.60	.45	.85	.70	.55
Initiative	.55	.30	.55	.45	.35
Confidentiality of Data	.65	.55	.70	.40	.50
Working Conditions	.25	.20	.15	.20	.15
Interactions with Others	.60	.30	.70	.25	.30
Physical Effort	.15	.45	.15	.30	.35
Wage Rate	$4.35	$3.15	$4.80	$3.25	$3.40

of $.95 is selected. This procedure is followed for the rest of the factors until all factors have been priced. They are then totaled and a wage rate for the job established.

One advantage of the factor comparison method is that it directly establishes a rate for the job. With the point method, the points have to be converted into pay grades.

Variations of the point system and the factor comparison methods are common. Regardless, all of them attempt to break the job down into separate dimensions. Some kind of numerical assessment is made for each dimension and a final total derived.

Formalized job evaluation plans have the advantage of providing a systematic, step-by-step approach to the problem of ranking jobs by their worth to the organization. This is also their major drawback. Their use of numerics gives them an aura of precision which really does not exist. Unavoidable subjective judgments are involved throughout. Thus, they provoke controversy when only a point or two prevents someone from entering a higher pay classification.

Informal Job Evaluation Plans

Informal job evaluation systems serve the same purposes as do the more formal plans. Rarely, though, do they establish separate factors or dimensions on which to measure the job. Ranking takes place by looking at the job as a whole.

One common informal method is to establish key or benchmark jobs which are familiar to everyone in the organization. Truck loader and driver would be examples in a warehouse classification. These key or benchmark jobs are then placed in rank order based on a global (or overall) judgment of their worth to the organization. The other jobs are then looked at one by one. Comparisons are made of the demands and requirements of these jobs compared to the key or benchmark jobs. The end result is a ranking of the jobs on a vertical scale.

Informal systems have the advantage of being simpler and less costly to operate than formal systems. A permanent staff who do nothing but job evaluations is usually not necessary. A major disadvantage of informal systems is the subjective manner in which rankings are derived. They may be more difficult to defend to employees who question their classification.

Regardless of how formal and systematic or how informal and subjective, ranking jobs on a vertical scale is still a judgmental process. It may be obvious that a custodian sweeping the laboratory floor should be paid less than the technician analyzing virus cultures. But most job evaluations are not this clear-cut. Consistency of application of whatever methods are used is essential. For this reason, job evaluation is a function that is almost always centralized in the staff personnel department. This way, uniform application across the entire organization is better assured.

DETERMINING THE ACTUAL WAGE STRUCTURE

The process of determining the general wage level and the process of determining the vertical wage structure come together in deciding how much a given job is to be paid. The *actual wage* is the dollar amount the organization will pay for each job. This is usually expressed as an average rate in hourly, daily, weekly, or even monthly terms.

The method used for actual pricing of the job depends upon the method of job evaluation used. For informal job ranking systems, it is customary to compare average rates being paid present job holders to see if they conform to the vertical ranking assigned and to the going rate as revealed by the wage and salary survey. Jobs below what they should be are usually brought into line. Jobs priced too high are noted or "red circled" as it is customarily referred to. Present jobholders are not reduced, but new hires are brought in at the proper rate.

With the formal job evaluation plans the factor comparison method provides a rate structure. For point systems, the organization establishes a wage curve as shown in Figure 11-1. The dots can represent either current rates for jobs as revealed by a wage and salary survey or the rates of current job holders in the organization. A wage line is then drawn, which should leave approximately half of the dots above and half below the line. This line indicates the relationship between the points assigned and the proper rate

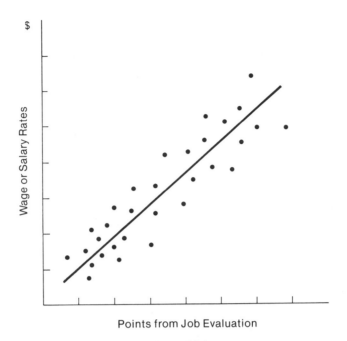

Figure 11-1
Wage Curve for Relating Internal Job Structure to
External Wage Rates

for the job. Jobs below the line should be brought up, and jobs above the line should be circled.

Organizations customarily group closely ranked jobs into pay grades or classifications. The organization might have 100 jobs but would condense these down into eight pay grades to avoid the unwieldiness that would result from attempting to separately price each job. It is also customary to establish a range for each pay grade to permit increases for seniority and merit. This is shown in Figure 11-2.

HANDLING SPECIAL PROBLEMS
A common problem occurs when the external market rate is out of line with the internal wage structure. A wage survey for a hospital shows that pathology technicians are paid more than radiology technicians. But the hospital's job evaluation plan places radiology technicians in a higher classification. It establishes a pay scale for pathology technicians below the market rate. This is obviously going to make it difficult to attract and retain persons with this skill.

This is not an easy problem to resolve. (It is commonly found when the

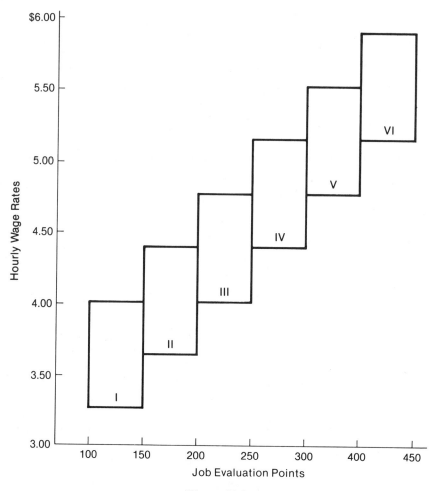

Figure 11-2
Pay Grades with Ranges

market rate for college recruits equals or exceeds the salaries of experienced college graduates.) It is possible that other organizational features may compensate for the wage rate which is out of line. More likely the organization will have to distort its internal structure to meet the realities of the market. This can create internal problems, but flexibility is essential in compensation programs.

Wage and salary programs also create problems by their inevitable rigidity. This rigidity is necessary if the program is to maintain control over personnel costs. But it can frustrate other goals.

A talented secretary may willingly take on additional duties and responsibilities delegated by the superior. Ideally this should result in additional compensation commensurate with the additional contribution. This is true even though the individual may be at the top of the rate range for secretaries.

The dilemma, though, is that if this practice is permitted to go unchecked, personnel costs get completely out of hand. This is commonly referred to as "upward wage drift." Permitting unlimited movement of positions into higher pay classifications eliminates any effective cost control.

It is not always understood that many jobs should not be performed beyond a certain level. Additional creativity is not worth the extra money to the organization. When talented and ambitious individuals are in these jobs, it is often best to promote them to higher classifications where their talents can be put to better use.

An ideal wage and salary program would recognize individual merit and contribution. It would not penalize initiative, extra effort, and achievement. At the same time it must provide structure so costs do not get out of line. This means that wage and salary administrators must strike a balance between rigidity and flexibility.

WAGE INCENTIVES

Wage incentive plans which tie compensation directly to output go back to the beginning of the twentieth century. Pioneered by the early industrial engineers, wage incentives were once considered the answer to problems of worker motivation. While still found, their use has declined in the last few decades.

The simplest incentive system is that of straight piecework. Workers are paid a straight amount for each unit produced. Variations include paying a premium for amounts above a certain level or paying variable amounts for production above and below a prescribed standard.

Piecework relates the wage directly to output. Other systems establish time standards. Output is translated into standard time units. Pay is based upon the time savings realized by the worker.

There are many reasons for the decline of incentive systems. The nature of industry is such that fewer jobs today permit a distinguishable unit of output from one employee. They also require careful setting of standards which is a continual source of friction and conflict. It has also been found that workers will establish group norms to limit output and thus reduce the effectiveness of the system.

Group incentive plans have been developed and tried. They are used where distinguishable output cannot be attributed to an individual. They are designed with the hope they will foster team spirit and substitute positive group discipline for the discipline imposed by management. Some job enrichment programs have utilized group incentive pay plans. The reported results have been mixed.

It is a common practice to pay persons in sales a commission based on volume. This is a form of wage incentive. At one time it was not unusual to pay completely by commission. This method is still used but has given way to a base salary plus commission.

At the managerial level there are a variety of incentives. These include bonuses, profit sharing, and stock options, all designed to foster greater productivity and output. Some managerial compensation plans tie a portion of income directly to organizational results. As would be expected, these plans are more common in the private sector than the public sector.

Incentive plans will always have their place in wage and salary administration. Many years of experience have taught that simply tying earnings to output does not resolve problems of motivation. In many situations it simply increases them.

PUBLIC POLICY AND COMPENSATION

Fair Labor Standards Act   The most important law dealing with compensation is the Fair Labor Standards Act (1938), also known as the Wage-Hour Act. It is a complex measure dealing with several matters not strictly related to compensation such as child labor standards. But its principal focus is on minimum wages and overtime pay.

The act covers employees in the private sector involved in interstate commerce. Exempt from its provisions on the minimum wage and overtime pay are executive, administrative, and professional employees as well as outside salespersons. Prior to July, 1976, the act covered employees of the federal, state, and local governments. In that year the Supreme Court ruled that the federal government could not impose the Fair Labor Standards Act on state and local governments.

When the act was passed in 1938, the first minimum wage was $.25 an hour. It has been amended numerous times over the years. As a result of legislation enacted in 1977, the minimum wage increased on January 1 of each of the following four years: 1978, $2.65 an hour; 1979, $2.90; 1980, $3.10; and 1981, $3.35. In previous years there was a separate schedule for farm and nonfarm workers. This became a single rate beginning January 1, 1978.

The act requires that all employees covered must be paid at the rate of time-and-one-half of regular pay for all hours in excess of forty in any week. The regular rate of pay may not be the same as the hourly rate. Included in the regular pay are all bonuses, commissions, special incentives, and other payments. Also, the act does not require that overtime payments be made for extra hours in a day. It only refers to hours in excess of forty in a week. Some other federal acts as well as many union contracts require this, but not the Fair Labor Standards Act.

The Equal Pay Act of 1963, which is usually thought of as a separate measure, is actually an amendment to the Fair Labor Standards Act. Its basic provision is that the employer cannot discriminate on the basis of sex in paying employees. While designed primarily to protect females, it prohibits discrimination against males as well. One sex can be paid a higher rate if the payment is based on merit or seniority or other factors that exclude sex, such as output.

Under the act's enforcement provisions, administrative agencies of the Wage and Hour Division of the Department of Labor have the right to investigate organizations. They can obtain injunctions to prohibit violations of the law. Willful violaters face fines of up to $10,000 and possible imprisonment.

Davis–Bacon Act

The first federal minimum wage law was the Davis–Bacon Act of 1931. It is not nearly so comprehensive as the Fair Labor Standards Act. It deals with construction on federal buildings and public works for contracts in excess of $2,000. It requires organizations which have federal construction contracts to pay workers the prevailing wages of the locality in which the work is being performed. In recent years this has been expanded to include supplementary benefits as well as hourly rates.

Walsh–Healey Act

The Walsh–Healey (or Public Contracts) Act was passed in 1936 in an effort to extend the provisions of Davis–Bacon to other types of federal contracts. It applies to nonconstruction work for the federal government where the value of materials and supplies exceeds $10,000. Unlike Davis–Bacon it prescribes industry minimum wage standards rather than prevailing wages in the local area. These are set by the Secretary of Labor.

This act also provides pay at the rate of time-and-one-half for hours in excess of eight in a day, or forty in one week.

Copeland Act

The Copeland Act was passed in 1934. It authorizes the Secretary of Labor to make regulations on wage deductions for contractors and sub-contractors under federal contracts. Deductions which are taken out of the worker's pay must be shown to be proper and authorized. Its purpose is to protect workers from having to pay "kickbacks" to obtain their jobs. Violations are punishable by fines and imprisonment.

173

Contract Work–Hours Standards Act The Contract Work–Hours Standards Act was enacted in 1962. It was passed to extend certain protections afforded construction workers to employees who work under contracts which supply services and manufactured goods to the federal government. Its primary provision not duplicated in the Fair Labor Standards Act is that employees must receive time-and-one-half for any hours in a day in excess of eight.

Service Contract Act The Service Contract Act also deals with employees under contracts supplying goods and services to the federal government. It was enacted in 1965. If the employer has a contract in excess of $2500 then wages and fringe benefits must be equal to locally prevailing rates but no less than the minimum wage. Enforcement includes withholding of payments by the government and possible suit. Violaters can also be put on a "blacklist" and prohibited from doing business with the government for three years.

Consumer Credit Protection Act Title III of the Consumer Credit Protection Act, enacted in 1968, is a federal measure dealing with wage garnishments. These are legal attachments of the employee's pay by individuals or organizations to whom the employee owes money. Prior to 1968 wage garnishments were covered by state legislation only.

Title III prohibits discharge for garnishments resulting from one debt. The amount which can be garnished is related to take-home pay. Only amounts of pay above $48 are subject to garnishment. If take-home pay exceeds $64, the total garnishment is limited to 25 percent.

State Laws In addition to federal measures dealing with compensation, all of the states have enacted legislation in this area. The Fair Labor Standards Act permits states to enact minimum wages higher than the federal level. Employers in interstate commerce must comply with the state minimum wage law if it is higher. The same is also true if states require a shorter work week to qualify for overtime pay.

There are also numerous state laws dealing with such matters as the frequency and method of wage payments. Garnishments are also covered by state law and approximately one-half the states have equal pay statutes.

SUMMARY

The general wage level is the average of the absolute dollars paid in wages and salaries. The vertical wage structure is the worth of jobs within the organization in comparison with each other. In devising wages and salaries for an organization, both structures must be considered.

Goals of the wage and salary administration should be: to establish a wage level sufficient to attract and retain workers without incurring unnecessary costs, to encourage advancement, to motivate greater effort and channel it in desired directions, to maintain equity, and to conform with government regulations.

The general wage level is determined by wage surveys. This compares the organization's pay scales with pay scales of other organizations. The general wage level is a function of the "going rate," the organization's ability to pay and the desire to pay.

The vertical wage structure is established by job evaluation. These plans are either formal or informal. The most common formal plans are the point system and the factor comparison method. Both establish factors or dimensions for jobs and evaluate jobs based on these factors. Informal plans look at the job as a whole.

The general wage and the vertical wage structure come together in establishing actual pay levels. Wage curves accomplish this with point systems. It is done automatically by the factor comparison method. One special problem occurs when the vertical wage structure is not in agreement with the market rate. Another is the constant push of wages upward as jobs are moved into higher classifications.

Primary legislation dealing with wage and salary administration is the Fair Labor Standards Act. It prescribes a minimum wage for employees involved in interstate commerce and overtime pay for hours in a week in excess of forty. There are numerous other federal measures dealing with minimum wages and overtime pay, primarily in federal construction projects. More recent legislation has extended protection to workers in firms supplying the federal government with goods and services as well as construction.

SELECTED REFERENCES

BELCHER, DAVID W., *Compensation Administration.* Englewood Cliffs, N.J.: Prentice-Hall, 1974.

BERG, J. GARY, *Managing Compensation.* New York: AMACOM, American Management Association, 1976.

HENDERSON, RICHARD, *Compensation Management: Rewarding Performance in the Modern Organization.* Reston, Va.: Reston Publishing Co., 1976.

NASH, ALLAN N. and STEPHEN J. CARROLL, JR., *The Management of Compensation.* Monterey, Calif.: Brooks/Cole Publishing Co., 1975.

PATTEN, THOMAS H., JR., *Pay: Employee Compensation and Incentive Plans.* New York: The Free Press, 1977.

ROCK, MILTON L., ed., *Handbook of Wage and Salary Administration.* New York: McGraw-Hill, 1972.

PRODUCTIVITY AND LABOR COSTS

◀══ IDEAS TO BE FOUND ══▶
IN THIS CHAPTER

- Importance of productivity
- Measuring productivity and the unit labor cost
- Uses of the unit labor cost measure
- New approaches to productivity improvement
- Job enrichment, behavior modification, organizational
   development, and work scheduling

Productivity is important, both for society and for the organization. Improvements in productivity are the means by which society raises the standard of living. Its importance is attested to by the ninety-fourth Congress which, in 1975 in an effort to promote continued economic growth, created the National Center for Productivity and Quality of Working Life as an independent agency within the Executive Branch.

Closely related to productivity is the issue of labor costs. Labor (or personnel) costs are one of the largest expense categories for most organizations. Customarily measured in absolute terms, labor costs are the actual dollars spent on wages, salaries, and economic supplements.

Thought of only in this fashion, labor costs can be quite misleading. The crucial issue is not just the dollar amount paid in wages, salaries, and supplements; rather, it is what the organization receives for the dollars spent. This is what productivity and its corollary measure, the unit labor cost, are concerned with.

There is a large body of literature dealing with productivity for the economy as a whole. Less has been written about the use of productivity and unit labor cost measures for the organization. In this chapter these topics are examined along with a discussion of some of the newer programs for improving productivity.

WHAT IS PRODUCTIVITY?   Productivity is a ratio. It is a ratio of some unit of output to some unit of input. It is not production, though the two are often confused. Production refers to output by itself, such as 500 payroll checks processed. Productivity relates that output to some unit of input, such as 500 checks processed in two hours.

Productivity is a measure of efficiency. Probably the most familiar productivity measure is miles per gallon. How many miles can an automobile be driven for each gallon of gasoline it consumes? This does not mean the gasoline itself is the only factor involved in mileage. Other factors such as engine timing, quality of spark plugs, cleanliness of the air filter, and driving technique are more important. It is a measure of the engine's efficiency, not the efficiency of the gasoline itself.

Productivity measures are possible on numerous dimensions. Patients recovered per total operated on, hits per times at bat, sales per employee, policies renewed per policies sold—all of these are forms of productivity. The most familiar productivity measure for the economy as a whole is that of labor productivity. This is found by dividing Gross National Product, a measure of the economy's output of goods and services, by the hours utilized in their production.

$$\frac{\text{Gross National Product}}{\text{Hours of all persons*}} = \frac{\text{Output per hour}}{\text{of all persons}} = \text{Labor Productivity}$$

Just as in the automobile example, this does not mean that labor input alone is responsible for the goods and services. Capital equipment, work methods, quality of raw materials, availability of transportation—all of these and more play an important role. But labor productivity or output per hour of all persons is one measure of the efficiency with which the economy utilizes its labor force.

One of the factors limiting the use of productivity measures is the complexity of their computation. Ideally productivity should be measured in standardized physical units. Because this is impossible with the wide variety of goods and services the nation produces, the Gross National Product expressed in constant dollars is used as an approximation.

A manufacturing firm producing one product which never changes

---

*Formerly known as man-hours. It designates hours worked by payroll workers, self-employed persons, and unpaid family workers in a family business.

would have little difficulty in measuring productivity. As the variety of goods increases and as the quality changes from period to period, the problem of standardizing the units increases. For the service sectors where the output can be quite intangible, the complexity of the measurement problem is increased that much more.

In recent years much progress has been made in coming to grips with the problems raised in measuring productivity. Ways are being found to measure sectors of the economy once thought impervious to productivity measurement. Leon Greenberg has presented some helpful techniques for measuring productivity in a variety of situations.[1]

For measuring plant output, Greenberg suggests the use of labor-hour equivalents as a way of expressing the physical value of the products produced. All products are expressed in terms of the hours required in their production for a specified time period. This avoids the problem of using dollar measures which can be influenced by price changes and distort the extent to which real productivity changes are occurring.

More work is required for the service sector, but progress is also being made in this area. For some service organizations output can be measured by actual units, such as telephone calls in communications, haircuts for a barbershop, and units of electric power for a utility. Those with intangible services pose more difficulties. Greenberg suggests that multiple weighting systems may be most appropriate for these kinds of organizations. For trash removal, items such as volume collected, frequency of collection, cleanliness of the streets, and population density might be combined and weighted.

THE UNIT LABOR COST

Labor productivity for the organization is not the same thing as labor productivity for the economy as a whole. For the economy improvements in labor productivity mean an improvement in the standard of living. Increasing the output of goods and services for the same hours means greater material abundance. Producing the same output with fewer hours means extra leisure time. Either result benefits society.

For the organization improved labor productivity does not necessarily mean a corresponding improvement in the organization's condition. The organization is not concerned with just output and input. The organization is also concerned with the prices it receives for its goods and services and the costs it incurs in producing those goods and services. Sales, labor costs, material costs, profits, return on investment, and budgetary appropriations are just some of the financial indicators important for the organization.

Though by itself the labor productivity measure is of limited value to the organization, its value is enhanced when used in conjunction with other

[1]Leon Greenberg, *A Practical Guide to Productivity Measurement*. (Washington, D.C.: Bureau of National Affairs, 1973).

measurements. One such additional measure is the *unit labor cost*. The unit labor cost is a ratio of the cost of the labor input to the output per hour of all persons. The Bureau of Labor Statistics computes it along with labor productivity. For the economy it helps determine how competitive American goods are in world markets.

The unit labor cost is a valuable indicator for the organization, though its use is not wide spread. It is derived as shown.

$$\frac{\text{Output}}{\text{Hours of all persons}} = \text{Output per hour}$$

$$\frac{\text{Compensation per hour}}{\text{Output per hour}} = \text{Unit labor cost}$$

The unit labor cost gives a more realistic picture of labor costs than actual dollars spent because it relates those dollars to the output achieved. It should be noted that compensation per hour does not refer to the wage or salary alone. It includes wages, salaries, overtime payments, bonuses, pension contributions, health insurance fees, Social Security taxes, and all other direct and indirect personnel expenses.

How the organization can use the unit labor cost is shown in the example which follows. The three items the organization must compete are output, hours of all persons, and compensation per hour. With these three items it can determine the unit labor cost. In the example shown the unit labor cost is $1.20.

$$\frac{250 \text{ Units output}}{50 \text{ Hours of all persons}} = 5 \text{ Output per hour}$$

$$\frac{\$6.00 \text{ Compensation per hour}}{5 \text{ Output per hour}} = \$1.20 \text{ Unit labor cost}$$

By portraying labor costs this way, it is possible to see their interrelationship with other elements of the production process. If the organization wishes to reduce labor costs, it can conceptualize this in three ways instead of just the one of reducing payroll dollars. These three ways will be shown in turn.

Increasing Output   By increasing output and holding everything else constant, the organization effectively reduces its unit labor costs. In this example, output is increased to 300 units.

$$\frac{300 \text{ Units output}}{50 \text{ Hours of all persons}} \quad = \quad 6 \quad \text{Output per hour}$$

$$\frac{\$6.00 \text{ Compensation per hour}}{6 \text{ Output per hour}} \quad = \$1.00 \quad \text{Unit labor cost}$$

As shown, output per hour has increased from five units to six units. The result is to lower the unit labor cost from $1.20 to $1.00. The improved output may have been obtained by such things as improved work methods, better quality raw materials, or greater effort on the part of employees. This is what is meant by the often heard statement that to avoid inflation, increases in wages must be offset by increases in productivity.

Decreasing Hours
of All Persons

The organization can accomplish the same result by reducing hours of all persons to 42 (rounded off). Holding everything else constant, this is shown below.

$$\frac{250 \text{ Units output}}{42 \text{ Hours of all persons}} \quad = \quad 6 \quad \text{Output per hour}$$

$$\frac{\$6.00 \text{ Compensation per hour}}{6 \text{ Output per hour}} \quad = \$1.00 \quad \text{Unit labor cost}$$

This result could have been achieved by the same actions as in increasing output.

Decreasing
Compensation

Decreasing compensation from $6.00 per hour to $5.00 per hour is the third way for reducing unit labor costs. It is reduced by $1.00 as shown:

$$\frac{250 \text{ Units output}}{50 \text{ Hours of all persons}} \quad = \quad 5 \quad \text{Output per hour}$$

$$\frac{\$5.00 \text{ Compensation per hour}}{5 \text{ Output per hour}} \quad = \$1.00 \quad \text{Unit labor cost}$$

It might be thought that it is impossible to cut anyone's wages. But compensation here means all the dollars paid divided by hours. By such actions as reducing overtime payments, getting a better rate for health insurance, or reducing workers' compensation costs by safety programs, the organization can conceivably reduce its compensation per hour without cutting any individual's rate.

For purposes of illustration each of these methods has been shown separately. Obviously they can be performed in conjunction. Like all organizational indicators, the unit labor cost can give a distorted picture when seen in isolation. If the organization reduces unit labor costs by adding expensive capital equipment on which the return is poor, it may only be raising capital costs by the same amount it is reducing labor costs and is no better off than before.

PROGRAMS FOR IMPROVING PRODUCTIVITY

There are two major implications which stem from the creation of the National Center for Productivity and Quality of Working Life. One is concern over the nation's productivity, now and in the future. The other is that productivity is linked with something called the "quality of working life."

It is this latter implication which is reflected in many current productivity improvement efforts. The assumption is that languishing productivity reflects a general malaise and discontent with work itself. Work is seen as dehumanizing, monotonous, repetitious, with little opportunity for creativity and personal expression. It is said to provide ample satisfaction of basic needs for food and shelter but little satisfaction of higher needs such as autonomy and fulfillment.

The typical work environment is seen as an outgrowth of the turn-of-the-century industrial engineers who pioneered something called "Scientific Management." This movement was also concerned with improving productivity. But it showed little concern for the individual psyche. Its basic assumption was the worker's lack of intelligence. Work had to be made as simple as possible. Tight management control was essential. Workers had to perform tasks in the one best way devised by the engineer. For its time it had tremendous impact in improving the productivity of American industry.

Current programs can be seen as a swing away from both the techniques and assumptions of Scientific Management. Instead of making work simpler, it should be made more challenging. Instead of tight management control, there should be more autonomy and freedom. Workers are assumed capable of making intelligent choices of how work should be performed. New programs such as *job enrichment, behavior modification, organizational development,* and new concepts in *work scheduling* reflect these new assumptions.

Before discussing each in turn, it should be noted that opinion is not unanimous that changes are needed in work climate. Critics of these programs assert that reports of worker discontent and malaise are greatly exaggerated. Even if they are not, there are reservations that, regardless of effects on worker attitudes, the programs are no more productive than the methods they replace. And the charge is also made that in using tools of modern psychology, they are merely substituting one form of coercion for another.

Job Enrichment　　　　　　Job enrichment is an outgrowth of an earlier program called job enlargement. Job enlargement attempts to reduce work monotony by rotation and other methods that permit employees to work at a greater variety of tasks. This is known as expanding the horizontal dimension.

Job enrichment goes beyond this by adding a vertical dimension. In addition to variety it permits greater autonomy and independent decision-making. Work methods, production schedules, and output quotas are decided upon by work groups or work teams. Group decision-making is substituted for that of a supervisor. Group norms are utilized for control instead of imposed managerial authority.

The assumption is that permitting workers greater discretion and independence will result in better attitudes and job behavior. Many large organizations have become strong proponents of job enrichment in recent years. American Telephone and Telegraph has been a pioneer in this area and has claimed great success for its programs. Other organizations such as Texas Instruments have been equally enthusiastic.

As is true of so many of the new programs, it is impossible to offer any definitive assessment of their success. Most of the evidence has been of a testimonial nature. Studies have been conducted indicating success, but many are of questionable value. "Hawthorne effect," the effect of change itself, has seldom been effectively controlled for.* This is not to say job enrichment is not working. The premises on which it is based are sound and plausible. But hard evidence is still limited. And the nature of the production process in some industries, such as automobile manufacturing, makes introducing a job enrichment program difficult without greatly adding to costs.

Job enrichment programs require a drastic change in management's philosophy and style. Managers developed in a tradition of tight managerial control often experience difficulty relinquishing authority. Installation of such programs is therefore not just a matter of new techniques for the worker. A critical aspect of their success or failure is the ability of supervisors and managers to work in such a climate.

Behavior Modification　　　　　Behavior modification programs are based on the reinforcement concepts associated with B. F. Skinner. They are based on the law of effect. This principle says that behavior which is rewarded tends to be repeated. Behavior which is not rewarded tends not to be repeated. Behavior modifica-

---

*"Hawthorne effect" comes from the famous experiments of the 1920s at the Hawthorne Works of Western Electric. In testing for the effects of environment upon worker performance, the experimenters found that knowledge by the workers that they were participating in an experiment affected (and thereby contaminated) the results.

tion programs stress the use of positive reinforcement as a substitute for the aversive reinforcements of the traditional work environment.

Certain steps are followed in these programs. Work is broken down into identifiable behavior units. Goals are established and feedback provided to permit self-reinforcement. This self-reinforcement concept is one of the important features of behavior modification. (Lack of feedback is considered a deterrent in other types of motivation programs.) Periodic positive reinforcement from the supervisor is also stressed.

Behavior modification programs have become widespread in recent years. Great success has been claimed in terms of productivity measures such as increased output, fewer errors, less absenteeism, and reduced turnover. Studies have been offered to support these claims; unfortunately many of the studies lacked the rigorous controls desired in these kinds of investigations. But many organizations which have adopted such programs are enthusiastic about the results.

In addition to questioning the results, critics of behavior modification say such programs are dehumanizing. They supposedly treat humans like so many of Skinner's pigeons whose behavior is shaped by rewarding them with food. In this view humans are seen as organisms to be manipulated.

Behavior modification techniques have not been restricted to the work environment. An entire school of psychotherapy has developed which utilizes behavior modification. This approach rejects the traditional Freudian approach of insight and analysis. It concentrates on changing behavior by rewards and penalties. Success has been claimed in many areas of human functioning.

Organizational Development Of the new approaches dealing with productivity, organizational development (better known as OD) is the most difficult to define with precision. It encompasses many different philosophies, ideologies, methods, and techniques. Its main concern is the quality of working life.

OD deals with all aspects of the organization. It includes such things as communications patterns, hierarchical structures, formal organization patterns, and organization direction. It attempts to provide more open, noncompetitive, and trusting interpersonal relationships instead of the prevalent ones of competition, secrecy, and distrust. It borrows many of the concepts of earlier attempts in this direction such as sensitivity training and encounter group interactions.

OD customarily begins with a diagnostic phase. Feedback obtained through questionnaires, interviews, observations, and other means provides the diagnostician (typically an outside consultant) with an understanding of the organization and its problems. The next step is an action program to deal with the problems. Work groups are customarily asked to make recommendations and implement changes. These changes can range from revisions in the appraisal process to increased participation in goal setting. The focus is on change devised by the work group itself, not from directives issued by the formal hierarchy. Once begun, the process becomes a continual one for meeting OD goals.

Many work climate improvements have been attributed to OD. Testimonials also abound to its impact upon organizational productivity. As with the other methods, hard evidence is sparse. Because of the general nature of the changes proposed by OD, it is difficult to define what exactly is being modified. Most of the studies to date lack rigorous methodology to control for all the variables under examination.

Critics of OD decry its lack of theoretical and empirical base. In this view it is nothing more than old-fashioned problem solving dressed up in a modern psychological idiom. It is said to be just as coercive in its own way as traditional managerial methods.

But proponents have a much different view. They see it as providing ways to tap reservoirs of human potential untouched by present managerial methods. That this untapped potential exists is difficult to debate. The extent to which OD actually helps release it in constructive ways for the organization and the individual will undoubtedly be the subject of continued investigation in the future.

Work Schedules

Less ambitious than the previous programs are changes in work schedules. Rather than concern for directly modifying behavior or changing the organizational climate, these approaches are more limited. They attempt in modest fashion to treat workers more like adults by providing more independence and autonomy. The two major efforts in this area are *flexi-time* and the *four-day week*.

Flexi-time can only work under conditions where the nature of the work permits flexibility in scheduling. Workers are permitted discretion as to how they schedule their hours, provided they work the required number of hours in a week or a month. Some organizations permit discretionary arrival times between 7:00 and 9:00 A.M. and departures between 3:00 and 5:00 P.M. Some forms of flexi-time permit daily changes and others require a fixed schedule for one week at a time. Other variations include half days and days off with time to be made up later (providing there is no conflict with the Wage–Hour Act).

Obviously not all work environments permit this kind of latitude. Work flow operations where there is great interdependence impose limitations. Even here, though, some organizations have experimented with group decision-making permitting the entire group to decide upon a schedule all will follow.

The four-day week has also been experimented with in recent years.

This involves the worker putting in the traditional forty hours of work in four days instead of five. It permits more continuous time off and has met with favor by some workers and employers. Others find it too fatiguing since it calls for a ten-hour work day. And there are some indications workers use the extra days off not for leisure pursuits but to hold second jobs.

Since work scheduling changes are less ambitious, fewer claims are made for their impact upon organizational productivity. It is still too early to tell what the long-range impact will be upon quantity and quality of output as well as absenteeism and tardiness. But they do recognize that today's work force is probably less suited to regimentation that was customary in previous years. If enough employers permit their employees more discretion and autonomy in various areas of their working life, other employers will probably have no choice but to follow.

SUMMARY Productivity is a matter of great concern to society and the organization. Improvements in productivity are how a society achieves a higher standard of living. Productivity is a ratio of output to input. The most common productivity measure for the economy is labor productivity: Gross National Product divided by the hours of all persons, equals output per hour of all persons.

The unit labor cost is a valuable measure for the organization. It is derived from the productivity measure and is a ratio of compensation per hour to output per hour of all persons. Labor (or personnel) costs can be conceptualized in three ways. Unit labor costs can be reduced by increasing output, by decreasing hours of all persons, or by decreasing compensation per hour.

Newer approaches to improving productivity focus upon improvements in the quality of working life. *Job enrichment* expands the job on both horizontal (variety of tasks) and vertical (more autonomy and decision making) dimensions. *Behavior modification* programs attempt to motivate workers by the use of positive reinforcements. *Organizational development* represents an attempt through diagnosis and group interactions to change the work climate, particularly in the area of interpersonal relationships. *Flexitime* permits workers greater latitude in scheduling their work. Some organizations have also experimented with working the traditional forty hours in four days. Claims of improved worker attitudes and productivity have been made for all these approaches, but hard empirical evidence from rigorous studies is still lacking.

SELECTED REFERENCES

BUREAU OF LABOR STATISTICS, *Meaning and Measurement of Productivity*. BLS Bulletin 1714, 1971.

DUNNETTE, M. D., ed., *Work and Nonwork in the Year 2001*. Monterey, Calif.: Brooks/Cole, 1973.

GOLDBERG, J. and others, *Collective Bargaining and Productivity*. Madison, Wis.: Industrial Relations Research Association, 1975.

GREENBERG, LEON, *A Practical Guide To Productivity Measurement*. Washington, D.C.: Bureau of National Affairs, 1973.

PENYER, WILLIAM N., *Productivity and Motivation Through Job Engineering*. New York: AMACOM, American Management Association, 1973.

WALTERS, RORY, *Job Enrichment for Results: Strategies for Successful Implementation*. Reading, Mass.: Addison-Wesley, 1975.

EMPLOYEE
MAINTENANCE

EMPLOYEE BENEFITS AND SERVICES

← IDEAS TO BE FOUND →
IN THIS CHAPTER

- Development of benefit programs
- Protection against death, illness, and injury
- Retirement benefits
- Protection against job loss
- Pay for time not worked

Becoming increasingly important in personnel administration are programs of employee benefits and services. Once restricted to only the largest employers, they have become practically universal today. Referred to for many years as *fringe benefits,* other terms have come into use such as *economic supplements* and *supplementary benefits.* "Fringe" hardly describes these benefits now since they have become such a large and integral part of the wage and salary package.

Employee benefits and services range from coffee breaks, to paid vacations, to elaborate health and retirement plans. The distinction between benefits and services is somewhat arbitrary. Benefits are usually thought of as things purchased for the employee, such as life insurance. Services are those things provided directly to the employee, such as athletic equipment and recreation facilities.

Benefits and services are of two types. Some, such as workers' compensation, are provided by the employer because of statutory requirements. Others, such as paid holidays, are offered either voluntarily or through collective bargaining. This chapter examines the main features of both.

DEVELOPMENT OF BENEFITS AND SERVICES

The development and evolution of private benefits and services goes back to an earlier era of paternalism. This was a stance adopted by many large industrial employers from the turn of the century through the 1920s. During and after the depression of the 1930s this type of employer behavior declined and is almost nonexistent today.

Paternalism was the employer acting "in loco parentis." Acting from a variety of motives, not excluding the self-serving, paternalistic employers provided as much as possible for their employees' needs. The world of the company and the personal world were often hard to distinguish. Everything from company-provided housing to employee cafeterias to special recreation areas were common during this era. In return, employees were expected to give total allegiance to the employer including a willingness to not join labor unions and to accept employer-determined wage levels without complaint.

Paternalistic employers concentrated on services rather than benefits as they are known today. Instead of health insurance, company doctors and nurses were available for medical care. Employee benefits as we know them today received their biggest boost during World War II from 1940 to 1945. During this period, wages and salaries of private employers were put under government regulation. While direct payments of wages and salaries were frozen by the government to prevent inflation, the same was not true of indirect payments in the form of benefits.

Labor unions played a big role in the movement toward benefit packages. Unions were in a difficult position during the war years. For patriotic reasons most of them relinquished the right to strike. Because of government controls they also surrendered their major collective bargaining function of securing higher wages. The result was a push on their part for indirect wage payments in the form of such unregulated items as pensions, medical care plans, and life and accident insurance.

Because these benefits proved popular with workers, unions found themselves bargaining over more of these items following the end of the war. While large wage increases were still attractive, union leaders found they could enhance the union's position with the membership through innovative benefit programs. They also provided an extra dimension in the union's attempts to attract new members.

Organizations without unions were also encouraged to provide these benefits. The tremendous economic growth after World War II meant shortages of labor, particularly in the skilled categories. Benefit programs proved to be a strong recruiting tool. An attractive benefits program enabled the organization to compete more effectively for new workers as well as to retain those already on the payroll. They also provided tax advantages for the employer.

Another factor encouraging the expansion of benefit programs was recognition of the maintenance goal in developing a productive work force. Employers realized that a worker who was worried about mounting hospital bills might be less effective on the job. The same might be true of the worker who was concerned about financing his or her retirement someday. Benefit plans could thus make their contribution to worker productivity.

While benefits were a relatively modest part of wages as recently as two decades ago, they have become a costly part of the wage package today. Estimates vary as to how much benefits add to payroll costs, but most estimates place the average at approximately 33 percent. This varies considerably among industries and organizations. For some industries which are historically low paying, such as restaurants and lodging, the benefit package may be quite modest. In other industries such as petroleum refining and automobile manufacturing, the amount added by benefits is typically greater than the average.

PROTECTION AGAINST DEATH AND DISABILITY

Almost all organizations of any size today provide some protection for employees against the hazards of death, illness, and injury. Some of these are a result of private arrangements between employer and employee. Many are required as a matter of public policy.

Private Benefit Plans

In order to protect the worker's family against loss of either the principle or secondary wage earner, many organizations today provide life insurance. These are provided under group plans and are usually in the form of term insurance. Amounts vary, but typically coverage is not adequate without the worker purchasing additional insurance privately. One big advantage is that coverage is usually provided without requiring the worker to take a physical examination.

For protection against injury, organizations provide several forms of benefits. One of these is accident insurance which provides specified amounts in the event of injury on or off the job. The amount paid is usually related to the injury's severity.

Illness is covered by various forms of health insurance, either through Blue Cross–Blue Shield plans or from private insurance companies. Benefits vary widely but they provide at least partial reimbursement of hospital costs as well as physician fees. Many organizations also offer major medical insurance which protects the worker against the cost of catastrophic illness of long duration such as cancer or heart disease.

Sick leave is another form of illness protection. This provides the employee with a certain number of days per year for absences caused by illness. For these days there is no loss of pay. Five- to ten-days sick leave is common for organizations which have this benefit. Some permit the accumulation of sick days from year to year while others do not.

Protection against loss of income for relatively long periods of illness such as recuperation from surgery is covered by disability insurance which many organizations provide. This provides partial reimbursement of lost wages during time off the job. Usually this insurance is written for a maximum time period such as twelve or twenty-four months. More expensive forms provide for longer time periods including lifetime benefits in case of permanent disability.

Financing of these plans varies. Some are contributory with the employee paying part of the costs, usually up to a maximum of one-half. Other plans are noncontributory with the employer bearing the full expense.

Public Policy There is much legislation protecting the employee in the event of death, illness, or injury. Social Security is often thought of as providing only retirement benefits, but it is also a form of life insurance. For a fully insured worker who dies, benefits are paid to the surviving spouse and dependent children under eighteen, or until twenty-two if they are full-time students. When the children come of age benefits cease for them and the spouse, but are resumed under certain conditions when the spouse reaches retirement age. Dependent parents and disabled children can also qualify for benefits. At one time benefits were paid only to surviving widows, but recent court rulings concerning equal rights suggest widowers are also eligible under certain conditions.

Social Security also provides benefits if the worker becomes totally or partially disabled. Benefits continue until the employee is able to resume work. In cases of permanent disability, the benefits continue for life.

The *Medicare* program was added to Social Security in 1965. This provides hospital and medical insurance for persons over sixty-five who are covered by Social Security. Those not covered by Social Security previously can also apply for the program. It pays a major portion of the costs of hospitalization as well as physician fees and other medical costs such as out-patient care and laboratory services.

Disability and health insurance features of Social Security are financed by the same system which provides for retirement. Financing is by matching employer and employee contributions of a percentage of wages or salary. Coverage is mandatory for those covered by the Social Security Act.

Injuries on the job are covered by workers' compensation programs. These programs are under state jurisdiction, with all states having such laws. Provisions vary widely among the states in terms of types of injuries covered, benefit amounts, length of coverage, and other provisions. In cases of death from work-related causes, benefits are paid to surviving dependents.

Employees injured on the job are entitled to compensation without regard to fault and without having to sue. Benefits are usually a percentage of the wage. Disability benefits to replace a portion of lost income are paid as well as medical costs. Occupationally related diseases are also covered in some cases, but state handling of this area is quite diverse.

Financing of workers' compensation is almost completely by the employer. The two major methods are through state insurance systems or by obtaining coverage from private companies. Some states make state systems elective while others make it compulsory. A few states also permit self-financing by the employer.

RETIREMENT

Retirement planning and benefits have become increasingly important. With life spans becoming longer, more and more people can anticipate living many years after retiring. A marked increase in the general standard of living also means less willingness to greatly reduce that during the retirement years.

Private Plans

Pensions and other retirement benefits were once almost the exclusive province of executives and salaried personnel. While a few industries and the federal government pioneered retirement benefits in the form of pensions, they were not generally available for non-managerial employees until after World War II.

After the war years unions bargained strongly for inclusion of pension benefits in the contracts they signed with management. This trend was accelerated in 1948 when the Supreme Court upheld an NLRB ruling that companies under the Labor–Management Relations Act were required to bargain with unions over pension benefits. With this legal boost pension plans spread rapidly among organized firms. The unorganized sector followed the trend.

Even with new federal standards there is wide variation in the benefits the plans offer as well as vesting rights, financing, investment policies, and length of employment to qualify. Vesting refers to the number of years required before the employee "owns" the pension (retains pension rights even though leaving the employer). Financing can be either contributory—with the employee sharing the cost, or noncontributory—with the employer bearing the full expense. Benefits are usually based on some formula reflecting the employee's earnings.

Public Policy   Social Security is the older and better known of the two government measures dealing with retirement. Enacted in 1935, Social Security has been greatly expanded and modified over the years. It was never intended to provide totally for a worker's retirement needs. But for the vast majority of American workers who come under its provisions, it is intended to provide payments during the retirement years that afford some minimum standard of living.

Social Security is financed by matching employer–employee contributions which is a statutorily prescribed percentage of earnings. To qualify for benefits upon retirement, a worker must have worked a certain number of quarters under Social Security coverage. The benefits formula is a function of the worker's average earnings during the working years. A certain number of low earnings years are dropped off in computing the benefit.

In 1974 many years of Congressional investigation of private pension plans culminated in the passage of the Employee Retirement Income Security Act (ERISA). This is a very complex measure which provides standards to better insure that workers will actually receive their promised pension benefits upon retirement. New vesting rights are provided for as well as periodic certifications that the funding of the pension plan is sound. To provide for cases of plan failures, the Pension Benefit Guaranty Corporation was formed and is funded by premiums from employers.

PROTECTION AGAINST JOB LOSS

Financial aid during periods of unemployment is almost solely a matter of public policy. Some few industries have benefit plans related to layoffs. But these are quite limited in number.

Private Plans   Supplemental unemployment benefits are one of the few measures that employers have for protecting employees against job loss for economic (not health) reasons. Some unions such as the United Automobile Workers have such provisions included in their contracts. These supplemental benefits are added to regular unemployment insurance payments. They can either provide extra amounts during the period of government-provided unemployment payments or they can extend the period during which benefits are collected.

Those plans of supplemental payments which have been established are financed by company contributions. Benefits are limited to amounts accumulated at any given time, thus limiting the company's liability. In some cases of prolonged unemployment workers have exhausted these funds.

Some organizations also provide severance pay for workers who are permanently discharged for economic reasons. In some cases this is written into union contracts. In other cases it is simply a matter of company policy. Oftentimes such severance allowances are not provided for by company policy but are rewarded on an ad hoc basis. This is especially true for discharges that are unusual in nature such as closing a facility permanently.

Public Policy

All states have unemployment insurance programs which were established as part of the Social Security Act of 1935. Programs are under state control with wide latitude permitted in their administration provided minimum federal standards are met. Unemployment insurance is financed solely by the employer through a tax on payrolls. The percentage is adjusted up or down depending upon the unemployment claims filed by the organization's employees.

Unemployment benefits are determined by formulas related to the amount of earnings and in many cases upon the number of dependents claimed by the unemployed worker. They are designed to provide assistance during relatively short periods of unemployment such as for one year or less. This varies by state. Unemployment insurance is not designed to protect the worker against permanent unemployment. In certain cases of severe national unemployment, the federal government has allocated emergency funds to extend benefits when state benefits have been exhausted.

PAY FOR TIME NOT WORKED

One of the fastest growing segments of the benefits package is that of pay for time not worked that is not illness or injury connected. A productive economy can offer its citizens either increased goods or additional leisure. Such things as paid vacations and paid holidays provide a means for having both. Additional leisure is gained without sacrificing income, a combination that has made this category of benefits especially attractive to workers.

Private Plans

A certain amount of time away from the job can be of benefit to the employer. This assumes that the rest and relaxation it provides is returned in the form of increased productivity on the job. When the amount away becomes excessive it becomes dysfunctional and adds to costs. There is little evidence available to suggest exactly where the dividing line is.

Some paid time off the job is practically universal today. Few organizations do not offer a paid vacation. A common feature of vacations is their increase in length with organizational longevity. One week vacation after a year is common for new employees, with two weeks for one to five years of service also quite common. Many organizations now provide vacations of three, four, and five weeks for longer-service employees.

Paid vacations are only rarely a function of rank in the organization. Vacation time is usually based solely on organizational tenure. Various restrictions are found. Some organizations require vacation time to be taken during certain time periods only. Some restrict the number of weeks away at one time. Others permit some accumulation from one year to the next while others prohibit this entirely.

The number of paid holidays has increased dramatically in recent years. Such holidays as Christmas, New Year's Day, Thanksgiving, Memorial Day, Independence Day, Labor Day, and the birthdays of Washington and Lincoln have long been standard. Added to these are paid days off for the employee's birthday, the day before and after Christmas (and sometimes the entire week), the day after Thanksgiving, the day before and after New Year's, religious holidays such as Yom Kippur, Martin Luther King's birthday, and Good Friday, and "bonus" days which the employee can take any time. Employees who must work during these times are usually given extra compensation. Vacations are often extended if a holiday falls during the vacation time. It is not unusual to find organizations giving their employees ten and more paid holidays per year.

There are numerous miscellaneous forms of paid time off. Unions have innovated many of these in collective bargaining. Sick days off have already been mentioned. Paid rest breaks of certain time duration during the day are taken for granted today. Bereavement leave of three days for attending the funeral of a family member is quite common. Compensation to make up the difference between military pay and regular pay during periods of reserve training is also found regularly. Many organizations continue regular pay during periods of jury duty. Many union contracts provide for paid clean-up time before the end of the working day or shift. Paid lunch periods are also quite prevalent.

Public Policy

Public policy has little impact on the area of pay for time not worked. Paid vacations are voluntary on the part of the employer. They may be put into labor contracts because of union bargaining power, but they are not required by law. Legal holidays are enacted under federal and state legislation, but there is no law requiring the employer to grant paid time off for employees to observe them.

Some states have laws requiring rest periods for female workers. Because of civil rights legislation, the constitutionality of these are in question. Legislation also requires that the employer grant time off for military reserve training, but it says nothing about compensation for this time away from the job.

EMPLOYEE SERVICES Special services and unique benefits come in wide variety and show much imagination. Many of the unique benefits are offered because of the nature of the industry. Airlines, for example, offer substantial discounts on air travel to employees, often with the stipulation that this type of travel is done on a stand-by basis only. Among retail firms employee discounts on merchandise are quite commonly found.

Many manufacturing organizations follow the practice of providing employees with the goods produced by the firm at substantial discounts, or in some cases with no charge at all. Some breweries provide free beer for their employees. There are few organizations producing consumer goods that do not offer the goods to their employees at lower-than-market price.

Credit unions are widespread in large organizations. They offer many financial services such as car loans and high interest rates on savings deposits. Tuition reimbursements are provided to encourage employees to continue their education in night and weekend programs. Some organizations offer college scholarships for the offspring of employees.

Recreation areas owned by the organization are often available for employees and their families. Company-provided housing is not as common as it used to be, but in remote areas it can still be found. Some organizations assist employees in financing home purchases. Others will arrange for the sale of the home when the employee is transferred.

As part of their civic responsibility, many organizations buy blocks of season tickets to athletic and cultural events. These are often available at no charge to employees. Payment of fees for professional association memberships is not uncommon. Company cafeterias with low cost meals are so much taken for granted they are often not thought of as a special service. For employees who must wear special clothing, free uniforms and cleaning are often provided.

Regular medical services are often available from health personnel employed by the organization. In this area one of the services that is growing is that of personal and family counseling. These programs can involve everything from psychotherapy for emotional problems to alcoholism, drug abuse, and marriage counseling. Sometimes these services are provided by professionals employed by the organization. In other cases an arrangement is made with local private and public clinics. Confidentiality has to be maintained for these programs to be effective.

A very special category of services are the executive perquisites, or "perks" as they are often called. These are usually restricted to executives at the highest levels. Free use of automobiles, chauffeured limousines, private airplanes, country club memberships, and executive dining rooms are some of the items included in this category.

ADMINISTRATION OF BENEFIT PROGRAMS In organizations of any size administration of benefit programs is almost always centralized in the staff personnel department. Benefit programs involve considerable administrative work. There are endless forms for medical insurance, workers' compensation, retirement plans, and similar programs. It is much less expensive to centralize this function than to have duplicate staffs performing this work. This also helps insure uniform and consistent implementation.

Counseling with regard to benefits is also provided by the personnel department. Many of the programs are complex and need clear explanation. Retirement is a good example where the different options available must be clarified and outlined carefully so that sound decisions can be made. Good counseling programs do more than just aid in completing the paperwork. Their main value is assistance in the planning process.

FLEXIBLE COMPENSATION One innovative approach that has received considerable attention in recent years is that of "cafeteria" style benefit programs—programs of flexible compensation. The assumption is that workers have different needs for benefits based upon their individual circumstances. The descriptive reference of cafeteria style refers to employees making a selection from many different options as to the package best suited for their individual needs.

Older workers may prefer more health protection and have little need for life insurance. Young single workers may be less concerned about insurance generally and more interested in a profit-sharing program which provides more immediate returns. Married workers with large families may want large amounts of term insurance that does not build up cash value instead of smaller amounts of whole life which does. Those who have spouses working may find overlapping coverage in many benefit programs which they would like to eliminate. All of this suggests a more flexible approach.

Flexible benefit programs, though, do provide problems for the organization. They can be quite costly to administer. Tailoring a benefits program to the needs of the individual almost inevitably adds to administrative costs. Additional personnel are usually required. The low rates that go with large numbers may not be available. Maintaining equity among the workers can also prove bothersome.

But flexible approaches do have many compensating advantages despite the extra costs involved. They recognize that people are individuals and that everyone does not fit the same mold. Organizations which have experimented with such programs have generally had a favorable response from employees.

SUMMARY Private benefit programs are of two types, those required by law and those provided either voluntarily or through collective bargaining. They go back to an earlier era of paternalism. They received their biggest boost during World War II when wages were controlled and increases could only be given indirectly in the form of benefits. After the war unions continued to push benefit programs. Organizations without unions also began to provide these benefits. Today they represent about 33 percent of payroll costs.

Private plans for protection against death, illness, and injury include life, medical, and disability insurance. Government programs include Social Security, which provides protection against disability and provides survivor's benefits as well. Medicare is health insurance for persons over 65. Injuries on the job are covered under state-administered workers' compensation programs.

Retirement benefits are both private and a matter of public policy. Pensions provided by organizations are extremely common today. They are regulated by a new law, the Employee Retirement Income Security Act of 1974. Social Security also provides retirement benefits for the vast majority of American workers who are covered.

With the exception of a limited number of supplemental unemployment benefit programs, protection against job loss is almost exclusively a matter of public policy. Unemployment insurance administered by the states is the method for dealing with relatively short periods of job loss. One of the fastest growing benefit areas is pay for time not worked. Paid vacations, paid holidays, and bereavement leave are increasing rapidly. Vacations of three, four, and even five weeks are becoming more and more common. Ten and more paid holidays per year is not at all unusual.

Organizations also provide a variety of services to their employees including merchandise discounts, credit unions, medical services, recreation areas, tuition allowances, and college scholarships. Programs of benefits and services are almost always administered by the centralized personnel staff department. Flexible (or "cafeteria" style) benefit programs let employees select from different options for a package of benefits that suits their individual needs.

SELECTED REFERENCES

BABSON, STANLEY M., JR., Fringe Benefits—*The Depreciation, Obsolescence, and Transience of Man.* New York: John Wiley & Sons, 1974.

BUREAU OF NATIONAL AFFAIRS, *Services for Employees,* Personnel Policies Forum Survey 105. Washington, D.C.: BNA, 1974.

CHAPMAN, J. B. and R. OTTEMAN, *Employee Preference for Various Compensation and Fringe Benefit Options.* Berea, Ohio: ASPA Foundation, 1975.

COFFIN, RICHARD M. and MICHAEL S. SHAW, *Effective Communication of Employee Benefits.* New York: American Management Association, 1971.

McCAFFERY, R. M., *Managing the Employee Benefits Program.* New York: American Management Association, 1972.

PAUL, ROBERT, *Employee Benefits Factbook.* New York: Martin Segal, 1976.

EMPLOYEE SAFETY AND HEALTH

◄══ IDEAS TO BE FOUND ══►
IN THIS CHAPTER

- Extent of the safety and health problem
- How the safety and health functions are organized
- Measurement of organizational safety and health costs
- Compilation of accident and illness statistics
- Major provisions of OSHA

Because of attention created by passage of the Occupational Safety and Health Act (OSHA) in 1970, it may be assumed that concern for employee safety and health began in that year. This is not the case at all. Public and private efforts to cope with this problem began well before the turn of the century.

In the latter part of the nineteenth century Massachusetts became the first state to enact a law providing for inspection of factories. Primarily concerned with improving working conditions for women and children, the law provided for the elimination of certain hazards as well as the maintenance of proper ventilation and sanitation. Workers' compensation laws were enacted in the early part of the twentieth century. Safety programs were established in many private industrial concerns during this period as well.

But there is no question that OSHA reflects public concern over this issue in a way that has not been seen in the past. One of the most ambitious measures ever passed dealing with employer–employee relations, the act has received both wide acclaim and intense denunciation. While difficult to assess because of its relative newness, its impact in focusing public attention on worker safety and health is unquestioned.

The distinction between safety and health is somewhat arbitrary. Safety generally refers to hazards resulting in direct injuries such as cuts, bruises, sprains, impaired hearing, loss of eyesight, and broken and lost limbs. Health refers more to the role of the working environment in producing disease and illness. This chapter examines some of the issues in safety and health management and also takes a look at the Occupational Safety and Health Act.

EXTENT OF THE SAFETY AND HEALTH PROBLEM

In comparing today's industrial facilities with those of several generations ago, it might seem that strict enforcement of safety and health requirements would be a thing of the past. The cleanliness and attractiveness of many modern facilities would appear to have made such problems obsolete. This, though, would be a false impression.

Despite many decades of effort, worker safety and health remain a serious problem. The accuracy of the various statistics is always suspect, but estimates of the National Safety Council still place the annual death rate from injuries and accidents in the range of 14,000, and disabling injuries at approximately 2.5 million. In addition government estimates of death and disabling disease from exposure to toxic materials alone run into the hundreds of thousands.

Regardless of how such figures are derived, there seems little question that annual fatalities, injuries, and disabling disease from work-related conditions take a toll into the millions. Inhalation of coal dust with its resultant black lung disease still cripples thousands each year. The same is true of asbestos dust. Noise is still a problem in many environments. Various industrial chemicals have been linked to birth defects and sterility. Work-related stress may be a contributing factor to cardiac ailments.

It is ironic that the increasing life span of the population may be contributing to belated recognition of the incidence of occupational disease. Many problems created by long exposure to unsafe materials do not show up until late in life. Thus in years past many of the worst effects of debilitating illness may have been hidden by earlier mortality. Persons may live longer now, and the pernicious effects of occupationally connected disease may show up as chronic disabilities in later life.

It is difficult to derive any accurate figure of what all this costs the nation. But the figure must run into the billions of dollars annually. Thus safety and health at the workplace are still serious matters of concern. Undoubtedly this is what spurred Congressional action in 1970, after many years of investigation.

ORGANIZING THE SAFETY AND HEALTH FUNCTIONS

Organizing for Safety   While this will undoubtedly change as a result of OSHA, concern for safety over the years has been limited largely to industrial concerns. Methods for handling this issue could be characterized as diverse. Should it be centralized in a separate staff department? Should it be centralized as a line function? Or should it be decentralized with each line or operating manager responsible for safety in the individual units?

Nothing approaching unanimity has emerged in handling this area. Centralizing the function in a staff department has been the practice in many organizations. The safety director under these circumstances usually reports to the director of industrial relations. This has the advantage of making a specific individual responsible for safety and placing the function in the department which deals with other personnel matters.

The disadvantage is that this often makes operating managers feel that safety is a staff function and not their responsibility. It brings to the forefront all of the normal line and staff conflicts. This can result in questions of authority and responsibility and control becoming more important than the function of safety itself.

For this reason some organizations have appointed a safety director and have then had this person report to a top line executive. This has the advantage of giving the safety director greater authority. But there is one big proviso that goes with this method. The line official must be someone who is intensely concerned with safety. If the top operating executive has little interest in this area, it can restrict any positive efforts of the safety director.

Another method that is found less frequently is to decentralize the function entirely. Each line manager acts as safety director along with all other responsibilities. Because having everyone responsible usually means that no one is responsible, it has not found wide acceptance. But it does recognize that ultimately individual operating managers must take responsibility for implementing safety programs.

Because of the problems inherent in each of the above approaches, the majority of industrial organizations have adopted the practice of forming safety committees. These committees are usually composed of representatives from the various sectors of the organization. Staff safety personnel, worker representatives, union representatives, first line supervisors, and higher level operating managers are involved. These committees have the advantage of giving voice to the many segments of the organization which must share responsibility for safety. They act as a review body for safety practices and make recommendations to reduce accidents and injuries.

It is not easy to assess the effectiveness of such committees. As with so many organizational functions, the committee itself and its composition is less important than the attitudes of top management. Where top management makes it clear that safety is a critical matter, such committees probably have more impact upon reducing accidents and injuries.

With the advent of OSHA it seems obvious that government agencies, service firms, financial institutions, retail organizations, and similar sectors of the economy will have to become much more safety conscious. There is probably no one system of organization that will work best for everyone. The critical factor is less the organizational method than the commitment to safety.

Organizing for Health

Industrial medicine has not been a notable contributor to making the organizational environment a safer place in which to work. For most organizations the function of medical services has been to provide pre-employment physical examinations, to review claims for workers' compensation, and to offer first aid and other routine medical services. With a few exceptions, there have not been many large-scale programs of preventive medicine including research into the effects of the working environment upon employee health.

Just as specialists are beginning to appear in such fields as sports medicine, so industrial medicine is beginning to develop. A preventive medicine program within the organization can make a big contribution to the goal of keeping workers healthy. A starting point is the pre-employment screening process. This not only screens out individuals who might be a liability, but assists in proper job placement. This function has traditionally been performed by medical departments.

Another function is to insure the maintenance of good health by members of the organization. Periodic examinations, either performed by the organization's medical personnel or in consultation with private physicians and clinics, can help serve this purpose. Many organizations have done this with top ranking executive personnel but have not followed the practice with lower level supervisors and hourly personnel.

Consultation on job transfers is another important function for the medical unit. This has usually been done with regard to physical aspects of the job. A growing area will be that of ascertaining the varied effects of different work environments upon the mental and emotional health of employees. Little is known about this area at present.

An area due for growth and expansion is research into the effects of the working environment upon health. This will include investigations into toxic substances, levels of permissable exposure to hazardous agents, and more general research such as the effects of exercise in preventing heart disease.

Organizations will have to maintain close contact with other private investigations as well as those from government laboratories and universities. This will be a major responsibility of the medical department.

Combining Safety and Health   It is doubtful that the present practice of having separate safety and medical departments will continue in the future, at least as presently constituted. The growing importance of safety and health mandates change. The best way to insure a safe and healthful working environment will probably be by combining the two functions and having them report to the highest level staff personnel executive in the organization.

With the already high degree of expertise required, and with the degree of such expertise bound to increase, most organizations will find it best to make safety and health a staff function. It is doubtful that operating executives without considerable staff assistance can give the attention to this area it will require. Within the overall personnel function, safety and health can be subdivided into various classifications.

MEASURING SAFETY AND HEALTH COSTS

Determining how much accidents and occupational illnesses cost the organization is not a simple task. After obtaining the necessary data, which is only a small part of the problem, the major difficulty is finding an acceptable methodology that is both internally and externally consistent.

It is important for the organization to know such costs. It provides data on which to base the value of safety and health programs. It offers a basis for internal comparisons of improvement or decline among units and from one year to the next. And it is of value in comparisons with other organizations.

For many years the most common way of classifying accident and injury costs was by labeling them either "direct" or "indirect." This terminology may still be found, but Simonds has suggested labeling direct costs as *insured* and indirect costs as *uninsured*. [1] This has the psychological advantage of focusing management attention on accident costs not covered by insurance. While this classification has been largely restricted to accidents and injuries, the same concepts could be applied to occupational illnesses.

Insured costs are those involving payments under workers' compensation and medical expenses usually covered by insurance such as physician

[1]John V. Grimaldi and Rollin H. Simonds, *Safety Management,* 3rd edition (Homewood, Ill.: Richard D. Irwin, 1975), pp. 395–396.

fees and replacement of income. These costs are available from organizational records. Uninsured costs are largely based on estimates and thus pose more problems.

There are several items in the uninsured costs. The wages of workers who lose time on the job because of injury to another worker must be included. Costs of materials wasted and equipment damaged must be estimated. Any pay continued prior to collection of insurance benefits must be accounted for. The same is true if overtime is necessitated by the employee's absence as well as supervisory wages for the time devoted to the accident. An accounting must be made of decreased output after the worker returns to the job. The cost of the learning period by any replacements must also be added in.

It is important for the organization to know its safety and health costs. But there must be a balance between the costs of obtaining such information and the value it supplies. It may be dysfunctional if the expense becomes excessive. But some reasonable and consistent tabulation can be of value in assessing the contribution of the safety and health program.

MEASURING ACCIDENTS AND ILLNESSES

One of the problems in the safety and health field has been the compilation of reliable data to determine the extent of the problem. Various formulas for computing and compiling accident and illness data have been used by different organizations and agencies. In recent years progress has been made in standardizing the reporting systems.

The current measure used by the Bureau of Labor Statistics to comply with new regulations is the *incidence rate* of occupational injuries and illnesses. It represents the number of injuries and illnesses, or lost workdays, per 100 full-time employees. The formula is:

$$\frac{\text{Number of injuries and illnesses or lost workdays}}{\text{Total hours worked by all employees during calendar year}} \times 200,000$$

The figure of 200,000 is the base for 100 full-time equivalent workers who work a full forty hours per week, fifty weeks per year. The statistics are tabulated for all sectors of the economy by use of a stratified random sample.

The incidence rate replaces previous statistical series based on the American National Standards Institute's Standard Method of Recording and Measuring Work Injury Experience (Z16.1). These measures are for the *frequency rate* and *severity rate*. They are still used by many companies. The formula for the frequency rate is as follows.

$$\text{Frequency rate} = \frac{(\text{Number of injuries}) \times (1,000,000)}{\text{Employee-hours of exposure}}$$

This is the number of injuries that would be expected if the employees of an organization worked 1,000,000 hours instead of the actual number. Injuries counted are those severe enough to keep a person from a regular job which has not been especially created to accommodate the injury.

The severity rate evaluates injuries in terms of the number of days which the injured person is unable to work. The formula is:

$$\text{Severity rate} = \frac{(\text{Total time - lost charges}) \times (1,000,000)}{\text{Employee-hours of exposure}}$$

Deaths and permanent total disability are assigned a time charge of 6,000 days. A scale is established for permanent partial disability to determine time-charges.

THE OCCUPATIONAL SAFETY AND HEALTH ACT OF 1970

A new era began in 1970 when the Occupational Safety and Health Act was passed. A complex and controversial law, it has been praised for its far-reaching attempts to bring massive reform to matters of personnel safety and health. It has also been roundly condemned for saddling industry with extra costs without first establishing the necessary knowledge and technology. Harrassment on the part of OSHA officials has also been an often-heard complaint.

The purpose of the act can be stated simply: to provide a safe working environment for private sector employees involved in interstate commerce. It does not apply to public employees. Nor does it apply to working conditions covered by other legislation such as the Coal Mine Health and Safety Act.

Organization for Administering OSHA

Primary responsibility for administration of OSHA rests with the Secretary of Labor through the Assistant Secretary of Labor for Occupational Safety and Health, a position established by the act. While principle responsibility resides with the Department of Labor, the Secretary of Health, Education and Welfare (HEW) also is charged with certain duties and responsibilities. The act also establishes a number of commissions and committees.

The body which hears appeals from enforcement proceedings is the Occupational Safety and Review Commission. This is a quasi-judicial body of three members who function in similar fashion to the National Labor Relations Board. They are appointed by the President with the approval of the Senate.

The twelve-person National Advisory Committee on Occupational Safety and Health is an advisory body with no actual authority. This group is composed of representatives of management, labor, the public, and the occupational safety and health professions. They are supposed to make recommendations to the Secretary of Labor.

Another group established by the act is the National Institute for Occupational Safety and Health (NIOSH). This body works primarily with the Secretary of HEW. It is charged with developing standards for occupational safety and health and making recommendations in this area. It helps fulfill the research and training mission and conducts informational and educational programs.

The Assistant Secretary of Labor for Occupational Safety and Health is charged with establishing safety and health standards through inspections of workplaces. It is this official's responsibility to issue citations for standard violations and for failure to provide a safe and healthful work environment. An additional responsibility is developing training programs which provide information about unsafe and unhealthful working conditions.

Developing Safety and Health Standards

An integral part of the act are provisions dealing with the establishment of occupational safety and health standards. A standard is a rule which requires that certain specified conditions be met or which requires the adoption or use of one or more practices, means, methods, operations, or processes that are needed to provide a safe and healthful environment. Interim or temporary standards were to be issued within two years after the act was passed. These were made up of standards already in existence, either from established federal standards or from the American National Standards Institute.

Emergency temporary standards are those issued by publication in the Federal Register when the Secretary of Labor feels employees are exposed to serious danger from harmful substances or from other causes. Permanent standards are also provided for which are to replace the interim standards. The establishment of permanent standards follows a procedure which includes publication in the Federal Register with interested parties having the right to file objections or request public hearings. The act prescribes procedures for judicial review of standards.

Dealing with Violations   OSHA provides for six types of violations. *Minor* violations have no direct relationship to safety and health. *Non-serious* violations have a direct relationship, but would probably not cause death or serious physical injury. *Serious* violations could result in death or serious injury. *Willful* violations indicate the employer is intentionally disregarding unsafe conditions. *Repeated* violations indicate a previously cited violation that has not been corrected. And *imminent danger* violations reveal conditions where it is reasonable to assume that the possibility of death or serious injury exists immediately.

To determine violations of the act, compliance inspections are ordered by the Secretary of Labor. Priorities have been established ranging from situations with the potential for catastrophes down to random selection. These inspections are made by compliance safety and health officers and industrial hygienists. They have created much of the controversy surrounding the act. Many managers and owners feel the inspections have been conducted in a high-handed manner and amount to little more than harassment. Since advance notices of inspections do not have to be given, this has undoubtedly contributed to the antagonism. The inspections are essentially "walk around" visits with all aspects of the working environment subject to review by the compliance officers.

Citations are issued for violations. The citation must be posted, though this can be delayed if an appeal is made. The appeal process begins with a hearing before an Administrative Law Judge. The Occupational Safety and Health Review Commission hears appeals of decisions made by the Administrative Law Judge. Decisions of the Review Commission are subject to review by the federal courts.

Employer–Employee Rights   Employees have certain rights that are prescribed under OSHA. They can request that safety and health inspections of the work place be made. They have the right to have a representative accompany the inspector during an inspection. The employer is required to maintain accurate records on exposures to dangerous materials or agents. Dangerous substances must be identified by labeling. Employees must be informed of any exposures to harmful agents in excess of prescribed standards. Employer violations must be posted in a prominent spot.

Employer rights are also set forth in the act. The employer has the right to be advised of the reason for an inspection. OSHA personnel must properly identify themselves. The employer cannot be barred from participating in inspections. The employer has the right to contest and appeal citations and to request temporary variances from standards. Permanent variances can also be applied for. And OSHA must assure the confidentiality of any trade secrets observed during inspection.

OSHA and Workers' Compensation

OSHA does not affect programs of workers' compensation (discussed in Chapter 13 on employee benefits). Actually the two programs are quite compatible. OSHA prescribes standards for a safer working environment and penalizes employers who violate the standards. Workers' compensation provides financial compensation to employees for occupationally related injury or illness.

SUMMARY

Work connected deaths, injuries, and disabling illnesses remain a serious problem today. The number of workers affected annually runs into the millions, with costs estimated in the billions. In the past safety and health have been organized as separate functions. Safety has been centralized as a staff function, centralized as a line function, and decentralized. Industrial medicine has been limited largely to pre-employment physical examinations and routine first aid. Growth is expected for both these areas and the likelihood is that they will be combined in one department as a staff function.

One recommended method of measuring organizational safety and health costs is to classify them as either insured or uninsured. Insured costs can be obtained from records; uninsured costs must be estimated. In compiling statistics on accidents and illnesses the newest measure is the *incidence rate*. The frequency and severity rates of accidents are older measures, discarded by the Bureau of Labor Statistics but still used by many organizations.

The Occupational Safety and Health Act (OSHA) is a complex measure designed to provide a safer working environment for private sector employees. Primary responsibility for administering and enforcing the act rests with the Secretary of Labor. Numerous commissions and committees have been established to help implement its provisions.

The development of safety and health standards for the work environment is an integral feature of OSHA. Various levels of violations are prescribed, ranging from minor to willful to imminent danger. Compliance inspections are ordered by the Secretary of Labor to determine violations of the act and civil and criminal penalties are provided for. There is an appeals procedure for violations with final review by the federal courts. Both employers and employees have certain rights enumerated. OSHA does not affect programs of workers' compensation. OSHA stresses preventive safety for the worker; workers' compensation provides financial compensation in case of injury or occupationally related illness.

SELECTED REFERENCES

ASHFORD, NICHOLAS, *Crisis in the Workplace: Occupational Disease and Injury: A Report to the Ford Foundation.* Cambridge, Mass.: MIT Press, 1976.

BUREAU OF LABOR STATISTICS, *Occupational Safety and Health Statistics: Concepts and Methods* (Report 438). Washington, D.C.: Government Printing Office, 1975.

GRIMALDI, JOHN V. and ROLLIN H. SIMONDS, *Safety Management*, 3rd edition. Homewood, Ill.: Richard D. Irwin, 1975.

HAMNER, WILLIE, *Occupational Safety Management and Engineering.* Englewood Cliffs, N.J.: Prentice-Hall, 1975.

MARGOLIS, BRUCE L. and WILLIAM H. KROES, *The Human Side of Accident Prevention: Psychological Concepts and Principles Which Bear on Industrial Safety,* Springfield, Ill.: Charles C. Thomas, 1975.

PETERSON, DAN, *The OSHA Compliance Manual.* New York: McGraw-Hill, 1974.

PART

7

LABOR
ORGANIZATIONS

LABOR–MANAGEMENT RELATIONS

⟸   IDEAS TO BE FOUND   ⟹
IN THIS CHAPTER

- Structure and government of labor organizations
- The role of law
- Collective bargaining and agreement administration
- Political and institutional nature of labor organizations
- Evaluating the labor relations function

An organization which must bargain with one or more labor organizations has an extra dimension added to its personnel function. Unions greatly restrict managerial discretion. Much decision-making is bilateral instead of unilateral. Actions appropriate for an unorganized work force may be quite inappropriate if employees are organized.

It is almost universal for organizations to establish the function of labor relations as a separate personnel subunit. It is highly specialized and is usually referred to as the labor relations (or industrial relations) department. It co-exists with units devoted to personnel relations with unorganized workers, since it is uncommon for an organization to have all of its nonsupervisory personnel organized.

This chapter looks at some of the problems and challenges a labor organization brings to the organization. Generalizations will be made, but they are always subject to qualification since labor organizations and managements exist in so many varieties and forms. A labor–management relationship is unique in many respects. The parties are adversaries. But the organization needs the workers. The workers need the organization. It is the mutual dependence that ultimately leads to resolution of conflict.

A successful labor–management relationship does not come easily. The parties may not even agree on the definition of "successful." It requires great skill, good faith, and continual effort from both sides. Concession and compromise are inevitable. But with integrity and hard work the parties can achieve a relationship that serves the needs of both.

THE EXTENT OF ORGANIZED LABOR TODAY

It is difficult to obtain a precise picture of the current size of organized labor. Statistics on membership are not noted for their reliability. Complicating the matter is that it is more difficult today to define exactly what a labor organization is.

Until recent times labor organizations could be identified by their role in society and by their referring to themselves as unions. But recently, other groups such as professional associations have undertaken collective bargaining functions for their members and perform like unions in practically everything but name. These include the National Education Association (NEA) which represents teachers and the American Association of University Professors (AAUP) which bargains for college instructors.

Combining unions and those associations which bargain collectively, membership is approximately twenty-three million. This represents approximately 25 percent of the total labor force and 30 percent of employees in non-agricultural establishments. More important perhaps than numbers is that this represents a decline in union penetration over the past two decades. Unions alone represented approximately one-quarter of the total labor force in 1958. Excluding associations, this had dwindled to approximately one-fifth two decades later. With association membership added, unions have grown slightly, but not enough to keep pace with growth in the labor force as a whole.

Membership in unions and associations is widely dispersed. Public sector labor organizations have been the fastest growing, but transportation, construction, mining, and manufacturing remain the strongest sectors of union strength. Approximately half of the nation's blue-collar workers are in unions. This includes approximately 75 percent in construction and mining and about two-thirds in such manufacturing industries as automobiles, steel, and rubber.

There are major geographical differences in union strength. States with the fewest union members are in the South. Approximately one-half of union membership is accounted for by five states alone, New York, California, Pennsylvania, Ohio, and Illinois. Unions are also heavily concentrated in several key cities such as Pittsburgh, Seattle, and Detroit.

It is risky to draw firm conclusions about labor's strength from membership figures alone. Labor organizations are heavily concentrated in key and critical industries. But they are being hurt by the continued movement in the economy from a blue-collar to a white-collar work force. White-collar workers have proved resistant to organization. When they bargain collectively they have often selected professional associations as opposed to traditional unions. Women have not historically been attracted to labor unions, and the increasing number of females in the labor force has been a deterrent to growth. Stodgy leadership and poor public image have also hurt organized labor.

But organized labor activity in the United States has always been marked by cycles of growth and decline. Despite current problems, it would be very shortsighted to overlook the still formidable power and strength of organized labor. As an institution it still exerts great influence.

STRUCTURE AND GOVERNMENT   There are between 150 and 160 national or international (to indicate Canadian members) unions in the United States today. They range in size from the Granite Cutters' International Association with approximately 2,500 members to the huge International Brotherhood of Teamsters with over two million. These nationals in turn charter local unions which remain affiliated with that national. Over 100 of these national unions belong to the AFL–CIO.

Strictly speaking, the AFL–CIO is not actually a union itself since it does not have a collective bargaining function. It is, rather, a union of unions, which looks out for the interests of organized labor as a whole. Union structure and government is best understood by looking at this body first.

The AFL–CIO

The AFL–CIO came about as a result of the 1955 merger between two organizations, the old American Federation of Labor and the Congress of Industrial Organizations. It is a federation composed of highly autonomous national unions. Membership is voluntary, and while the majority of labor organizations are members, two of the largest, the Teamsters and the United Automobile Workers, are not affiliated.

The AFL–CIO is headquartered in Washington, D.C. It looks after the interests of organized labor in Congress and the other agencies of government. It has an extensive lobbying function which it performs at the national, state, and local levels. The state and local levels are served by state and city bodies. These are composed of delegates from local unions whose national unions are themselves affiliated with the AFL–CIO.

One of the chief functions performed by the AFL–CIO for its affiliates is that of giving unions exclusive jurisdiction in a particular industry or craft. This is to prevent dual unionism, which is unions competing with each other for members. Jurisdictional disputes between unions are resolved by an internal process with arbitration as the final step.

The AFL–CIO has little real power; its strength comes from its considerable influence, particularly in the political arena. Its authority over its national unions is limited since they relinquish little autonomy when they affiliate. Its one sanction when member unions engage in actions of which it disapproves is expulsion. The Teamsters were expelled for corrupt practices in the 1950s.

The National Union

The real power of the labor movement lies in the hands of the national unions. It is through these national unions, which carve out jurisdictions for themselves largely on the basis of craft or industry, that collective bargaining takes place. Actual negotiations may take place through the local union. But it is the national which charters the local and which oversees its activities.

National unions administer their relations with locals through staff representatives who are paid employees of the national. They assist the local union in its function of enrolling members, conducting negotiations, and handling grievances. The staff representatives are themselves responsible to the national president who is an elected and paid official in all national unions.

National unions are highly varied in their collective bargaining procedures. In such unions as the United Steelworkers of America, negotiations on major issues including wages are conducted at the national level with representatives of the major steel companies. Negotiations over local matters are conducted separately through the individual locals. In the construction industry there are no national negotiations. Negotiating is done either locally or regionally.

One of the main functions of the national union is conducting organizing drives to obtain new members. This is carried out by the staff representatives who attempt to sign up enough workers in nonunion organizations so that a representation election can be held. Once the election is authorized through the National Labor Relations Board, the union attempts to win a majority vote.

The Local Union

It is the local union which actually enrolls the individual worker and which collects dues. In addition to contract negotiations where these have been authorized by the national union, the local's main function for its members is that of administering the agreement and processing grievances. It does this through union stewards or other designated officials who are typically elected to office. They carry worker complaints to management and attempt to resolve disputes at the place of work.

The local has a president, vice-president, and other officials who are elected to office and who typically are not paid. It is their responsibility to look out for the interests of the members and to work with national head-quarters. Bargaining and grievance committees are common in local unions.

Professional
Associations

In recent years, a new element has been added to organized labor in the form of professional associations which bargain for their members. There is some controversy over whether they are actually part of organized labor. Organizations such as the National Education Association through its state and local affiliates engage in collective bargaining with school boards and sign contracts which bind members to its terms.

In addition to their normal professional activities the associations enroll members, conduct negotiations, and process grievances just as traditional unions do. The controversy over their roll in the union movement is that they compete with traditional labor unions for representation rights. Both the National Education Association and the American Association of University Professors compete with the American Federation of Teachers (an AFL–CIO affiliate) for the right to represent teachers and college instructors.

THE ROLE OF LAW

Public policy has great impact upon labor–management relations in the private sector. The modern period of regulation began in 1935 with passage of the *National Labor Relations Act*, better known as the *Wagner Act.* Amended by the *Taft–Hartley Act* in 1947 and the *Landrum–Griffin Act* in 1959, it is still very much in force today. Now officially called the *Labor–Management Relations Act*, it is usually referred to as Taft–Hartley.

Under this act, which applies to firms engaged in interstate commerce, workers are guaranteed the right to select representatives of their own choosing for purposes of collective bargaining. Certain practices of employers which infringe upon that right as well as other employee rights are prohibited. Workers are also guaranteed the right to refrain from joining labor organizations. Practices of labor organizations which infringe upon that and related rights are also prohibited. These practices of employers and labor organizations are referred to as unfair labor practices.

Taft–Hartley is a complex measure. Its principal provisions are administered by a quasi-judicial body, the *National Labor Relations Board* (NLRB). The NLRB has two major functions. One is to conduct representation elections in units designated for that purpose to see if workers wish to be represented by a labor organization. If a majority vote "yes" then the employer legally must grant recognition and bargain with it in good faith. The labor organization is obliged to represent all the workers in the unit even if they do not become members. The NLRB also conducts decertification elections if the labor organization loses majority support.

The NLRB's other major function is to hear and adjudicate charges of unfair labor practices by employers or labor organizations. It does this through the General Counsel and the regional offices throughout the country. Cases which are not settled satisfactorily through NLRB proceedings can be appealed to the federal courts.

There is no equivalent of the Labor–Management Relations Act in the public sector. Several executive orders establish procedures for federal government employees to form labor organizations and bargain collectively. State and municipal employees are covered by state legislation which varies considerably among the states.

COLLECTIVE BARGAINING

A primary function of labor organizations is to bargain collectively with employers on behalf of their members. Collective bargaining is the negotiation process by which labor and management decide upon the wages, hours, and working conditions of employees. This is a deceptively simple sounding phrase. Over the years it has been defined to include such diverse items as subcontracting, profit sharing, and rental of company housing.

The process of collective bargaining is divided into two areas. One consists of *labor contract negotiations*. It is well known because of publicity in the media when large management and labor organizations bargain over a new contract. The other is equally if not more important. But it receives little media attention. This is the day-to-day *contract administration* after the contract has been negotiated.

The purpose of negotiations is to reach agreement on a *labor contract*. Contract is somewhat misleading, even though it is enforceable in the courts, since the real contract is between the worker and the organization. The labor organization does not contract with management to supply labor. Nor does the organization contract with the labor organization to supply work. Another term for the document is *labor agreement*. So long as work is offered and accepted, both parties agree to be bound by the terms decided upon in negotiations. Because of popular usage, it is customary to use the terms contract and agreement interchangeably.

Negotiating the Agreement

Negotiations to decide the terms of a new agreement take place when the old agreement expires. The parties start preparing for this long in advance. The labor organization prepares a list of demands it wants included in the new agreement. Management commonly develops its own list. For both parties some of the items are actually wanted and others are camouflage to use as bait.

The whole process is highly ritualized, with both parties playing roles they know are expected. The labor organization paints a dire picture of what the members will do if demands are ignored. Management offers an equally bleak forecast of the inevitable insolvency meeting such demands will bring.

To the outsider negotiations appear to be exciting and stimulating. While there may be such moments, much tedium is involved in reviewing the numerous proposals and counterproposals. Some items such as starting and quitting times are not too difficult. Others such as cost-of-living clauses and revisions in the pension and insurance plans can be extremely complex and require careful scrutiny.

The end result of this process, which may include a work stoppage if there is a breakdown in negotiations, is a document which will govern relations between the parties during its life. Agreements are signed for periods up to five years, with three years being the most common. Too frequent negotiations create unwanted stress for both sides. Three years is enough to bring stability to the relationship without locking the parties into provisions that unforeseen changes may make undesirable.

Administering the Agreement

While receiving less publicity than negotiations, the day-to-day administration of the agreement is extremely important. It is here that the parties define the terms on which they will live and work together day after day. If the agreement permits the organization to discharge for "just cause," this abstract provision must be made concrete in actual situations. If two persons vie for the same job and the agreement says seniority shall govern where ability is equal, then "equal ability" must be made explicit so that a fair decision can be made.

The primary mechanism for administering the agreement and resolving disputes is the grievance procedure. It sounds negative because of its name, but the grievance procedure is actually a positive device for affirming the rights of workers. It is the mechanism by which meaning is given to the contract. It is a valuable communications system for management to learn what is bothering the workers.

Most grievance procedures have several steps or stages at which disputes can be resolved. Step one usually takes place between the worker, the union representative, and the first line supervisor. Subsequent steps take place at higher levels with higher level officials from management and the labor organization.

If the dispute cannot be resolved by this procedure, approximately 95 percent of American labor agreements provide for dispute resolution through final and binding arbitration. This is a voluntary process which permits a third party acceptable to both sides to make a decision which both agree to abide by.

Arbitration is one of the great accomplishments of American industrial relations. It substitutes reason for force in resolving conflict. The term "final and binding" is somewhat of a misnomer since arbitration decisions can be appealed to the courts. The courts as a general rule are reluctant to set aside arbitration decisions and several important Supreme Court decisions have affirmed that concept. But since contracts are enforceable by the courts, they do retain a review function once the parties have agreed to an arbitration clause in the labor agreement.

POLITICAL AND INSTITUTIONAL NATURE OF LABOR ORGANIZATIONS

There are two aspects about labor organizations which are easy to overlook. One is the nature of the *institution with a life of its own.* The other is its *political nature.* These two aspects help explain much behavior that might otherwise be difficult to understand.

Labor Organizations as Institutions

The labor organization as an institution has an existence that is something more than that which is associated with its present members. It is an organization with a past, present, and future life. Decisions must take into account those who helped build it but are no longer present plus those who will join it in the future. This cannot be judged as either good or bad but is a fact of life which must be reckoned with. It is true of most organizations in society including corporations, universities, civic clubs, and government agencies.

For example a choice must be made in bargaining demands. Management will accept either a dues checkoff (automatic payroll deduction of dues) or an extra fifteen cents per hour in the wage package. The labor organization can't have both. For the immediate members a dues checkoff promises no personal gain. But from the standpoint of strengthening the organization automatic dues collection will make the union financially stronger.

Thus labor leaders often must make such decisions which make them appear indifferent and even irresponsible to the interests of their members. But actually, such behavior may be very responsible on the leader's part. It may represent a sincere conviction that strengthening the organization for the future must take precedence even if present members must make some sacrifices.

The same phenomenon is often at work during labor disputes. The media often ridicule organized labor by pointing out that wages lost during a lengthy strike will never be made up even if demands are won. What is overlooked is that the strike is not just about today's wages. All actions must be weighed with consideration not just for the present but for tomorrow and all the tomorrows which follow. Even though present members sacrifice, future members will benefit because management knows the labor organization is willing to fight for what it wants.

Managements which overlook these institutional factors will always be limited in their understanding of labor organizations. This is why tactics such as offering the workers Christmas bonuses without first obtaining union or association consent will often produce a negative response from labor officials. Assuming no ulterior motive, management may be perplexed why officials object so strenuously. Whether intended or not, labor leaders can easily see this as weakening the labor organization's hold on its members, an action they must protest in protecting the interests of the organization.

Political Nature of Labor Organizations

Labor organizations are also predominantly political institutions. Management is responsible to senior officials in an upward chain of command. The labor leader's position is just the opposite. The labor leader is responsible to persons downward in the hierarchy. The management official is *appointed* by superiors. The labor official is *elected* by a constituency.

This places labor officials from shop steward up to national president in a continual dilemma. It is common to all elected officials in parliamentary democracies. Labor officers are supposed to be responsible leaders. It is their responsibility to see that the agreement is lived up to, that the members do not harass management with frivolous grievances, that bargaining demands are reasonable, and that the rules and laws of society are obeyed.

This means that wildcat (unauthorized) strikers must be disciplined. Petty and unjustified grievances must be turned down. Bargaining demands must be compatible with the realities of the economic environment. Racial and sex discrimination must be eliminated even if members object.

But at the same time the labor official wants to get re-elected. These very actions that society labels as responsible leadership provide an opportunity for political challengers to discredit the incumbent. Accusations of not looking out for interests of the members are difficult to answer in a heated and emotional campaign for office. Thus, the labor leader is in a dilemma between taking actions to insure getting re-elected and taking stands which may be unpopular but which are morally and legally right. It is not an easy position. Stances that may seem outrageous to management may reflect a labor official facing a tough political challenge.

MANAGEMENT ORGANIZATION FOR LABOR RELATIONS

Organizations which bargain with labor organizations customarily centralize a great deal of authority in their staff labor relations departments. The labor organization reduces the permissible margin of error in personnel decision-making. An unwarranted reprimand of an unorganized worker can result in antagonism on the part of one person and possibly other members of the informal work group. The same action against a labor organization member can escalate into a major confrontation. There is the possibility of a time-consuming and costly grievance as well as greater potential for group retaliation.

Thus the organization must control its own supervisors more closely, especially when discipline is involved. The terms of the labor agreement must be applied uniformly and consistently. Even grievances which seem simple and trivial have the potential for serious disruptions.

Seeing that the agreement is applied fairly and consistently is a major responsibility of staff labor relations personnel. Their presence is usually required at each step of the grievance process. They look out for the organization's interests in labor relations matters. Sometimes this can place them in an adversary relationship with supervisors and managers if they feel the organization has violated the contract. (The same is true of the labor organization steward or other official, who has a dual responsibility for seeing that members are treated fairly and also that they themselves live up to the terms of the agreement.)

Another important role for staff labor relations is in contract negotiations. In many cases the organization's top labor relations official at whatever level negotiations are taking place will head the bargaining team. Exceptions to this are when a senior operating official performs this duty.

Regardless of the degree to which staff personnel are involved in actual across-the-table bargaining, they will have an important role in information and data gathering. Accurate data is essential if the negotiations are to be conducted on a sound basis. Items the labor organization is expected to ask for must be costed out. If it requests a cost-of-living increase, its financial impact must be estimated. This estimate must be compared with estimates of other possible proposals including those management will make as possible tradeoff items.

Costing out such things as cost-of-living increases, pension or health insurance plans in actual dollar terms is not too difficult compared with many items the parties will bargain over. The labor organization may want to switch from departmental seniority to plant-wide seniority. This means for layoffs that senior persons in one department can displace or "bump" junior employees in other departments. Even where ability to perform the job is required before bumping takes place, a certain loss in efficiency is almost inevitable when employees are shifted to different jobs. What impact will such a change have? What does the organization's past experience tell about the likelihood of layoffs? What kind of cost figure can be attached to such a proposal?

Estimates must also be made of labor organization intent. Here the staff department acts as an intelligence unit. How serious is it about certain of its proposals? Is a strike a serious possibility or is it bluffing? If management takes a certain stance will this push the labor organization toward settlement? Or will it inflame the membership and solidify their resistance? The bargaining game is being played for high stakes and miscalculations can be costly. Staff labor relations personnel must be prepared to deal with such issues.

PUBLIC SECTOR COLLECTIVE BARGAINING

While private sector labor organizations have seen a decline in percentage of employees organized, the same cannot be said for the public sector. The past two decades have seen rapid growth of both traditional unions and professional and civil service associations which bargain for public employees. From less than one million in the 1950s, estimates today place membership in government unions at approximately 2.5 million, and association membership in excess of three million.[1]

As indicated earlier the Labor–Management Relations Act governing the private sector does not apply to public employees. Federal employees are covered by two executive orders: E.O. 10988 which was issued in 1962 by President John F. Kennedy, and E.O. 11491 which became effective in 1970 and was issued by President Richard M. Nixon.

The original order by President Kennedy was the first federal recognition that government employees had the right to organize and to bargain collectively. The order was deficient in many respects, but it did provide for different types of labor organization recognition and methods for resolving contract disputes.

The 1970 order by President Nixon modified the original order and removed many of its deficiencies. It provided for exclusive recognition if a labor organization won bargaining rights by winning a majority in a representation election. It created a Federal Labor Relations Council to administer and interpret the order. It provided for another official, the Assistant Secretary of Labor for Labor–Management Relations, to handle such functions as deciding upon bargaining units and supervising representation elections.

[1]Data adapted from Arthur A. Sloane and Fred Witney, *Labor Relations*, 3rd ed. (Englewood Cliffs, N.J.: Prentice-Hall, 1977), pp. 37–39.

It also dealt with a major problem in public sector bargaining. To resolve contract disputes it created an impartial Federal Services Impasses Panel. This body can order binding arbitration if necessary.

Action by the federal government apparently had impact upon the states. Prior to the 1962 Kennedy order only one state had a law permitting public employees to organize. Today practically all states have legislation which gives at least some public sector employees collective bargaining rights.

The most difficult problem in the public sector has been the strike issue. Employees of the federal government and most of the states are not legally given the right to strike. This is a major difference between private sector and public sector bargaining. In the private sector there generally are substitutes for goods and services not available due to strikes (though this is not necessarily true in the short run).

Public sector services constitute a monopoly. There are no realistic alternatives when fire personnel, police officers, teachers, or sanitation workers go on strike. And yet without the right to strike labor organizations have no effective power to exert in contract negotiations.

Resolving this problem remains one of the big challenges in the public sector. As all citizens know, prohibitions against striking have proved ineffective when public employees have felt their rights abridged. Various types of arbitration and other resolution mechanisms have been suggested and in some cases tried. Future years will show if orderly procedures can be substituted for strikes in the public sector.

There is no way of knowing if public employee unions and associations can continue the growth rates of the past two decades. What is certain is that they will continue to have major impact upon personnel relations in the public sector. The right of public employees to organize and bargain collectively has been affirmed. There is no reason to believe this will change.

EVALUATING THE LABOR RELATIONS FUNCTION

Evaluating the effectiveness of the labor relations function is not an easy task. It is not simply a matter of totaling the number of grievances, unfavorable arbitration awards, favorable arbitration awards, unauthorized work stoppages, or any other numerical indicators. An organization may have few grievances and work stoppages because it has lax supervisors who demand little from the workers. It may have numerous grievances because it insists the members of the bargaining unit provide a fair day's work for their pay.

The organization ultimately wants a productive work force that is a positive force in attaining organizational goals. This means it provides high quality and quantity of output in relation to its costs. Costs can be tangible such as dollar amounts paid for wages and supplements. They can be intangible such as the cost in customer relations brought about by indifferent workmanship. Output can be tangible such as the number of satisfactory units produced. It can be intangible such as a truck driver creating customer good will by helping unload a shipment even though the contract does not require it.

All labor relations decisions should be evaluated by their long-term impact upon the attainment of organizational goals. A strike that is costly in the short run may be good in the long run if the organization avoids getting saddled with unnecessary costs. Or a strike may cost little in the short run if the organization has a heavy inventory of finished goods it wants to deplete. But if it produces bitter feelings that are translated into indifferent workmanship, absenteeism, and slow downs, then it may prove costly in the long run.

There is no precise formula for evaluating the impact of labor relations decisions and policies upon goal attainment. Subjective judgment is always involved. But every labor relations decision, from deciding whether to settle a grievance at the first stage or to contest it all the way to arbitration, should be made with this principle in mind.

For organizations with insecure managers, this may be asking too much. A president whose job tenure depends upon this year's income statement may be inclined to forego a strike even though it means higher costs in the long run. A plant manager in the same situation may be inclined to settle grievances which should be contested in order to avoid having poor results show on the record for this year.

It is often thought that the presence of a labor organization automatically makes the organization less efficient. And it is probably true that given an unrestricted choice most organizations would prefer to direct their workers without labor organization intervention. But it is far from the truth that labor organizations and inefficiency are linked together. It is not a matter for which proof can be readily offered. But it is probably true that well-managed organizations with labor organizations function far more effectively than do poorly managed organizations without.

SUMMARY Membership in labor unions and professional associations which bargain collectively is approximately twenty-three million. This represents a declining proportion of the total labor force, currently about 25 percent. There are between 150 and 160 national unions in the United States. A little over 100 of these belong to the AFL–CIO, which looks out for labor's interests in the political arena. The collective bargaining function is performed by the national unions which charter affiliated local unions. National unions as a general rule exert much control over locals. The grievance process is largely handled by the locals. Professional associations which bargain collectively have grown rapidly in recent years.

Public policy in the private sector is regulated by the Labor–Management Relations Act, better known as Taft–Hartley. It provides for representation elections to secure recognition. Through the National Labor Relations Board established by the act, unfair labor practices on the part of labor organizations and management are adjudicated.

A primary function of labor organizations is to bargain collectively for their members. Negotiations are conducted to establish a labor contract (or agreement). Negotiations take place upon expiration of the old agreement. After the agreement has been signed, it must be administered during its life. The grievance procedure is the primary mechanism for administering the agreement. Approximately 95 percent of American labor agreements provide for binding arbitration to resolve disputes over terms of the agreement.

Labor organizations are political groups, since labor officials are elected to office. An important aspect of understanding labor organizations is their institutional nature. This means the organization has goals beyond those of the immediate membership. Management responds to the labor organization by giving much centralized authority to its staff labor relations department. Evaluating the labor relations function is not easy. All labor relations decisions and policies should take into consideration the long-term impact upon the attainment of organizational goals.

Unions and bargaining associations of public employees run counter to the membership trend in the private sector. Collective bargaining for public employees was given impetus by executive orders issued by President Kennedy and President Nixon giving federal employees many of the organizing rights enjoyed by private sector employees. The most difficult issue in public employee collective bargaining remains the question of strikes.

SELECTED REFERENCES

HAGBURG, EUGENE C. and MARVIN J. LEVINE, *Labor Relations*. St. Paul, Minn.: West Publishing Co., 1978.

MARSHALL, F. RAY, ALLAN M. CARTTER and ALLAN G. KING, *Labor Economics*, 3rd ed. Homewood, Ill.: Richard D. Irwin, 1976.

REYNOLDS, LLOYD G., *Labor Economics and Labor Relations*, 6th ed. Englewood Cliffs, N.J.: Prentice-Hall, 1974.

RICHARDSON, REED C., *Collective Bargaining by Objectives*. Englewood Cliffs, N.J.: Prentice-Hall, 1977.

SLOANE, ARTHUR A. and FRED WITNEY, *Labor Relations*, 3rd ed. Englewood Cliffs, N.J.: Prentice-Hall, 1977.

TAYLOR, BENJAMIN J. and FRED WITNEY, *Labor Relations Law*, 2nd ed., Englewood Cliffs, N.J.: Prentice-Hall, 1975.

PART

8

THE FUTURE

16

PERSONNEL MANAGEMENT IN THE FUTURE

⊂══ IDEAS TO BE FOUND ══▷
IN THIS CHAPTER

● Demographic changes and their impact
● Unevenness in population cohorts
● Continuing government regulation
● Continued movement for more fulfilling, satisfying work
● Increasing stature of personnel administration

There are a number of trends already visible which will have impact upon the management of personnel in the years to come. It is easier to outline these trends than to offer solutions to the problems and challenges they pose. But in order to devise practical solutions, we must understand what the problems are. This chapter examines some of the major forces at work today that are shaping the personnel administration of tomorrow.

DEMOGRAPHIC CHANGES AND THEIR IMPACT

The most significant trend which must be reckoned with is the changing nature of the American population. These are not projected changes based on *future* birth rates, these are actual changes based on persons already in existence.

Population Shifts

In simple terms the population is becoming older. By the year 2000 half of the population will be over thirty-five, a dramatic change from the youth culture caused by the baby boom following World War II. It is not just an aging population that poses the big challenge. Rather it is the unevenness of the various age group segments (or cohorts) that creates the major difficulties.

These changes for the decade 1980–1990 are shown in Table 16-1. Several things stand out upon examination of the data. During the decade beginning in 1980 the age group of 16- to 24-year-olds will decline by six million. This is occurring at the same time the age group just ahead, the 25- to 34-year olds, will increase by five million. And one of the most significant changes of all is in the ages thirty-five to forty-four which will show a jump of almost eleven million. These are the former members of the baby boom now moving into the prime earning years.

Another way to highlight these changes is by graphing them as shown in Figure 16-1. The chart shows the *changes* that will occur in each of the age cohorts during the 1980s. It illustrates the unevenness referred to. If one extends the trend into the 1990s, the 25- to 34-year-olds will go from an increase of approximately five million to a *decrease* of six million.

Impact of Population Changes One organizational impact of this in the 1980s will be the large number of 25- to 44-year-olds in comparison with the 45- to 64-year-old group. Since most senior management positions are held by this older segment, organizations may find themselves with large numbers of young managers and without large enough cadres of seasoned, mature managers to train them. It also could mean having to give difficult management assignments to persons at younger ages than has been the case

Table 16-1
United States Population Projections for 1980 and 1990
(Numbers in Thousands)

Age Groups	Actual	Projected	
	1970	*1980*	*1990*
5–15	44,774	37,851	41,235
16–24	32,459	37,590	31,512
25–34	29,294	36,157	41,062
35–44	23,142	25,702	36,545
45–54	23,310	22,640	25,213
55–64	18,664	21,047	20,479
65 and over	20,087	24,523	28,933

Source: Department of Labor, *Employment and Training Report of the President* (Statistical Appendix, Table E-1, p. 252), 1977.

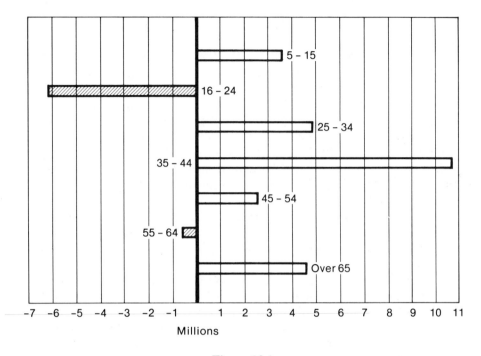

Millions

Figure 16-1
Population Changes by Age Group
of U.S. Population for the Decade
1980–1990

formerly. The unevenness of the age cohorts must be built into human resource planning structures to deal with this potential problem.

Starting in the 1980s and extending into the next decade is another problem with potential for social repercussions. Both the large numbers of younger persons and the unknown impact of extending retirement until age 70 means there are likely to be larger numbers of young persons seeking advanced positions than there will be openings available. This comes at a time when demands for equal opportunity for females and minorities will continue to be strong. Thus competition for choice positions and higher level incomes could become extremely fierce.

Dealing with large numbers of highly educated, highly qualified junior level managers who have no advancement possibilities is going to require great skill. This will have to be dealt with at the same time that large numbers of persons with college degrees are likely to find themselves frozen out of managerial careers completely. The eleven million increase of 35- to 44-year-olds includes the largest number of college graduates this country has ever had. Many of them will be forced to settle for routine clerical, service, and nonsupervisory positions. This too will require great sophistication in handling unmet expectations.

But in the 1990s this problem could shift. At this time the declining birth rates of recent years could actually spell labor shortages among younger workers. If the trend towards leisure time continues, with hours of work reduced and vacations and holidays increased, the labor supply in the 1990s and beyond may become too small to meet the economy's needs.

Going past the year 2000 another problem looms. This is the large number of retired persons in relation to the numbers working. This is a social problem that government will have to deal with, but it is not one that organizations can ignore. This group will insist upon retirement benefits that keep up with inflation. Not only will the Social Security system be affected, but there will be pressure upon organizational retirement plans to raise amounts being received by persons already retired. Many collective bargaining plans already have provisions providing for increased benefits for workers already retired.

These are some of the major impacts that a shifting population will have. For a variety of unknown reasons the scenarios sketched out may not occur. Attitudes, values, and behaviors are always subject to change. But as indicated earlier, the people being referred to are not future statistics in a demographer's forecast. They are people already in existence. That fact alone means that organizations must prepare for personnel situations that will undoubtedly be quite different from what existed in the past.

CONTINUING GOVERNMENT REGULATION To meet a variety of social needs government influence upon organizational personnel policies has greatly increased in recent years. It is difficult to make any assessment of the future that does not include a continuing role for government. It is possible that future developments may slow down the growth rate of government regulation, but the possibility of reduced governmental influence is practically nil.

Future court decisions may reduce the scope of affirmative action and other programs for equal employment opportunity. But whether reduced or not, the pressure for equality in the entire employment process including promotion, compensation, and job tenure will continue. Organizations will have to continue in some form programs that assure equal employment opportunities for females and minorities. This will have to be maintained in the face of increasing resistance from white males who find themselves increasingly shut off from opportunities once taken for granted.

OSHA will continue to make its impact. Whether there is any change in the labor laws or not, there is little chance that regulation of the collective bargaining process will decrease. There will be continued efforts to implement the reforms of the Employee Retirement Income Security Act. The minimum wage provisions are scheduled for increases which will be felt by many organizations.

DEMANDS FOR BETTER WORK PRACTICES

There is some controversy about whether work is frustrating and unfullfilling for most workers. Whether or not this is true, pressures for providing a work environment with less regimentation and greater autonomy will undoubtedly continue to grow. Increasing levels of education alone suggest that even if most workers are not discontent with their jobs, they will insist that organizations be more cognizant of individual needs and aspirations.

Greater job security, additional opportunities for advancement, and adequate levels of compensation will be sought. This will come when domestic and world competition will be forcing organizations to become more cost conscious. Accommodating these worker demands while meeting intensifying competitive pressures will require personnel strategies and programs not envisioned in the past.

Organizations will find that not only demographic changes will have to be considered. Changes in life styles will also have impact. Already the two-career family is making itself felt. In many organizations some of the most talented personnel will be married to persons who share an equal commitment to a career. Geographic relocation, which so often accompanies advancement in the organization, will have to be reconciled with this new development.

For the best-run organizations these problems will be transformed into opportunities. If employees demand more from their organizations, ways will be found to better utilize the available talent for the mutual benefit of both parties. This is the real challenge of the years ahead.

INCREASED ROLE FOR PERSONNEL MANAGEMENT

All trends today point to an increasing role for the function of personnel management and personnel managers. Forecasts from the Bureau of Labor Statistics for the 1980s indicate personnel administration being a growth area in terms of jobs available. There seems little reason to quarrel with this projection.

In addition to more jobs for personnel administrators, the influence of this group will undoubtedly continue to grow. Along with other staff specialists, personnel managers for many years were seen as individuals with little real power and authority. While this view has diminished in recent years, it is a stereotype that has persisted.

Any remaining vestiges of the viewpoint that personnel managers are impotent in terms of power and authority should vanish completely during the coming decade. Compliance with government regulations alone will require tighter control of personnel policies and practices. Of necessity personnel departments will have to assume more authority than ever before.

Line or operating managers will not be relieved of their personnel responsibilities. But personnel staff executives will have more say about decisions of all types. Who should be promoted? How should salary increases be allocated? Which of three candidates should be hired? Who should be sent to the university's management training program? What can be done to increase office productivity? How can necessary concessions be obtained from the union? Is the proposed job enrichment program worth the cost? How should the organization respond if the engineers authorize a union election? These decisions will involve personnel managers, even in organizations not accustomed to delegating authority to staff executives.

More so than in the past, personnel backgrounds are viewed as excellent training for high level responsibilities in general management. More organizations are also having their top personnel executive report to the chief administrative official. This insures that personnel matters receive the attention they deserve. Organizations that in the past have not followed this practice are doing so in greater numbers. This trend should continue.

Personnel administration will remain a staff function. Responsibilities will be shared with line and operating managers. But this sharing will take place with personnel managers on a footing equal to line and operating managers instead of in a subordinate staff position.

SUMMARY   Forces are at work posing new problems, challenges, and opportunities for personnel administration in the years to come. The major trend is the changing nature of the population. Age cohorts are uneven. Large numbers of workers are now entering the prime working years, and smaller numbers are behind them. This means that fewer seasoned managers will be available to train junior executives, and that greater competition for organization positions of high prestige and income will exist.

Government regulation will continue unabated. There is practically no likelihood of any decrease and much greater likelihood for increasing controls and regulation. Pressures for more freedom and autonomy at work will continue along with demands for greater job security. All this means that the role of personnel administration will expand, with greater power and authority being given to personnel executives.

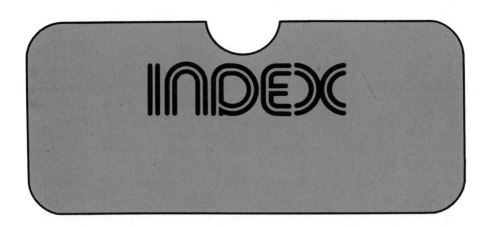

Absolute wage level (See General wage level)
Accident insurance, 193
Adkins v. Children's Hospital, 22–23
Administration of Veterans' Affairs, 96
Affirmative action:
  consent decree, 100
  Executive Order 11426, 100
  future and, 236
  handicapped and, 26, 96
  programs, 100–2, 135
  recruiting and, 65–66
  reverse discrimination, 101
AFL-CIO, 219–22
Age Discrimination in Employment Act, 26, 95
Albemarle Paper Co. v. Moody, 98–99
Alliance of Independent Telephone Unions, 102
American Association of University Professors, 218, 221
American Federation of Labor (See AFL-CIO)
American Federation of Teachers (AFT), 221
American Telephone and Telegraph Co., 100, 102, 128–31
Application forms, 81–82
Arbitration, 54–55, 223–24, 228
Assessment Center, 129–31
Audio-visual aids, 118

Bakke case, 102
Benefits and services, 191–202
  administration of, 200
  death and disability, 193–94
  development of, 192–93
  flexible benefits, 200–201
  job loss, 196–97
  pay for time not worked, 197–99
  personnel function and, 12, 191–201
  retirement, 12, 21, 23, 195–96, 200
Bennett Mechanical Aptitude Test, 97–98
Behavior modification:
  productivity and, 12, 183–84
  training and, 9, 110–11
Blue-Cross–Blue-Shield, 193
Bray, Douglas, 129
Budgeting process, 53–54
  training and, 118–19
Bureau of Labor Statistics, 237
Business games, 118

"Cafeteria" benefit programs (See Flexible compensation)
Career pathing, 135
Career planning (See also Management development), 10, 132–33
Carter, Jimmy, 95
Cases, in training, 117
Child labor laws, 6, 21–22, 26
Civilian Conservation Corp., 24
Civil Rights Act of 1964, 26, 65, 94, 130, 137, 154
Civil Service Act, 93
Civil Service Commission, 93, 96–97
Coal Mine Health and Safety Act, 209
Collective bargaining (See Labor-management relations)

College recruiting, 63–64
Communications Workers of America, 102
Compensation (See Wage and salary administration)
Comprehensive Employment and Training Act (CETA), 27, 122–23
Concurrent validity, 78–79
Conditioning (See also Behavior modification), 110–11
Congress of Industrial Organizations (See AFL-CIO)
Consent decree, 100
Consumer Credit Protection Act, 25, 174
Contract Work-Hours Standards Act, 25, 174
Copeland Act, 25, 173
Cummings, L. L., 148, 152

Davis-Bacon Act, 25, 173
Decision making in selection, 85–88
Defense, Department of, 96
Disability insurance, 194
Discrimination in employment (See Public policy; Selection)
Division of Negro Economics, 92
Duke Power Co., 97–98

Economic supplements (See Benefits and services)
Electrical Workers, International Brotherhood of, 102
Element, in job design, 71

Employee Retirement Income Security Act (ERISA), 28, 196
Employment (See Selection)
Employment Act of 1946, 23
Equal Employment Act of 1972, 26, 95
Equal Employment Opportunity (See Affirmative action; Public policy; Selection)
Equal Employment Opportunity Commission (EEOC), 26, 94–95
Equal Pay Act, 25, 93–94, 173
Empirical validity, 78
Executive orders:
 E. O. 11246, 96, 100
 E. O. 11375, 96
 E. O. 11478, 96–97
 E. O. 11141, 97
 E. O. 11701, 97
 E. O. 11914, 97
 E. O. 10988, 227
 E. O. 11491, 227
 labor relations and, 30, 222, 227–28
 selection and, 28, 96–97
External wage structure, 159, 161–64

Factor comparison, 166–67
Fair Employment Practice Committee, 92
Fair Labor Standards Act, 22, 25, 93, 172–74
Federal Labor Relations Council, 227
Flexible compensation, 200–201
Flexi-time, 185
Four day· week, 185
Fringe Benefits (See benefits and services)

Gilbreaths, 48
General Counsel, 222
General Electric Co. v. Gilbert, 99
General wage level, 159, 161–64
"Going" rate, 163–64
Government regulation (See Executive orders; Public policy; Selection; State

legislation; Wage and salary administration)
Granite Cutters' International Association, 219
Greenberg, Leon, 179
Grievances, 54–55, 223–24
Griggs v. Duke Power Company, 97–98, 103

Hammer v. Dagenhart, 22
Handicapped, discrimination and, 26, 96
Hawthorne experiments, 6, 183
Health (See Safety and health)
Health, Education and Welfare, Department of, 96
Health, Education and Welfare, Secretary of, 209–10
Holiday pay, 198
Human resource planning, 8, 35–46
 forecasting, 36–41
 labor, availability of, 42–44
 labor demand, 44
 labor supply, 42–44
 monitoring and, 44–45
 qualitative, 41–42
 quantitative, 36–41

In-basket exercise, 117
Incentive systems, 171–72
Incident process, 117
Industrial relations (See Labor-management relations)
Industrial relations director, 14, 110–11
Instrumental conditioning (See also Behavior modification), 110–11
Insurance:
 accident, 193
 disability, 194
 life, 193
 Social Security and, 194
 unemployment, 21, 23, 28–29, 197
Interview, 82

Job analysis:
 management development training and, 113–14

Job design, 71–72
 job defined, 71–72
Job enrichment, 12, 171–72, 182–83
Job evaluation, 164–68
 factor comparison, 166–67
 informal methods, 167–68
 point system, 164–66
Job specification, 46, 74–75
Job success criterion, 46, 73–74
Johnson, Lyndon B., 24, 26, 96

Kennedy, John F., 24, 30, 227, 228
King, Martin Luther's birthday, 198

Labor costs (See also Unit labor cost; Wage and salary administration), 11–12, 47–56, 160, 177–82
Labor, Department of, 92–93, 96, 173, 209
Labor force:
 demand for, 44
 future and, 233–36
 human resource planning and, 42–44
 labor market and, 60, 87–88
 participation rate, 43
 selection and, 87–88
 supply of, 42–44
 transformation of, 7
Labor market, 60, 87–88
Labor-management relations (See also Labor organizations):
 agreement, administration of, 13, 223–24
 arbitration, 54–55, 223–24
 collective bargaining, 29–30, 54–55, 222–24
 contract, 13, 55, 222–24
 evaluation, 228–29
 General Counsel, 222
 grievances, 54–55, 223–24
 labor unions, 13, 29–30, 217–30
 management organization, 226–27
 membership, 218–19
 National Labor Relations Board (NLRB), 221–22
 negotiations, 13, 54–55, 222–23

Labor-management relations
    (*continued*)
  personnel function and, 13
  public policy:
    Executive Order, 10988,
      30, 227–28
    Executive Order 11491, 30,
      227–28
    Labor-Management Rela-
      tions Act, 29–30, 221–22
    Landrum-Griffin, 29–30,
      221–22
    Railway Labor Act, 30
    Taft-Hartley, 29–30,
      221–22
    Wagner Act, 29–30, 221–22
  professional associations, 13,
    29–30, 218, 221
  public sector, 13, 29–30,
    227–28
  representation elections, 29,
    220–22
  staff function, relation to, 6
  staffing levels and, 54–55
  unfair labor practices, 29, 122
Labor-Management Relations,
  Assistant Secretary of
  Labor for, 227
Labor-Management Relations
  Act, 7, 29–30, 221–22
Labor organizations (See also
  Labor-management rela-
  tions; Professional associations):
  AFL-CIO, 219–20
  government, 219–21
  institutional nature of, 224–25
  local, 220–21
  membership, 218–19
  national, 220
  officers, 219–21
  political nature of, 225
  professional associations, 13,
    29–30, 218, 221
  staff function, relation to, 6
  staffing levels and, 54–55
  structure, 219–21
  wage and salary administra-
    tion and, 11
Labor, Secretary of, 96, 173,
  209–11
Labor unions (See Labor-
  management relations;
  Labor organizations)
Landrum-Griffin Act, 29–30,
  222
Lecture, 117

Lie detector (See Polygraph)
Life insurance, 193

McDonnell Douglas Corp. v.
  Green, 98
Major-medical insurance, 193
Management by objectives, 147
Management development:
  assessment center, 129–31
  candidate analysis, 131–32
  career pathing, 135
  career planning, 10, 132–33
  coaching, 135
  human resource planning
    and, 36, 41
  managerial job analysis,
    127–29
  objectives in, 133–34
  off-the-job, 135–36
  on-the-job, 135–36
  organization for, 126–27
  program monitoring, 136–37
  public policy and, 137
  rotation, 134–35
  selection of managers, 129–32
  special boards, 135
  staffing levels and, 30–51
  training and, 125–38
Manpower Development and
  Training Act, 27, 122
Manpower planning (See
  Human resources planning)
Medicare, 194
Minimum wage (See also Wage
  and salary administration),
  21–22, 24–26, 172–74
Minors, hiring of (See Child
  labor laws)

National Advisory Committee
  on Occupational Safety and
  Health, 210
National Apprenticeship Act,
  27, 123
National Center for Productivity
  and Quality of Working
  Life, 177, 182
National Education Association
  (NEA), 218, 221
National Foundation on Arts
  and Humanities Act, 25
National Institute for Occupa-
  tional Safety and Health
  (NIOSH), 210

National Labor Relations Board,
  29–30, 210, 220–22
Nixon, Richard M., 30, 227

Occupational Safety and Health,
  Assistant Secretary of
  Labor for, 209–10
Occupational Safety and Health
  Act (OSHA), 12, 27, 209–
  12, 236
Occupational Safety and Health,
  National Advisory Commit-
  tee on, 210
Occupational Safety and Health,
  National Institute for
  (NIOSH), 210
Occupational Safety and Review
  Commission, 209, 211
Office of Federal Contract
  Compliance (OFCC), 26,
  96
Operant conditioning (See also
  Behavior modification),
  110–11
Organizational development
  (OD), 12, 182, 184–85

Paternalism, 192
Pay for time not worked, 197
Pension Benefit Guaranty Corporation, 196
Pensions, 195
Performance appraisal, 11,
  139–55
  errors in, 141–42
  frequency of, 150
  goals in, 140
  innovations, 152–54
  methods, 143–49
    behavioral scales, 145
    conventional, 143
    direct indices, 147
    essay rating, 148
    forced choice, 144
    forced distribution, 143
    graphic scale, 143
    management by objectives,
    147
    straight ranking, 143
  performance and, 140
  performed by, 149–50
  public policy and, 154
Personnel costs (See Labor
  costs; Unit labor cost)

Personnel department:
benefits, services and, 200
development of, 5–7
functions of, 16
future of, 237–38
labor relations and, 13,
226–27
line-staff conflict, 14–16
management development
and, 136–37
nature of, 4–5
organizational maintenance
and, 18
organization of, 14–16
performance appraisal and,
151
productivity and, 12, 18
safety, health and, 205–07
selection and, 88–89
staff function, 6–7
staffing levels and, 9
structure, 14
training and, 121–22
Personnel manager, 14
Point system, 164–66
Polygraph, 85
Population:
changing nature of, 233–36
labor force trends and, 42–44
Position, in job design, 71
Productivity, 177–87
defined, 178–79
personnel functions and,
11–12
personnel management and,
17–18
programs for improving,
182–87
society and, 177–78
staffing levels and, 52
unit labor cost and, 179–82
Professional associations (See
also Labor management re-
lations), 13, 29–30, 63, 218,
221
Programmed learning, 117
Protective labor legislation:
child labor laws, 6, 21–22, 26
defined, 21
evolution of, 6–7, 21–24
minimum wage, 21–22,
25–26, 172–73
Social Security, 23, 28,
194–96
unemployment insurance, 21,
23, 28–29, 197

workers' compensation, 22,
27–28, 194–95, 203, 212
Public policy (See also Executive Orders: Labor-
management relations,
Selection; State legislation;
Wage and salary adminis-
tration):
benefits, services, and,
191–99
compensation, 25–26, 172–
75, 198–99
evolution of, 21–24
future and, 236–37
growth of, 7
labor-management relations
and, 29–30, 221–22, 227–28
management development
and, 137
performance appraisal and,
154
recruitment and, 65–66
retirement and, 28, 196
safety, health and, 27–28,
203, 209–13
selection and, 26, 92–105
training and, 27, 122–23

Railway Labor Act, 30
Rational validity, 79
Recruitment, 9, 59–67
internal, 64
labor market and, 60
methods:
college, 63–64
employment office, 61
employment agencies, 62
miscellaneous, 64
newspapers, 61–62
present employees, 63
professional associations,
63
U.S. Employment Service,
62–63
public policy and, 65–66
Reference checks, 83
Regents of the University of
California v. Allan Bakke,
102
Representation election, 29,
220–22
Retirement (See also Social Security; Employee Retire-
ment Income Security Act),
21, 23, 38, 195–96, 236

counseling, 12, 200
human resource planning
and, 38
private plans, 195, 236
public policy and, 21, 23, 196,
236
Reverse discrimination, 101
Right-to-work laws, 30
Role play, 117
Roosevelt, Franklin D., 92

Safety and health (See also Occupational Safety and
Health Act; Workers' com-
pensation), 203–13
accident insurance, 193
death, protection, 193–95
disability insurance, 194
disability, protection, 193–95
extent of problem, 204–5
illness, 193
measurement of, 207–9
organizing for, 205–7
personnel function and,
12–13
public policy and, 21–22,
27–28, 194–95, 209–13
Occupational Safety and
Health Act, 12, 27, 209–12
workers' compensation, 7, 22,
27–28, 194–95, 203, 212
Satisfaction, worker, 17, 182–
87, 236
Schwab, Donald P., 148, 152
Scientific Management, 48, 182
Selection, 9, 26, 68–105
costs in, 87–88
decision making, 85–88
job design, 71–72
job specification, 46, 74–75
job success criterion, 46,
73–74
labor market, 87–88
organizational goals and,
69–71
organizing for, 88–89
public policy and:
affirmative action, 65–66
100–02, 236
Age Discrimination in Em-
ployment Act, 26, 95
Civil Rights Act, 26, 65, 94,
130, 137, 154
consent decree, 100

Selection (*continued*)
development of, 92–93
Equal Employment Act,
26, 95
Equal Pay Act, 25, 93–94,
173
Executive Orders and, 26,
96–97
judicial decisions, 97–100
Selective Service Acts, 26
state legislation, 26, 97
systemic discrimination,
103
Veterans Readjustment
Act, 26, 96
Vocational Rehabilitation
Act, 26, 96
selection instruments:
application forms, 81–82
interview, 82
physical examinations, 83
polygraph, 85
references, 83
tests, 84–85
training, relation to, 109, 128
validation, 75–81, 88
Selective Service Acts, 26
Service Contract Act, 25, 174
Services (See Benefits and services)
Severance pay, 197
Sick leave, 193–94
Skinner, B. F., 110
Social Security, 23, 28, 194,
196, 236
Staff departments (See also Personnel department), 4, 6,
14–16
Staffing levels, 8–9, 47–56
budgeting and, 53–54
comparative data, 49–53
labor organizations and,
54–55
work measurement, 48–49
State legislation (See also Public
policy):
civil rights legislation, relation to, 198–99
compensation, 172–74
current, state of, 24–30
development of, 21–23
labor relations, 30, 208
safety, health and, 27–28,
195, 203
selection and, 26, 93–97
training and, 27, 123

Supplemental unemployment
benefits, 196
Supplementary benefits (See
Benefits and services)
Supreme Court, 21–23, 97–102
Systemic discrimination, 103

Taft-Hartley Act, 29, 221–22
Task, in job design, 71
Taylor, Frederick, 48, 182
Teamsters, International
Brotherhood of, 219
Teamsters v. United States, 99,
101
Tests in selection, 84–85
Thorndike, E. L., 110
Time and motion study (See
Work measurement)
Title VII (See Civil Rights Acts
of 1964)
Training, 9–10, 27, 109–24
apprenticeship training, 27,
123
behavior modification, 9,
110–11
budget and, 118–19
Comprehensive Employment
and Training Act, 27,
122–23
conditioning, 110–11
effect, law of, 110
evaluation, 119–20
formal, 111–20
informal, 110–11
instrumental conditioning,
110–11
Manpower Development and
Training Act, 27, 123
National Apprenticeship Act,
27, 123
objectives in, 114–15
off-the-job, 116–18
audio-visual aids, 118
business games, 118
cases, 117
in-basket, 117
incident process, 117
lecture, 117
programmed learning, 117
role play, 117
organization for, 121–22
public policy and, 27,
122–23
steps in, 111–20

*Trans World Airlines v. Hardi-
son*, 99

Unemployment insurance, 21,
23, 28–29, 197
Unfair labor practices, 29, 222
United Automobile Workers,
219
United States v. Darby, 22
United States Employment
Service, 62–63
United States Supreme Court
(See Supreme Court)
United Steelworkers of
America, 210
Unions (See Labor organiza-
tions; Labor-management
relations)
Unit labor costs, 179–82

Vacations, 197–98
Validation, 75–81, 88, 119–21
concurrent, 78–79
contaminating factors in,
79–80
continuing checks on, 80
criterion related, 78–79
empirical, 78–79
external, 120
generalization of, 81
internal, 120
predictive, 78
rational, 79
training and, 119–21
Vertical wage structure, 159–60,
164–68
Veterans' Employment Service,
96
Veterans Readjustment Act, 26,
96
Vocational Rehabilitation Act,
26, 96

Wage and salary administration,
11, 25–26, 159–76
absolute wage level, 159,
161–64
actual wage structure, 168–69
external wage structure, 159,
161–64
flexible compensation, 200–01

Wage and salary administration
(*continued*)
general wage level, 161–64
goals in, 160–61
going rate, 163–64
incentive systems, 171–72
job evaluation, 164–68
factor comparison, 166–67
informal methods, 167–68
point systems, 164–66
labor costs, 11–12, 47–56,
160, 179–82
minimum wage, 21–22,
24–26, 172–74
pay for time not worked, 198
productivity in, 179–82
public policy and:
Consumer Credit Protec-
tion Act, 25, 174
Contract Work-Hours

Standards Act, 25, 174
Copeland Act, 25, 173
Davis-Bacon Act, 25, 173
Equal Pay Act, 25, 93–94,
173
Fair Labor Standards Act,
22, 25, 93, 172–74
National Foundation on
Arts and Humanities Act,
25
Service Contract Act, 25,
174
state laws and, 25–26, 174
unit labor cost, 179–82
Walsh-Healey Public Con-
tracts Act, 25, 173
upward wage drift, 171
Wage-Hour Act (See Fair Labor
Standards Act)
Wage-Hour Division, 93, 173

Wagner Act (See Labor-
Management Relations Act)
Washington v. Davis, 99
West Coast Hotel v. Parrish, 23
Wonderlic Personnel Test,
97–98
Workers' compensation:
development of, 7, 22, 203
explained, 194–95
OSHA and, 212
public policy and, 27–28
Workmen's compensation (See
Workers' compensation)
Work measurement, 48–49
Work schedules, 12, 182,
185–86
Works Projects Administration,
24